'The definitive acc_____
   Ness Shankly

'No one ever said _____
Arriving with his team in New York at the start of
a short American tour (the Beatles weren't the only
Liverpudlians to make the Ed Sullivan show in the
mid-1960s), Shankly was asked by his assistant Bob
Paisley if he fancied adjourning to the bar. Shankly
said: "At this time of night?" Paisley pointed out that,
on account of the time difference, it was five hours
earlier than Shankly thought. "No Yank's going to tell
me what time it is," Shankly said, and went to bed.
That, you could say, was archetypal Shankly: stubborn,
funny, appalling and, above all, powerfully parochial.
Dave Bowler's authorised biography has a hundred
other stories that serve up the man just as crisply'
Daily Telegraph

'It's a great read'   Ivor Broadis

'A labour of love ... the level of Dave Bowler's research
into Shankly's early life and background make
this very much the Life and Times of Bill Shankly'
When Saturday Comes

'A fine, beautifully observed account of the life of the
most charismatic football manager ever ... A fantastic,
impeccably researched account'   *Total Football*

Dave Bowler has written various biographies.
He lives in Staffordshire.

SHANKS

The Authorised Biography of
BILL SHANKLY

Dave Bowler

ORION

An Orion paperback
First published in Great Britain by Orion in 1996
This paperback edition published in 1996 by Orion Books Ltd,
Orion House, 5 Upper St Martin's Lane, London WC2H 9EA

A CIP catalogue record for this book is available
from the British Library

ISBN 0 75280 246 1

Typeset by Selwood Systems, Midsomer Norton
Printed in Great Britain by
Clays Ltd, St Ives plc

To Mom and Dad

When I was twenty, I thought I knew so much more than you did. You caught up very quickly. Sorry.

And for Denise

If I am sinking, no-one will know it

Always

David

CONTENTS

ILLUSTRATIONS

ACKNOWLEDGEMENTS

Without the help of many, many people, this book would have been around half the size. Certainly without the permission, encouragement and remarkable generosity of Ness Shankly, the work would never have been undertaken. It is impossible to express the depth of my gratitude and I can only hope that the text goes some way to repaying her faith in me.

Once Mrs. Shankly confirmed me as the authorised biographer, the floodgates were opened and I was inundated with offers of help. Throughout the extensive research period, I was constantly amazed and fascinated to hear first-hand accounts of Bill's life and work. Everyone left me with a unique story of a man who loomed large in their lives, however brief their acquaintance. Roy Evans told me early on, 'Bill was just one of those great men that you count yourself fortunate to have met' and that sums up the attitude of all my interviewees.

I am very grateful to everyone who agreed to speak with me and would like to thank them and, in most cases, their families, for putting up with me. My heartfelt thanks go to Jean Roberts, Jack Mindel, Tom Finney, Tommy Docherty, Paddy Waters, Geoff Twentyman, Ivor Broadis, Eric Forster, Jim MacLaren, Jack Lindsay, Tom Wilkinson, Reg Scotson, Tom Daley, Clarry Williams, Wally Freeburn, Jackie Bertolini, Noel Hodgson, George Aitken, Ray Wilson, Dave Hickson, Sandy Kennon, Ronnie Moran, Roger Hunt, Tommy Smith, Ray Clemence, Emlyn Hughes, Kevin Keegan, Peter Thompson, Brian Hall, Peter Robinson, Jack Cross, Tom Saunders, Roy Evans, John Roberts, Billy O'Donnell, John King, Howard Kendall, Joe Royle, Brian Barwick and John Peel. Every interview was great fun for me and, I hope, not too much of a trial for my victims.

Billy Watson not only sat through two interviews but provided countless articles, photos and other pieces of information that were priceless. As a close friend of Bill's, he
dutifully read through the whole text as I was putting it
together and made a number of suggestions. James Forbes also
had much of the text inflicted on him and read it without
complaint and provided me with excellent background information on Glenbuck and its environs. Thanks also go to
Stuart Brownlee and John Laurenson at the Baird Institute in
Cumnock who provided me with enormous amounts of local
history material. I am grateful for their permission to quote
briefly from *The Cherrypickers* by Faulds & Tweedie, *Garan 1631
to Muirkirk 1950* by Thomas Findlay, *Muirkirk In Bygone Days*
by J.G.A. Baird, *Through The Parish Of Muirkirk* by J.M. Hodge
and *Muirkirk: A Miscellany* by Thomas Findlay.

The BBC Written Archives Centre were very helpful as was
Rachel at Radio City in Liverpool. I am most grateful to them
for providing me with the surviving cassettes of Bill's chat
show and for allowing me to quote from them.

Ken Hinks came to the rescue early on by allowing me
to use quotes from the interview album 'Shankly Speaks', a
marvellous record that bristles with Shankly magic. Two and
a quarter hours long, it's still available from Ken for £9 from
81 Long Lane, Tilehurst, Reading, Berkshire.

An appeal for local information in the *Huddersfield Shopper*
was a great success and the fanzine network was extremely
helpful in putting me in touch with those with stories to tell,
in particular *The Absolute Game*. Others of assistance were *One
Man And His Dog*, *The Cumberland Sausage*, *Watching From The
Warwick*, *Pie Muncher*, *Sing When We're Fishing*, *Nothing Borough
Park's Team*, *Hanging On The Telephone* and *A Slice Of Kilner Pie*.
The addresses for all these august chronicles can be found at
the back of the inestimable *When Saturday Comes* to which
everyone probably subscribes by now anyway.

Ed Horton's excellent *The Best World Cup Money Can Buy* –
available from Sportspages – was an indirect inspiration for
some of the text and I also pinched a bit from it. I also used

The People's Game by James Walvin quite extensively along with *The Juniors* by McGlone & McLure, the inevitable *Rothman's*, Paul Agnew and Ian Rigby's *North End*, *The Breedon Book of Football League Records* by Gordon Smailes, *McIlvanney On Football*, *Carlisle United Fifty Seasons On* by K. Wild, *Liverpool – A Complete Record 1892-1990* by Brian Pead and *Football League Players Records 1946-1992* by Barry Hugman. Highly recommended is Martin Wingfield's early league history of Workington, *So Sad, So Very Sad* and Tom Allen's *The Team Beyond The Hills* which provided excellent background to the Workington years.

I'd like to thank Caroline Benn for permission to quote from *Keir Hardie* and Arthur Barker Limited for permission to quote from *Shankly* by Bill Shankly, *Kevin Keegan* by Kevin Keegan and *Crazy Horse* by Emlyn Hughes. Telstar's video *Shankly – The Story Of A Soccer Legend* was invaluable as were *The Story of the Kop* and *The Centenary Of Liverpool Football Club* from the BBC. Mike Davage and David Steele were generous with their time and helped track down a number of interviewees.

Other help came via 'phone calls or letters from Brian Clough, Sir Walter Winterbottom, Bill Nicholson, Gordon Taylor, Bob Crampsey, Geoff Ford, John Litster, Sid Woodhead, Janet Clarkson, Stewart Davidson, J.P. Black at the SJFA, Janet Longden, James Castle, Robin Taylor, Les Triggs, Alex Douglas, John Townsend, Chris Balderstone, Robert Reid, Ginger Johnson, Bernard Robinson, Mrs. L. Walker, Alex Kitson, Ellis Robinson, Janette Millar, Diana Wong-Plomley, Andrew Roberts, Mrs. V. Gregson, Liverpool, East Fife, Workington, Huddersfield Town, Grimsby Town, Arsenal, Carlisle United, Preston North End, Norwich City, Partick Thistle.

After all that, I must thank everyone at Orion, particularly Jane Wood and Katie Pope, for their faith and encouragement. Thanks also to Tanja Howarth and Mark Hayward for taking care of business. Hackenbush would also like to offer greetings to Bryan Dray.

Denise had to put up with a great deal during the last year,

particularly my continual absence from home while inter-
viewing. She has the patience of a saint, which continually
amazes me. I'll try to be home more often this year, which
should require Job-like tolerance.

Finally, thanks to Dad for taking me to countless football
matches over many years and to Mom for letting us go.

AUTHOR'S NOTE

Anyone willing to read a biography has the right to know where the author stands on the subject before they invest their time and money. I believe that Bill Shankly is the pre-eminent club manager in post-war British football but that that is just part of the story.

Great success does not necessarily a great story make and nor are the successful always fascinating characters. For me, Shankly's life is compelling, his story unique.

As a football manager, others accumulated more trophies than he yet none has been able to construct a footballing dynasty. Matt Busby created a succession of dazzling teams at Old Trafford yet on his departure, the club waited a quarter of a century for worthy successors. Don Revie made Leeds the most feared team in the land yet after his departure they lived through a decade and a half of turmoil and under-achievement. Bill Nicholson won the double with verve and panache yet ever since, Tottenham have been little more than a good Cup team and, like the others, have suffered the ignominy of relegation. Even Brian Clough, builder of two great teams, could not bequeath success in perpetuity. Derby rallied on his departure but soon found themselves in the Third Division and facing extinction while Clough himself presided over a relatively barren period at Forest before taking them down himself in his season too far. But Liverpool are still Liverpool. How did Shankly, this straightforward man with the overwhelming personality, leave a club that, living by his principles and employing capable men who understood his methods, could seemingly do no wrong?

I've never liked saints, never trusted them. I don't think you'd want a saint lining up next to you at right half before a

Cup Semi-Final, for instance. It's rare that a man who makes an absolute virtue of complete honesty is well loved, for he must inevitably upset people along the way simply by speaking his mind. It could be argued therefore that Shankly's greatest success was to pass into folklore, to become a legend who not only eclipsed the popularity of his own players but transcended the barriers of club loyalty. Whatever the Kop felt about Hunt, St. John, Smith or Keegan, you could double that, treble it for Shankly. At opposing grounds, there was a genuine warmth in the welcome he received from opposing fans who instinctively recognised him as one of their own.

It's a moot point as to which was the more important achievement, building the greatest club in world football or becoming the most important and influential figure in the lives of 50,000 strangers. Whatever your opinion, there's no doubt that a man who can achieve both stands apart from the crowd and is well worth remembering.

Liberty's in every blow!
Let us do – or die!

Robert Burns

A working class hero is something to be.

John Lennon

FOREWORD

I'm delighted to be able to offer a few words of introduction to this book which I hope will be recognised as the definitive account of my husband's life.

It's difficult to imagine, but it's more than fifty years since I first saw Bill running out of the camp, keeping fit, when we were both stationed at Bishopbriggs in Glasgow. After he had convinced me to go out with him and then to marry him, the years that followed flew by. We had a good life and I have many very happy memories of our time together. In his research, Dave has uncovered people, places and stories that even I had forgotten, so reading the book has been like leafing through an old photograph album. It has been a pleasure to revisit old friends on every page.

Bill worked hard all his life but he felt that all the effort was worthwhile. If it was worth it for him, then it had to be worth it for me to see him so satisfied with what he achieved. Whatever he did at all the clubs, but especially at Liverpool, wasn't for himself but for the people who stood on the terraces. They were in his blood and it was for them that he put in those long hours looking for new players. I hope that they will read and enjoy this book for it will show them just how proud he was of them and how proud we all are of him.

NESS SHANKLY

A WORLD TO WIN

A Saturday at the end of April. Anfield readies itself for the final game of the season, the last opportunity before the interminable summer for club, players and supporters to engage in that peculiar communion that is only really understood by the football fanatic. As kick off time approaches, the Kop are in full cry. Thousands of voices come together in spontaneous song. 'Shankly, Shankly, Shankly, Shankly.' The tuneless drone goes on and on but the emotion it contains is real enough and never wavers. For them Bill Shankly represents everything that is great about their club and their game.

This particular Saturday came in April 1994, 'The Kop's Last Stand'. Almost twenty years had passed since Bill Shankly sent half of Liverpool into mourning with his shock decision to retire from football and from the club that were the most formidable in the land. Yet in all those years, despite all the great players that have passed through Anfield, the enormity of Bob Paisley's success as manager, the massive contributions made by men such as Fagan, Dalglish, Moran and Evans, the memory of Shankly remains the beating heart of Liverpool Football Club. One banner on the Kop said it all, a picture of Shankly headed with the words 'Lest We Forget'.

Some saw the end of the Kop as the final act of release for Shankly's spirit which continued to permeate every nook and cranny of Anfield. Nonsense, for his spirit has never been more alive among supporters than over the past two years; the upgrading of the ground necessitated by the tragedy of Hillsborough, which followed the numbing awfulness of that night at Heysel, would have found favour with Bill, the manager who had initially presided over massive improvements to the stadium in the 1960s and whose success had made such developments financially viable. Only the very best was good enough for those supporters who he termed 'the real people of football'. His love of the game and its traditions did not extend to the perpetuation of squalor, outdated facilities and potential danger – the very idea of fencing people into their patch of terracing would have been anathema to him and he would have forcibly argued that if you treat people like animals, you should not be surprised if they act in that way. The 'hot leg' and the pocketful of someone else's urine that were the staple of existence of an afternoon on the Kop might have made for an effective rites of passage tale for youngsters making their first forays into the bosom of the footballing family but British stadiums had to be brought into the 20th, never mind the 21st, century.

The Kopites celebrated the eternal verities of the Shankly way throughout the 1980s and into the 1990s until those values were upset under the stewardship of Graeme Souness. Observers noted that the age-old principles that had taken the club to the very pinnacle of world football were rejected in favour of new ideas and disciplines that did not always find favour with the players and which were not going to repeat the successes of the past. Murmurs of discontent grew louder, press and public alike grew more voluble in their con-demnation of the new regime, anguished at the betrayal of the Shankly legacy. The writing was on the wall and in January 1994, Souness became the first Liverpool manager to be dis-missed since Phil Taylor's enforced resignation 34 years pre-viously, which lead to Shankly's appointment. Souness was the first appointment to be made from outside the club since then, even if he was an Anfield old boy. Returning to first principles, the club chose to replace him with Roy Evans, a graduate of the Boot Room academy. Suddenly the talk was of Shanklyism, the atmosphere changed overnight and as 1994/95 illustrated, Liverpool was revitalised.

Over the years, the very name Shankly has become a tal-isman across Merseyside, the fanatical legions certain in the knowledge that the lesson according to Bill was football's own

Gospel. It's a conclusion with which it's hard to argue. Few, if any, have ever been so thoroughly obsessed with the game in all its minutiae. His encyclopedic knowledge of players, their strengths and weaknesses was rivalled only by those who worked alongside him. Few could match his ability to read an individual and administer the appropriate motivational charger. His devotion to work is legendary, yet could never be exaggerated. Allied to these skills was a charismatic personality so strong that players would follow him anywhere and a wit so sharp that few ever got the better of him.

This is not merely the story of Bill Shankly but an epitaph for a lost era. Younger readers with no first hand experience of the way he wove his spell across Liverpool can only wonder at the way such a miracle was performed. There's little doubt that the kind of transformation he wrought at Anfield and its environs would be virtually impossible today; Kenny Dalglish and Jack Walker may have spent their way to success, but they have not been midwives at the rebirth of a community, its confidence and its culture as Shankly and his lieutenants were back in the 1960s. Such a prize is now beyond them for the local football club is no longer the centre of a community as once it was.

It's all too easy and all too tempting to cast your mind back a few years to a golden age of dimly lit memory, conveniently forgetting that we were all doing the same thing then; we are living in what will be the good old days of 2020. Much of the evidence does point to a sport that is in crisis, not simply because of the transient if unsavoury incidents of the 1994–95 season – Cantona, Grobbelaar, Graham, Wise *et al* – but because of a far deeper, more insidious malaise. The indiscretions of a few individuals will soon be hazy memories, misdemeanours perpetrated by long forgotten individuals. Let's not be coy; football has always been a game whose beauty has been clouded by illegal payments, corruption, violent behaviour and rank stupidity. The threat that the game currently faces is far more serious which is why it is hidden beneath the sensational headlines penned by those seagulls

that follow Eric everywhere. The vested interests have too
much at stake to allow the public to receive accurate information on the way their game, the game that Shankly loved,
is being taken away from them. Those in higher office have
always been suspicious of football and its adherents, recognising its potential as an arena for radicalism and rabble-
rousing as long ago as the fifteenth century. Mrs. Thatcher was
not the first to attempt to kill the game for political ends.

It's not the game itself that's changed; football has evolved,
formations have changed, tactics moved on but as the
emblematic footballing cliché points out, 'at the end of the
day it's just eleven men against eleven and it's all about scoring
goals'. Intrinsically football is the same game that ever it was
and each Saturday, Sunday, Monday or whatever day football
is now played, it's quite possible to see feats of skill and
matches of extreme excitement which rank with those of any
cherished era of a past where bungs and bribes, fights and
follies were every bit as common as they are today. It's the
landscape into which football fits that has mutated. The committed supporters can still promote arguments as to Hunt's
superiority over Fowler, Bergkamp's suitability for the English
game, the escalating awfulness of goalkeeping attire and so
on. As Nick Hornby observed in *Fever Pitch*, football is possibly
the social lubricant, certainly in the stunted world of male
communication; if you know your football, you never have
any difficulty finding another nutcase who will share your
passion be it in a pub, club, factory, dole queue, office or
school playground. This incessant debate is the oxygen which
helps football maintain its premier position.

The context and content of that debate is changing. League
football's greatest strength has been the fierce hold it has on
those who watch. The loyalty of this constituency, the working
people for whom football was a safety valve, a badge of belonging and an expression of community spirit, is being tested to
the limit. These are not new observations of course, for anyone
who has picked up any club fanzine in the last decade will
have seen them rehearsed and rehashed *ad infinitum*, but the

voices of dissent are increasingly consigned to the wilderness, marginalised by the forces of capital exploitation that have devoured football and left it a very different game from the one which Bill Shankly knew and helped shape. The protesters are being forced into exile by the ever escalating cost of following the team. It is hard not to conclude that the decimation of football's traditional support is as much a political as an economic act – once people become engaged in any protest movement, they often find other causes that motivate them. If you can take away the focus of their first tentative steps into activism, you can prevent their discontent spreading.

Forces beyond the game itself have conspired with those that run football for their own interest to transform it from the working man's essential visceral release into another entertainment sideshow; once football becomes entertainment alone, it is nothing. Of course the term 'working man' has been rendered meaningless in anything but its broadest sense when compared with the way it was understood thirty years ago and beyond that to the roots of football's popularity in the last century. Allied to the pauperising of the working, now under, class that has gone on these last fifteen years, politicians spend their time polishing homilies on the non-existence of society and its attendant communities, on the virtues of the individual above the collective. Civic pride has been treated as an eccentric attachment to a buried past. In every town where he was manager, Shankly exploited local pride to the full; not only the fans at Carlisle, Grimsby, Workington and Huddersfield but the towns themselves responded to the man who was giving his all to the people, people who lived in close proximity to one another and to the football ground. As families are forced to move to out of town housing developments their ties to their home are inevitably weakened.

The geographical population drift has eroded the identification with the home town team and left many clubs cut adrift from the source of their support. Enormous numbers of children now take in their football from the TV rather than going to their local club and so, for example, we see the

Midlands awash with Blackburn Rovers and Manchester United replica shirts rather than those of Villa, Albion or Walsall. Ironically, Shankly's very achievements meant that Liverpool F.C. was taken away from the Kopites as the club sprouted fan clubs across the country, filled by those who wanted to be associated with the club's success, a development that found little favour with Shankly. Nevertheless the local fervour which he was able to tap into in those early days in Liverpool and then harnessed for the good of the club and then the city is a feat that would be almost impossible to match today. His triumph at Liverpool could not be measured in mere games won, points accumulated and trophies earned. Shankly's achievement was to make himself, his team and his club indivisible and indistinguishable from those that stood on the terraces and shouted themselves hoarse, transforming them from followers of a second division also ran into ambassadors of England's foremost club. Certainly money also came into the equation for he was able to convince his board of the need to speculate to accumulate yet most of their great players were either home grown – Phil Thompson, Hunt, Smith, Lawler – or came from the bargain basement – Milne, Clemence, Keegan, Heighway. Finance was nothing like as central to the ascent of Liverpool as it has been to Newcastle United or Blackburn Rovers.

While football rejects communities in the search for national and international revenue it does itself and the country a disservice. During the culturally turbulent years of the 1960s and 1970s, Bill had a dual role. Not only was he the manager of Liverpool, but he was also the most successful social worker in the city. Joe Mercer called him 'Liverpool's answer to vandalism and hooliganism because the kids came to see Liverpool ... [he] was their hero, their football god'. The standards of honesty and integrity that Shankly set, his insistence on decent values, provided a greater example to the youngsters of Liverpool than any teacher ever could. While Liverpool still had its share of professional criminals like every other city, Shankly's words and deeds did have an impact on many impressionable youths – many letters from local teachers testify to his commitment which saw him visiting local schools to preach the virtues of playing to win but living with integrity.

In this regard, Shankly was a true visionary just as, albeit in a different way, his friend and rival Matt Busby was at Old Trafford. History has it that it was Shankly who could only talk about football while Busby, committed though he was to Manchester United, had a range of interests beyond the playing field yet Busby only changed the face of British, particularly English football, while Shankly had an impact on the world beyond the game. Busby it was who ripped through the pathetically parochial vision that the Football League and Football Association had of the game, a view which held England up as the greatest nation in world football, a blinkered assessment which somehow persisted beyond England's humiliation at the hands of the Hungarians. After Chelsea had been persuaded not to enter the inaugural European Champions Cup, Busby pointed the way ahead for the domestic game by leading his babes into the competition, breaking down the insular thought processes that held back the development of our game.

Shankly took the game as his theme in an attempt to improve other aspects of society. This is not to suggest that he was a great philosopher or social engineer for that would be stretching the facts to breaking point. His gut instinct was that football could be the focal point of a community, that an entertaining and winning team could unite people behind a simple cause. His own experience proved that football could be a force for the good. Events at Liverpool bore out the truth of these beliefs though they were scarcely new. The difference was that for once, football was being used in benevolent rather than sinister fashion. Fascist dictators around the world had long since acknowledged the value of a successful national team, its impact on morale or its ability to divert attention from political problems. Mussolini spared no effort to ensure that the Italians were World Cup winners, the military junta engineered an orgy of nationalistic celebration when Argentina took the trophy in 1978, while in the wider sporting world, no further comment is required on Hitler's Olympics in 1936. For the ordinary people, particularly in depressed economies, sport provides the great release and as the people's game, football is more important than any other. If Bill could not have articulated that philosophy, he knew it in his bones and he built a great club at Anfield to help alleviate the misery of ordinary life.

Bill Shankly is remembered not simply as a great football manager but as the most vivid and honest example of the working class hero that the game has to offer. It is as well to remember that we shall not see his like again simply because there is no longer the scope for such a man to exist in the same way. Shankly could never betray the supporters of his club. Today it is expected. Consider the position of Manchester United, a team threatening Liverpool-like dominance of the English game. At the time of writing, their fans are up in arms, ostensibly because of the loss of favourites Ince, Hughes and Kanchelskis. The root of their frustration lies in the way the most successful English club of the decade is being run and the way in which the hard-core support is gradually being squeezed out of Old Trafford and replaced by higher income groups who are more easily controlled, are less likely to air their grievances, will buy more souvenirs, use the catering facilities and so on. The typical terrace supporter has been perfectly happy to roll up to the ground half an hour before kick off having had a drink with friends in their local, watch the game and go home. He's – for such support is predominantly male – not interested in buying United Cola, Fred The Red scarves or United burgers. He merely wants to shout at the referee for ninety minutes, see his team win and play well, in that order, and doesn't particularly care if he has to stand in pouring rain to do it. He wants to escape the drudgery of a working week. As Ed Horton points out in his excellent book *The Best World Cup Money Can Buy*, 'football is the sport of working people – who are lied to, exploited, manipulated in their working lives and then arrive in the stadium to see the liars, exploiters and manipulators sitting in the most expensive seats: complimentary, of course'.

The conventional argument among the biggest clubs in the land is that those fans represent the past, that football is a business, show business and they must cater for the 'family audience'. Anyone who has the future of the game at heart should be delighted if attendances rise and a wider cross-section of society goes to games. As casual racism is gradually being eradicated, we can be pleased with the progress, yet this progress has been made by the fans almost alone, with little assistance from the authorities, the PFA excepted. It is good to see the threatening atmosphere, oppressive in some stadia, being lifted, great to see that more women feel comfortable at the game without being subjected to the levels of harassment that were prevalent a few years ago.

Football should not be an exclusive pastime ruled by inverted snobbery. At its best, it can be a huge, inclusive celebration. The increasing number of families at our grounds is excellent news because the game's continuity is preserved, supporting your local club passed down the generations like an heirloom. Where the dangers of the Premiership lie is in its rules of natural selection; it wants the middle class family from the suburbs with no axe to grind, out for a day at the footballing theme park, with lots of income to dispose of, not the family from the local run down council estate struggling to survive on inadequate benefits.

It's absurd to suggest that families have never been part of English football. In the past when grounds featured both seats and terracing, young working families generally took their place in 'safer' sections of the terracing or in the cheaper seats while the more affluent might sit in the grandstand. Football supporters have always come from every sector of society, it's always been an egalitarian game in that respect. While the current crop of chairmen might complain that those who prefer the terracing are dinosaurs, that it is they who do not want the better off families taking their place at the club, the exact opposite is the case. It is the middle classes, prejudices hyped and hardened by the leader columns of the *Daily Express* that don't want the working class fans at the ground. Consequently, the hard-core, largely working class support that follows a club through thick and thin is being priced out of the game with the supposedly exorbitant cost of transferring to all-seater stadia used as justification for higher ticket prices; it's not just young working class males who are lost to the game with the loss of the terraces for as seat prices climb, the cost of a father taking his two children to the game each week is becoming harder to justify. In the climate of mass unemployment with which we've lived for the past two decades, this is a particularly vicious attack on those for whom football is their life, not a leisure pursuit. It is also a short-sighted betrayal of those who have put football on its pedestal as the nation's sport.

Manchester United's independent supporters association campaigned against another round of price increases at Old Trafford; the club's finance director, in a gesture of which Marie Antoinette would have been proud, suggested on *Newsnight* that if they can't afford to watch the first team they should go to the reserve and youth team games instead. Had such a comment been made at any club while Bill Shankly was manager, the explosion would have been heard for miles around yet Alex Ferguson is forced to accept the dictates of the board, forcing him to dip in and out of the transfer market at times best suited to the fiscal strategy of the club.

When today's top of the table team are tomorrow's also-rans or relegation candidates, when English league football becomes just another channel on Sky and when going to a game is merely a leisure choice rather than something that is in the blood and a compulsive act of allegiance, the future of the Premiership will look very bleak indeed as it already does for those, lower down the League pyramid, who have been deliberately starved of cash. All of this may seem to have little relevance to the life of Bill Shankly yet it is essential to accept that the football world that he inhabited is with us no longer, for from today's perspective the story of his life is beyond credulity. If he were with us now, he would devour the fanzines and rather than attempt to silence them as so many clubs have done, he'd welcome them with open arms as contributions from those 'real people' that he loved so well. He would understand the language of Hornby's *Fever Pitch*, empathise with the author's obsession with his team. The dilettante face of the footballing media would get short shrift, those who change their club colours for political favour and a job on the radio would be treated with withering contempt.

We must also remember that though he was a romantic, besotted by the glory of the boys own game, Bill Shankly was no sentimentalist. He knew that the Kop had its share of rogues, knew that the people who comprised that powerful choir were not all leading angelic, blameless lives. Unlike the 'intelligentsia' who condemn the thousands for the acts of a dozen, Shankly was smart enough to approach the problem from the other angle. He dedicated himself to the majority who worked hard during the week in factories or on the docks and desperately required the fortnightly escape into excitement that Anfield could provide. He had an affinity with these working lads, for those were his own roots. There could be no greater testament to his feelings than his decision to watch a number of games from the Kop after his retirement.

We all know about Shankly the footballing legend, the man for whom football was more important than life and death, whose every waking hour was channelled into the game he loved. Yet this is just one side of the man who had a lively and original mind, an interest in politics and was the head of a happy family unit. The domestic stability offered by his wife and children were crucial to his success, his home offering a haven where he could forget about the pressures of club football and recharge his batteries prior to the battles that lay ahead. That family ideal was perhaps the central tenet of Shanklyism. As a boy he was one of a large family and a member of an even greater community in the mining village of Glenbuck. His political ideas grew from that time, leaving him a lifelong socialist who played like a socialist and managed like a socialist. Everything about Shankly was geared to fostering a community, a powerful team spirit that acknowledged the fact that no individual component was more important than the greater good. It's ludicrous to suggest that Shankly loved football as some kind of Marxist intellectual exercise for he was no intellectual and had no time for theory above practice as he demonstrated on the training ground; in any case his love of the game came long before any political ideas had formed. It is not too outlandish to argue that the politics he embraced were shaped every bit as much by experiences on the football field as at the coal face where he first hewed his living. Ultimately his socialism and the way in which he lived his life and played his football became indivisible. He was absorbed by the game and its infinite variety. He was consumed by the sport, spoke of little else, but that gave a false impression. Football wasn't everything to him for he saw it in its context within society. It also provided him with a frame of reference, a window through which he saw the rest of the world. Everything that happened could be simplified into a footballing analogy. Football was a matter of life and death for to accept defeat was a living death.

The legacy of Shankly is one that will endure. In the midst of the mean spirit that has infected top flight football, Liverpool has of course to operate on the new playing field. Decisions are made at the club which would doubtless jar Shankly's principled sensibilities but much of the blame for that has to be laid at the door of changing times rather than an inept club. They tread the fine line between finance and respect for their supporters more successfully than most – price increases have generally been well managed and justified, the rebuilding of the ground has retained its atmosphere, marketing has not been allowed to bring the club into disrepute, public relations have been skilfully and sensitively managed with the Souness era representing the only dip in their reputation.

Much of the credit should be laid at the door of indefatigable Chief Executive Peter Robinson, regarded by most in football

as one of its unsung heroes. Since it was Shankly who recommended Robinson for the job as Liverpool's Secretary back
in the 1960s, much of the Shankly ethos was either shared by
or passed on to Robinson. Liverpool's dealings as a club have
the stamp of decency, honesty and an interest in the welfare
of the supporters, prizing ethical behaviour in an unethical
milieu. At times they have fallen short of the highest standards
just as the crowd have failed to learn from Shankly – he would
have been appalled by the moronic banana greeting handed
out to John Barnes or the ritual chants of 'Munich' that disfigured Anfield whenever Manchester United visit. Yet the
dignity which marked the club's bearing through the different
disasters of Heysel and Hillsborough held echoes of Shanklyism. Above all else, as the scenes on that April afternoon
showed, Liverpool F.C. is, quite genuinely, a family. Anfield
and its Shankly Gates are not the only lasting monument to
the work of Bill Shankly.

Winning prizes is one way of making a mark in life, concrete
evidence of excellence in the chosen field. Yet the way to
immortality is to live on in the hearts and minds of those who
carry on. When we come to remember the tigerish tackling and
will to win that earned him international caps, the captaincy
of his country and an F.A. Cup winners medal and which
characterised Shankly the footballer or the tactical acumen
and Svengali-like hold over his charges that made him such a
great manager, we would do well to recall that Bill Shankly
was, above all else, a good man who made a difference to the
lives of thousands who never even met him but felt his loss as
keenly as that of their own father or brother.

True greats should not be reduced to caricature for we are
not so rich in men of such stature that we can afford to
diminish them. As the years pass the Bill Shankly that we hear
of has been reduced to shorthand; the wise-cracking Scot with
a witticism for every occasion, a God-like genius who never
put a foot wrong when it came to football. In reality, Bill
Shankly was no saint, had a powerful temper at times, upset a
few along the way, made a few errors of judgment on and off

the field but finally left the world the richer for his presence and those whose lives he had touched grateful that they had come to know him. Such has been his effect that few can still come to terms with the fact that he has been gone some fourteen years now. Turn on *Match of the Day* and there is still an expectation that this seemingly indestructible man might be spitting out his opinions of the players of the day. 'Ryan Giggs? Aye, he's quick, good feet, but if you want to hear aboot wing play, now you start with Tommy Finney. Oh! What a player. He'd win this game without takin' off his overcoat.'

Bill Shankly lived life the only way he knew how. He lived it his way by the principles of honesty and integrity that were instilled in him as a child. This is an honest account of that life.

chapter one

GLENBUCK

Has there ever been a village like Glenbuck in all the history of British football? If there has, it doesn't come easily to mind. Tucked away off the main road from Muirkirk through to Ayr, on the edge of the Ayrshire coalfield, Glenbuck was the birthplace of Bill Shankly, his four elder brothers and five sisters. The boys all went on to play football professionally yet in Glenbuck that was a feat only marginally less common than going down the pit to graft for a living. If Yorkshire legend of the time suggested that you need only shout down the nearest mine shaft to come up with a fast bowler, then this passionate corner of Scotland could claim the self-same distinction where footballers were concerned. This tiny hamlet fostered the game of football as no other village before or since. Amid a population that rarely exceeded 1,000 and was generally around the 750 mark, Glenbuck provided association football with more than fifty professionals in something less than fifty years.

Shanks' memory is revered not simply for what he achieved, but for the manner in which he set about accomplishing it and for the man that he was. Though he won his fair share of the trophies that football can offer as player and then manager that is perhaps the smallest part of his story. Supporters love and respect the man not simply the winner. It is memories of his enthusiasm for the game, the intensity of his commitment, his insistence that his standards should be upheld and his undisguised feelings for the people who stood on the terraces that are most convincingly recalled when remembering his career. All these traits were legacies of his upbringing, the many formative experiences that shaped the way young Willie Shankly looked at the world.

Indeed it would be unforgivable not to delve into the richness of his early life and the development and character of the town of his birth. That very birthplace is steeped in footballing significance – Glenbuck, the home of the celebrated junior side the Glenbuck Cherrypickers, in the county of Ayrshire, the same mining territory that gave the game those other managerial giants Jock Stein and Matt Busby. Football provided the great escape for ambitious young men who wanted to leave the real hard work of the mine behind them, to flee from the enveloping darkness of the pit and go out to make a living in God's fresh air. Just as in some places today boxing is the way out of the working class ghettos, so football was the passport to a wider world for the young men of Glenbuck.

To concentrate solely on football would be to misunderstand Glenbuck and its environs, its people and their ilk in similar mining villages across Ayrshire. The communities of that time bred a certain kind of man; strong with native intelligence and an abiding sense of right and wrong, powerful yet with an empathy for their neighbours, idiosyncratic individuals who worked for the common good. Men like Stein, Busby and Shankly.

'His way of working was individualistic while yet commanding collectivity. He loved the common people en masse but often quarrelled with the single individual among them. He had difficulty with figures of authority but always encouraged the young.' Those words could have been written about Bill Shankly, yet in fact they refer to another great miner who first rose to national prominence in Cumnock, a town just a few miles from Glenbuck itself. The description comes from Caroline Benn's biography of Keir Hardie, one of the founding fathers of the Labour Party. The comparison with Shankly is neither as fanciful nor as highfalutin as it might first appear, for many of those that he went on to work with suggested that had football not been his passion, he too could have been a great socialist leader, perhaps in the trade union movement. Robert Burns, another kindred spirit and one of Shankly's heroes, a man that he described as 'poet, philosopher, prophet' was also born into poverty in Ayrshire. Just why so many great Scots should have been fostered in such an area requires examination for in the greatness of his fellows lies the key to Shankly's character.

The Glenbuck that the Shanklys came to know started to evolve around 1800, as the nation began its transformation from agriculture to industry, a move that was to culminate in the exploitation of the rich seams of coal that were soon discovered throughout Ayrshire. The New Mills Weaving Company opened for business in Glenbuck in 1760, allowing the village to expand to a population of almost 600 within just a few years, but it was as the industrial age gathered momentum that Glenbuck came into its own.

Rich mineral deposits were discovered in the area, exploited ironically enough in such a fiercely Scottish village, by English businessmen. Just a few years later at the turn of the century, Glenbuck was the home to 800 people with public housing having been built for the workforce. Industry comprised an ironworks with its foundry and blast furnace, a limestone quarry, two dedicated ironstone pits, two coal mines and two pits that gave up both coal and ironstone.

In the last decade, we've heard much about the special nature of coal mining communities, the close knit relationships engendered in a village built on dark, dangerous, claustrophobic work. That's perfectly true today in an industry with a vastly improved, if still imperfect, safety record. How much more important must it have been in the early nineteenth century to know that you could rely implicitly on your friends, family, workmates and neighbours at a time when private mine owners were notoriously reticent when it came to spending their brass on improving working conditions and standards of safety? Certainly when almost every family was dependent in some way or another on the mining industry, dependent on a way of life that forever flirted with the possibility of fatal accidents, it was inevitable that people would come together and accept their neighbours for what they were, rather than sniping at one another. In such communities, everyone had to pull their weight. Letting the side down could have had disastrous consequences. The people were further forced together by the closure of the ironworks in 1813, an event which had a traumatic economic effect on the town and led to the first great exodus through the following generation as people sought work elsewhere.

In the still novel surroundings of heavy industry, the people of Glenbuck were drawn together both in adversity and in the attempt to improve their lot; if the mines had brought heavy, back-breaking work to the village, they had also brought better money to a village that had hitherto been prey to disease on a terrible, if fairly typical scale. As Glenbuck expanded to take in nine pits with names like 'Spireslack', 'The Lady', 'Grasshill' and 'Galawhistle', the townspeople banded together to improve standards of cleanliness in the town, to clean up the gutters and the dunghills that had been at their doors. Over many years, things improved; although the village was inevitably grimy in appearance – the discharges from the coal-mines saw to that – the miners and particularly their wives became increasingly houseproud. By the 1880s, J.M. Hodge wrote in his *Through The Parish Of Muirkirk* that Glenbuck was filled with 'tidy little houses with garden plots in front or rear'. A contemporary of Bill Shankly's, Jean Roberts, then Jean Ferguson, remembers that by the 1920s, the 'women kept the houses like little palaces', a feat of industry when you remember that the men would come home from the pit caked in coal dust and would have to wash at home. Such was their dedication to their homes that they provided the only source of rivalry as 'the women were inclined to vie with one another about houses. Someone got a piano at one time, so then they all wanted one!'

In the homogenised world of today where one town is very much the same as another, living in communities that have long since fallen apart as people become ever more isolated from one another, it's desperately difficult to imagine that a place like Glenbuck ever existed. Glenbuck was not the ideal-ised vision of age old Britain that politicians like to conjure up when they discuss the erosion of the nation's values, values which they have done more than most to eradicate. It was not a village filled with old maids cycling to and fro distributing scones to clean and shiny children. Glenbuck was a raw, hard boned environment, a working town where everyone had a tough job to do but where they could be relied upon to do their bit without complaint, where everyone was entitled to go about their own business without incurring the displeasure of others and where people stuck together when the need arose. Again, Jean Roberts recalls that 'it was a very happy village. We probably had a little more money because my father was the station master, but it didn't make any difference to anyone, there were no comments, no nastiness, no petty jealousies at all. Even during the strike when my father was still earning money, no-one ever said "it's all right for you!".'

Essentially then, community and solidarity were the themes of life in Glenbuck and its inhabitants worked hard to improve their lot. Organised schooling was established in 1876 though there had been a schoolmaster giving some lessons there since 1806, while a church was built from funds of £2,000 raised by the villagers in 1882, an enormous sum in those days. Sport too played a part in the life of the village and those around it. In the village of Douglas for example, just a few miles to the east of Glenbuck, a young man by the name of John Shankly was causing quite a stir in the local athletics world as a middle distance runner through the 1890s, even beating the celebrated Canty Young over the half mile. Dedicated to maintaining his fitness, he was a strong man, powerfully built and useful at most distances; even in later life he would regularly walk the eight-mile round trip to Muirkirk, to visit the nearest cinema, his greatest form of relaxation.

A tailor by trade, as Glenbuck's coal mining industry continued healthily through the final years of the last century, it was no surprise that he should move there to look for work. Naturally enough given the circumstances of the miners, John found most of his work in repairing and altering a variety of garments for as his son Bill was to remark many years later in his autobiography 'if you could alter clothes you could make a bigger living out of that than making clothes'. It was a talent that ran in the family, particularly through the female line, and it probably accounts for Bill's own insistence on high standards of dress in later life; few could ever accuse Bill Shankly of being anything less than immaculately turned out throughout his life. Other good habits for a professional athlete were picked up from his father too – the Shankly house was teetotal and nor did they smoke.

All the boys took after their father in many ways. They were good athletes, strong on self-discipline; Bill was later to remark that it was a bad day for the world when boys were no longer frightened of their father. John Shankly was not an aggressive man however, but one who demanded and commanded respect, a stickler for standards of behaviour which he drummed into his children from an early age. Bill remembered that 'we were brought up to be 100% honest ... our father was a fiery fighting man with strong principles. Very strong principles indeed. He knew the Bible as well as anyone alive ... He had an unquenchable spirit which I luckily inherited.'

As in so many of Glenbuck's families however, it was John's wife, Barbara, who ran the household. Barbara came from one of Glenbuck's most celebrated families, the Blyths. Her brother Bob, who rejoiced in the nickname 'Reindeer', was reckoned to be the fastest sprinter in the village, timed at 11 seconds for the 100 yards dash. He went on to make his name further afield, playing top class football for Glasgow Rangers, Middlesbrough, Preston and Dundee before becoming player-manager and finally chairman at Portsmouth. A second brother, Billy, plied his footballing trade at Portsmouth, Preston and Carlisle before joining Bob as an administrator and director and then chairman of Carlisle. As we shall see later, Billy had a great influence on Bill Shankly's career in the game.

Bill, or Willie as he was more commonly known, was born on 2 September 1913, the ninth of ten children, youngest of five boys. Like the others before him, he was born in the family home, in Auchenstilloch Cottages, known locally as 'Miner's

Row' or 'Monkey Row'. Jean Roberts lived just outside the village with her parents at the local station, but she spent much of her childhood in Glenbuck and naturally enough attended the local school in a class below Willie Shankly who was a few years her senior. Her memory of the cottages is of 'very comfortable little houses and of course in winter they had warm fires from the coal. I think the Shanklys were one of the main families in the village because there were so many of them. In the Monkey Row they had two houses next to one another and knocked them into one so that they could all get in. The beds were built into the walls like bunks. Later on there were some new council places built, and the Shanklys got one of those.'

Inevitably with ten children to look after, life was sometimes a struggle for the Shankly clan, even if not all of them would be at home at any one time. Bill recalled later that his mother was his greatest inspiration in life and he would often marvel at her devotion to raising the family; he told journalists 'I told you that all the Shanklys were total abstainers. Well, I was wrong. We had a bottle of whisky in a cupboard. It came out of that cupboard ten times – once each time to help my wonderful mother in childbirth. She achieved a miracle of dedication. I try, but mine is nothing in comparison.'

His feelings for his mother were shared not only by the rest of the family, but by the rest of the villagers, Jean Roberts recalling her as 'a wonderful mother. She kept the whole family together and wherever they went to work, they'd always come back home. Mr. Shankly was kind of quiet, quite a small man but I can't remember him having all that much work to do sometimes. I don't know how they managed so well. She would make them tatties and neaps (potatoes and turnips) and they were never deprived. I always looked forward to seeing her. You were never left outside on the doorstep, you always went in for a cup of tea, though that was true of the whole village.' Bill's memory of his childhood was similar, though he maintained: 'our father earned quite a good wage for the times but with such a big family to feed and clothe and such primitive conditions in the village we had to fight for everything ... How did my mother feed ten of us on a humble tailor's income in a little mining village? Imagine your wife bathing the children in front of the fire. All the water from this primitive house had to be brought from outside. I never saw a bathroom until I left Glenbuck.'

Barbara Shankly couldn't have brought up such a hungry brood on a shoestring without having her wits about her though. 'We kept a few hens,' Jean remembers, 'so we would take a few eggs up to Mrs. Shankly. She'd always give me a penny for myself for bringing the eggs up to her, but she always knew exactly what price the eggs should be even before my mother did!' Undeniably sharp, Barbara Shankly was universally liked throughout the village for her willingness to help anyone in trouble and for the way in which she and her husband John brought up their family.

The Shankly boys all managed to avoid the preordained path of a lifetime down the pits by virtue of their footballing skills. Alec, or Sandy as the family knew him, was the eldest boy. He had played football at inside forward for Ayr United prior to the outbreak of the Great War, whereupon he went into the Royal Scots Fusiliers and then the Royal Flying Corps. With his career over, he found himself a miner once more. Jimmy played as centre half and then centre forward, taking in spells at Portsmouth, Halifax, Carlisle United, Sheffield United, Southend and Barrow, his final club before retirement in 1933. He was a particular inspiration to the young Willie, though not for his masculine achievements on the football field; he felt that Jimmy was perhaps the finest man he ever knew because when he was away at his various clubs, he never forgot his parents, brothers and sisters back home. In the summer he'd come back to Scotland to help out and in the winter, whatever he could spare from his wage packet went back to Glenbuck to support his family, a dedication to duty that Bill was to prize above all else in later life.

The middle brother, John, was an outside right for Portsmouth, Luton Town, Alloa, Blackpool and Greenock Morton. Not so hardy as the rest of the family, he trained too hard during his time at Portsmouth and was out of the game for three years at Luton with a strained heart muscle. He had to return to Glenbuck to recover and again, when his career was over, he went back to the village and the pit, while his mother continued to watch over his failing health. Tragically, if somehow appropriately, John's death in 1960 came in footballing surroundings, after suffering a severe heart attack at Hampden Park during the Real Madrid versus Eintracht Frankfurt European Cup Final, finally passing away that night in hospital. The fourth brother, Bob, was closest to Bill in every way, going on to have a very successful career in football management, notably with Dundee, who he took into the later stages of the European Cup, and Falkirk after having played there and with Alloa.

The boys didn't get things all their own way at home though, for there were five sisters to contend with, girls who were perhaps more high-spirited than their brothers. In much the same way as the boys were predestined for work as coal-miners, the girls saw careers in domestic service ahead of them; the difference was, of course, that football did not offer them an escape route! Because there were so many men in the house, usually with one or more of the boys working down the mines, Jean Roberts remembers that the Shanklys followed the tradition of the larger village families. 'Generally, there would be an older daughter kept at home to help her mother with the house, to look after the younger children and the men when they came home from the pit. There was a lot of work, washing all the clothes. Of course there was no way of washing the clothes at home so they had to carry all those heavy pit things out to the wash house and clean them there. If your father was a miner, there was always plenty to do at home. The Shankly girls took turn about. One would go away to service because there was just no other work for them to do – the minister's wife would get work for them with her well-to-do sisters in Edinburgh. I do know that they were all very highly thought of when they went away, they were great workers.'

The five sisters, Netta, Elizabeth, Isobel, Barbara and Jean, all had parts to play in village life and in the life of young Bill. Netta and Isobel for instance were the girls with the responsibility for washing the boys' footballing clothes. Elizabeth was the life and soul of Glenbuck, 'she could always give you the news' according to Jean Roberts. 'They were all very outgoing, but we used to call Liz the loudspeaker. She'd come down to the station to pick up the newspapers for the village – Willie would sometimes come with her – but she'd a loud voice and you could hear her long before you could see her! She was as good as a local paper too, collecting news from the houses and passing it on as she went.'

Jean was equally animated. 'She was in the same two-class classroom that I was in. She was always being told to "sit still" which was just impossible for her. She had fiery red hair like her sister Bel, a real character, full of mischief but good fun. She was the only one in the family who went on to Higher Grade school in Muirkirk, perhaps because she was the youngest. We had to go by bus and on the first morning, we new ones had to put up with a bit of ragging and we were rather intimidated by it all, but not Jean! She and her friend Mary Tait always gave as good as they got. They always sat at the back of the bus and one day Mary fell out when the door burst open; she wasn't hurt but Jean made quite sure the bus company knew all about it and replaced the stockings she damaged in the fall!' With a sharp wit, the young Jean was obviously similar to the Bill Shankly who later became a national figure through his TV appearances. As Jean Roberts continues, 'She was very funny when the class photos came, her remarks were really rich. She didn't spare herself, she'd say things like "Look at me! I've got eyes like peas in a bottle!"'

Young Willie naturally held his family in the very highest esteem and it's easy to see why. His parents were able to create a warm and comforting home despite the privations of the time and his mother in particular seems to have had endless patience to help her deal with the children. Recognising that they would probably be all too soon cast into lives of hard work with little respite, she indulged them whenever she could, even when Bob and Willie would play football indoors. Each Sunday at the tea table, they would blow up balloons and play head tennis, breaking vases as they went, yet Barbara Shankly would never reproach them for it. Perhaps, with Sandy and Jimmy already having played the game for a living, she felt that supporting her younger children in their love of football might be the best way of providing them with a better life for themselves. Whatever the reasons, the Shankly boys were never short of encouragement, surely the most important nourishment a child can receive.

Back in the 1910s and 1920s, social life in most small industrialised villages was centred around three things: the church, the pub and the school. As already noted, the local church was opened in 1882 having been paid for by public subscription. It was established in the Protestant Church of Scotland faith but by the time Willie Shankly was growing up, the church was no longer central to village life, Jean Roberts confirming that 'it wasn't a lively church. The minister and his wife were very nice but the miners weren't inclined to go to church. I suppose they were glad of the rest on a Sunday. It was the farmers and a few of the miners' wives that went.'

In fact, Glenbuck mirrored the way in which organised religion was fragmenting across the country in the early days of the century for many reasons. The strict regime of Calvinist Presbyterianism imposed restrictions of behaviour that hardworking men no longer had any time for. They believed, perfectly understandably, that their enormous efforts to earn a living for their families meant that they were entitled to some rewards – perhaps to take a drink every now and again, to gamble a little money on card games, to enjoy a day's rest before the working week started. While Mr. McKenzie, Glenbuck's minister, was well liked, the church that he represented had begun to mean less and less to his potential congregation. The miners may well have thought that their whole-hearted acceptance of the Protestant work ethic was evidence enough of their spiritual integrity. A failure to attend church did not necessarily mean that the people were atheists or agnostics of course. In fact, their behaviour is very similar to that of millions today who have evolved their own form of Christianity. In later life for instance, Mrs. Shankly, then alone at home with her son John, liked to spend her evenings having Bill Smith, of the Christian Brethren, come to the family home and read to her from the Bible. She brought up her children in the Christian faith, even if churchgoing wasn't always on the agenda.

One characteristic of the people was their distaste for imposed sectarian barriers. Rather than try to classify people by their beliefs and exclude one another from any kind of social gathering on that basis, Glenbuck was a community that believed in bringing people together, that they should concentrate on the ideals that brought them together rather than minor disagreements on emphasis that might drive them apart. It is little wonder then that there was a Christian Brethren hall in the village. Today, the Brethren's importance has been severely diminished, but its philosophy is pertinent to the way in which Bill Shankly thought about life. It sought to create a unity or fellowship, standing firmly against the practice of alienating any particular branch of faith by the imposition of strict, dogmatic rules. Brethren ideology frowned on organised religion and doctrinal formulations, seeing the Bible itself as the only word by which people should live. It's been compared with Southern Baptist sensibilities in America, the idea of no smoking, no drinking, no enjoying yourself, but the reality is far more complex than that. Central is the concept of social service and in the last century they took a pivotal role in the establishment of orphanages and charitable institutions throughout Britain, and particularly in Scotland. In order to achieve their ends, the Brethren community is more than willing to join forces not only with other congregations but with other denominations when the need arises. In Glenbuck for instance, the Brethren Sunday School would organise annual outings on which all were welcome: 'We might get to the seaside at Ayr by train,' remembers Jean Roberts, 'or if we weren't so affluent that year, we'd go out to a local farmer's field by horse and cart and have a picnic.' Once more, the pattern of life in Glenbuck, the pattern which so influenced Bill Shankly, is clear – do not judge others, help the community, act as a unified group.

Alongside the Brethren, the Rechabites were particularly strong in the area. In essence, the Rechabite ideal was quintessential behaviour for that community; the establishment of a friendly society. It is significant that one of the few stores in town was a co-operative. Those who subscribed to the Rechabite methods gave money to a general fund against which they could draw in future for funeral expenses, or a wage if the man of the house was injured or taken ill. Effectively, they were a local insurance company. There were other facets to the Rechabites' operations though as Jean Roberts recalls. 'There were big certificates up on the wall in a lot of the houses for the Rechabites to show that they were teetotal. I suppose that's how they managed so well, they didn't spend money on anything else but the house and the family. They were awful against drink most of them.'

Many argue that the problems of alcohol in the final quarter of the nineteenth century afflicted our cities every bit as savagely as the drug culture does today and the Temperance movement continued its work well into the new century, spurred on by memories and graphic accounts of the effect of the demon drink on family life. Inevitably, it had been the poor, seeking recreation and a means of retreat from their dismal working lives and appalling conditions of dirt and squalor in the industrial towns who had become besotted with drink. Consequently, the family's earnings found their way to the local brewery while a man's wife and children might live in fear of his violent temper, exacerbated by drink; it sounds a little like some quaint melodrama, but a hundred years ago it was a very real and increasing social problem. In modern terms, the Rechabites created self-help groups where the victims of alcoholism could find refuge and assistance in over-coming their difficulties. Their work had a great impact. By the 1920s, by Jean Roberts' testament there was 'only the odd problem where a father might drink'. Even so, Glenbuck did have its own pub, The Royal Arms, and it could become rather boisterous at the end of the week. This was the only side of the town that Bill did not take to for some of the inhabitants would criticise the miners for taking too much drink on a Saturday night. Inevitably Bill stood up for the rights of those workers to relax in whatever way they saw fit after putting in a hard week's work.

The Temperance movement was especially important in Scotland, having roots in strict Calvinist doctrine, but it also grew from increased levels of political activity. Ironically it was this that helped advance the cause of socialism in Scotland to the detriment of religion. It must be remembered that the years surrounding Bill's birth were times of great political radicalism, where ordinary people were beginning to question their status as mere chattels in the hands of land or factory owners and were starting to organise, to fight in a unified manner for improved rights. It was also a time in which sectarianism was being questioned and re-evaluated as another means by which the working classes could be divided. Around the country, politics was regarded as a vehicle for change. The working people had begun to turn away from the church as union activity and the march of socialism seemed to provide them with a more potent voice. While the church might seek to mitigate the awfulness of their circumstances, political engagement was a means of breaking the stranglehold which locked them into that depressing way of life. It was a lesson that the Shanklys learned the hard way and throughout his life, Bill continued his political self-education, reading up on the subject when time would allow though he became increasingly disenchanted with the behaviour of MPs – what he would make of the current crop does not bear thinking about.

With its standards of equality, Glenbuck can seem to

resemble some kind of socialist utopia but in reality it was far from that. People were forced to help one another out because their very existence meant that someone would always be in trouble, perhaps due to a mining accident, illness in the family and so on. Mining work was terribly hard physically, 'an awful job' as Jean Roberts makes clear. 'They'd come home covered in coal dust and there were no baths at the pit until very late on. Before then the men had to come and have a bath in the house; there was no water in the houses so it all had to be carried in from a pump outside and then heated on the range.' Small wonder that the miners wanted social change to come and come quickly.

According to Hodge in his *Through The Parish Of Muirkirk*, there had always been a communist element in Glenbuck for 'ground here was given to a few communists to work out their pet ideas'. While it would be inaccurate to suggest that Glenbuck was some kind of Marxist hotbed, there was plenty of evidence that the village was on the move towards the political left and the headmaster's report as late as June 1929 suggested that 'there seems to be a spirit of "Bolshevism" in the village and some children would "kick" against any attempt at discipline'; this minor change in the atmosphere might be ascribed to the sense of hopelessness that was by then enveloping a dying village as well as feelings engendered by the miners' strike three years previously. Jean Roberts again remembers that 'they were very strongly Labour. James Brown was the candidate for South Ayrshire for many years and he always got in because they wouldn't vote Conservative but I know he was too mild for some of them, he wasn't a keen socialist. There was a communist element there, they called themselves red hot socialists which was a bit stronger than just Labour. It was around the time of Keir Hardie and they supported him very strongly, I remember that there was some celebration in Cumnock where he was speaking and some of the men went on the train to hear him.'

It came to be something of a motif of Bill Shankly's career that he found some directors difficult to tolerate at his various clubs. There was a general feeling of animosity that could clearly be traced back to his youth and the atmosphere in which he grew up, one where mistrust for the mine owners and the ruling classes was rife. In particular Shankly found it hard to disguise his contempt for men who might espouse their Christian values on a Sunday having spent the week trying to swindle their workforce, condemning them to live in what we would now regard as abject poverty: 'You are born what you are, born a socialist. The politics that are in me is me. Your politics have to reflect what your religious beliefs tell you. How can a man vote for one party at one election and then change his mind to vote for another?'

Certainly his politics were heavily ingrained for he never lost those beliefs. Jack Mindel, with whom he served in the R.A.F. during the Second World War, remembers that 'his attitude to the Conservatives was very simple. He objected to them. He knew all about capitalism, he'd seen the poverty in Ayrshire, grown up in it. Whenever there was a scandal about the treatment of working people, Bill was ready to stand up for them. Those politics came from experience, working in the mines, seeing the conditions people lived and worked in. He couldn't understand anyone from that area being anything but Labour.'

As well as the political edge to the village, Bill received further socialist education at school where he immediately took to the works of Robert Burns. Combining the two strands of influence on his personal philosophy, he later remarked that 'Burns was an early socialist – the first was Jesus Christ of course. He didn't think that God made people to be unequal, he thought everyone should share in the work and the rewards.' His interest extended to a wide knowledge of Burns' life and the respect paid to his memory – 'he was a great favourite in Russia, they even brought out postage stamps in his honour'. When his time came to appear as a castaway on *Desert Island Discs*, the book he selected was *The Life Of Robert Burns* by James Back. He was aware of his failings too, such as his eye for the ladies. 'In his day,' Bill remarked, 'if a man committed fornication, the local minister would humiliate him in front of the congregation by sitting him on the Cutty Stool. Burns had a season ticket!' Such an interest in the minutiae of his hero's life, in his works and in his ideals gives the lie to the commonly held belief that Bill Shankly was solely devoted to football with time for nothing else. His was a bigger spirit than football alone could contain.

Paradoxically, football's greatest evangelist, its biggest fanatic, was moulded and driven by forces beyond the game to such an extent that his footballing philosophy was his philosophy on life in microcosm. This was shown when, on his retirement, Bill was given his own chat show on Radio City in Liverpool where one of his guests was Harold Wilson, then still the Prime Minister. A Merseyside MP, Wilson's decision to make time for the programme speaks volumes for the esteem in which Bill was held in the country and the two enjoyed a fascinating conversation in which Shankly's grasp of political philosophy was not found wanting. The conversation inevitably turned to Burns and Wilson's thoughts on the poet echoed those which many held of Shankly: 'he was not a theoretical socialist, but was a socialist because he felt it was right, felt a bond with his fellow man and wanted to see their lot improved'. With such an attitude to life, it's obvious why Shankly was so loved by spectators around the country for he was clearly one of their own.

The study of Burns was of course an integral part of school life just as the school was central to the life of Glenbuck. 'The headmistress, Miss Bain, was very nice. She was one of four teachers who lived in a big house that was built for them, a kind of hostel. She arranged concerts in the village hall with the children,' recollects Jean Roberts. It was important that the teachers had excellent relations with their pupils for good attendance records contributed to the size of education grant that the school received. In the severe winters that the village fell prey to, often the majority of the children would be kept at home and there are records which note that those that made it in would be 'crying with the cold'. Conditions at the school were primitive, though probably little different from most schools at the time – in May 1920 for example, two members of the school board made mention of 'the most unsatisfactory sanitary arrangements' and seven months later recommended that 'scholars should be given facilities to wash their hands etc.'. It wasn't until September of the following year that 'the pail system had disappeared and up to date flush closets introduced'. Growing up in such humiliating conditions while hearing from his sisters of the comparative splendour of the houses in which they were in service, it's small wonder that Bill Shankly had little time for the upper classes.

School could be great fun for the children too, though as Jean Roberts points out 'no-one really made any stir but they didn't dare then. Mr. Rodger, the headmaster, was a great one for the strap, boys or girls.' Though young Willie Shankly was a quiet boy in keeping with such discipline, he had his moments as he recalled later. 'One morning, the teacher went out for a minute so I got up the ladder by the clock and put it forward from half eleven to twelve o'clock so it would be time for dinner and just as I was on top, the teacher got back. I thought "Good God, this is it, I'm gonna get killed" but he kept his head and said "Right Shankly, you're so keen on the clock, you can sit up there with it for half an hour." I was stuck up that ladder for ever and all the class were killing themselves laughing, it was terrible.'

Generally at school 'the children all got on very well' according to Jean Roberts. 'Nobody was neglected and the teachers were very good, they created a lovely atmosphere. A lot of the children did well and would have done a lot better if they'd had the chance but they usually had to leave so young. You'd go up to the equivalent of the Eleven Plus and then if you wanted further education you had to leave to go to Muirkirk. You'd have maybe three each year doing that and the rest stayed at Glenbuck until they were fourteen, school leaving age. Most of the boys went down the pit. Some went even earlier, they got exemptions from school if they got a job.

There was nothing else for them really.' The problem for all the families was money and being able to send their children on to Muirkirk – not only would they be incurring the expense of educating their child, they would have to forgo the all-important wage packet that that child might be able to bring into the house. 'I think that the Shanklys were all reasonably clever at school and could have gone to Higher Grade. Mr. Rodger did his best to encourage the children to stay on but most of the families in the village just couldn't see a way to do it.' It's a sentiment with which Jack Mindel concurs: 'Bill wasn't an educated man but given the opportunity he had the natural ability to understand things.' Bill himself put it more simply: 'Me havin' no education, I had to use my brains.'

However, even as early as 1922 with Willie just nine years old, the boys were having to question their future as Glenbuck was down to just one operational pit and as employment prospects looked increasingly bleak, people began to drift away from the town. There had been a miners' strike the previous year when 'necessitous scholars' had been fed breakfast and a mid-day meal at the school following arrangements made by the Miners Union and the School Management Committee. This help was extended to Saturday and Sunday too, another example of the way people would all muck in together. It was becoming more and more obvious that Glenbuck was in terminal decline yet there was, short of migration, little on offer but the possibility of a life down the pit, an opportunity that also seemed likely to be taken away from him.

Nevertheless the miners bore their hardship with fortitude even if the spirit was being beaten out of them. Throughout the 1920s, the mining industry was systematically attacked by both the mine owners and the Baldwin Government. In July 1925, miners had been brought to the brink of another strike when, thanks to inadequate investment and a currency crisis, the industry was on its knees. The owners' solution was longer hours, wage cuts, closure of pits and general rationalisation of the trade – effectively forcing the workers to bear the entire cost of improving the industry's position. Under the slogan 'not a penny off the pay, not an hour on the day' the miners won a subsidy from the Government with the threat of strike action. The subsidy was removed nine months later – by which time the Government had had the time to acquire a position of strength by stockpiling coal, shades of 1984 – and the Government demanded wage reductions of ten per cent and an extension of the seven-hour working day among other measures. This led to the nine-day wonder of the General Strike of May 1926. When that resistance was crushed, the miners were forced to strike alone for a further seven months until they were eventually starved back to work on worse conditions. In Parliament, George Hardie, Keir's brother, claimed that the Government 'were going to risk smashing British industry and commerce in an effort to smash the Miners' Federation', but in general the Labour Party and the rest of the union movement turned its back on the strikers. Perhaps this was the reason for Bill Shankly's mistrust of MPs.

Certainly it allowed him to see extreme hardship close up, coming as it did the year before he was due to leave school for good. Soup kitchens operated in the school, the local co-operative gave credit and the villagers tried to eke out their resources as far as they could. Bill remembered having to go hungry on occasion but again, it was an experience that he later regarded as character building. As a manager, he would often seemingly talk in riddles, some of his more outlandish statements rarely seeming to make a great deal of sense. One of his more famous comments was 'I never cheated. If I played against my wife, I might break her leg, but I wouldn't cheat her.' The view of John Roberts, who helped him write his autobiography, was that 'he had a code which not everybody would agree with, in football and in life. It was simply that you had to be totally hard but within the rules, to win fairly but at the limits. It was something that I think evolved from his past and the challenges he'd faced. In the book he talked about himself as a boy stealing a bag of poor quality coal from the tons that weren't going to be used. He passed it off as just mischief, which it was, but at the same time he'd think how unfair it was that his family had no coal during a very harsh winter while there were mountains of it going to waste. When you remember the very hard conditions of the 1920s and 1930s, and the sense of grievance that the miners and their families had against the mine owners, it's easy to see how you could come to look at life in that way.'

Some of the miners tried to get their hands on some meat by keeping lurchers according to Jean Roberts. 'They went out on the hills after rabbits, though it wasn't just during the strike! Of course they were poaching, but the farmers turned a blind eye and I suppose they were glad to get rid of the rabbits!' Strong, powerful men, as they had to be for their trade, the miners were 'great ones for meat and the butcher's cart would have to come around two or three times a week in normal times. Whatever shift they came off, they'd have a full meal waiting for them at home. Later on when Willie was on television talking about looking after his teams and feeding them well, I used to think about those times.'

By 1927, Willie was ready to leave school and was lucky enough to find work in the mines at the princely sum of 2s 6d ($12\frac{1}{2}$ pence) per day – the exodus from the village meant that there was still little or no unemployment. Already similar in type to those that toiled underground, this close working proximity forged even stronger ties that were to stay with him through his life. Initially working at the pit top, emptying coal trucks, after six months he found himself working at the bottom. His job was one of extreme physical exertion as he recalled in his autobiography: 'I would shift full trucks and put them into the cages and then take out empty trucks and run them along to where they were loaded ... at the end of an eight-hour shift, I'd probably run ten or twelve miles.' Terribly hard at the time, it undoubtedly helped him build that granite-like physique that played such a prominent part in his career as a player.

Finally, young Willie worked his way to the back of the pit, locked away from the world above for eight hours at a stretch as the coal face was blasted away before him. Though too young to actually dig the coal, he had to endure the same hardships and became part of the family in those terribly primitive conditions. Bill Shankly was later described by many of his colleagues as having a fetish for fresh air. It's easy to see why. It's also easy to understand just why he demanded absolute commitment and honesty from his team mates and players once he had carved out a niche for himself in professional football. He had already worked alongside men who were the salt of the earth, who did an awful job for poor rewards. His view was simply that once you've been a miner, lived with the threat of imminent disaster, lived with the threat of contracting bronchitis or silicosis and any number of other occupational illnesses, everything else in life is easy. Life itself becomes a privilege that should not be abused. One of Shankly's greatest lieutenants at Liverpool, Emlyn Hughes, remembers that aside from football, he was a great enthusiast for life itself. 'When we were in for training, he'd go outside and say to us "Beautiful morning boys. Great to be alive, breathing in God's air." '

As already shown, the miners might enliven their hard lives with a drink or two after work but gambling was another of their favourite pastimes and the one 'vice' which Willie Shankly indulged in. Jean Roberts was aware that 'they had card schools out in the hills just outside the village and they were great ones for gambling but there was no badness attached to it', while in his autobiography Bill confirmed that while the stakes could be high 'there were no cheats'. Taking after his father, Willie also had a passion for the cinema, sometimes walking with him to Muirkirk. The gangster movies were a real favourite and in later years he used his voice like Jimmy Cagney used a machine gun, blasting those around him with withering, staccato outbursts. Visits to the cinema could be eventful though in those pioneering days – he recalled later that he went to see Al Jolson in *The Singing Fool*. The projector broke down so frequently that the screening wasn't completed until 3 a.m.

An isolated town, Glenbuck was quite insular and trips such

as those Sunday School outings were a big thing. Though some of the men occasionally made it to Glasgow to watch Rangers play at Ibrox, the people were rather naive. In spite of that, perhaps because of it, the village was full of characters and in later life Bill loved to talk about them; men like Barlinnie Swell and Bomber Brown. Down the pit, Bill would have heard many tall tales and it's more than likely that it was this, alongside his own natural razor sharp wit, that helped him become the highly quotable figure who was to delight pressmen thirty years later.

His tenure as a miner was short lived, however, for by 1930, he was unemployed. The oncoming depression that savaged the world was in full spate in Glenbuck, the demand for coal so low that only one or two shifts might be required per week. Drawing the dole was another harsh lesson that he assimilated quickly and never forgot when life improved.

Even in the midst of the village's deprivation, though, there was always a game of football to take you away from your worries. The virtuous circle that enveloped football and Glenbuck is a chapter in itself.

chapter two

THE NURSERY

Organised football was one of the great success stories of the second half of the nineteenth century. In Scotland in particular, the game grew at an exponential rate and, by the 1880s, if your town or village didn't have its own competitive team there was something seriously wrong with your civic priorities. It was ironic indeed that football became the game of the ordinary people during the latter half of the century for a hundred years earlier the working classes had forsaken it. It had very strong roots in their own culture, yet it was the public schools which kept football alive in varying forms and degrees through the first half of the nineteenth century.

Football had often been used as a forum for political agitation in previous eras but with the introduction of well organised law enforcement agencies, such activity was stamped out and football itself no longer seemed to fulfil any function. Naturally enough, this development was to the liking of the establishment and not merely because it helped protect the status quo. As Britain became a heavily industrialised, urban nation in the Victorian age, the agricultural system, in which workers were allowed time off, began to break down. The extensive investment made in plant, machinery, factory buildings and so on required employers to operate at intense levels and to exploit the productive capacity to the full. In order to facilitate this, they began to deny workers any leisure time. Allied to that, the voracious manner in which industrial buildings ate up the available space in our towns meant there was little space to play football even when the opportunity and the desire still existed.

Mention has already been made of Bill Shankly as unintentional social engineer but it was this very turn of mind that brought football back to the masses sixty years before his birth. Though the literature of the period portrays vividly the squalor that abounded in the new towns, not all employers were exploitative and some philanthropists were keen to do something to help their workforce, understanding too the economic advantages – healthier employees might well become more productive. As James Walvin makes clear in his thorough study of the unfolding story of British football, *The People's Game*, these middle class, public school educated reformers felt that the ordinary working man would benefit both physically and mentally from regular recreation. Just as the first wave of football teams came from the privileged school system, the latter part of the century belonged to clubs who were initially little more than works outfits – Manchester United and West Bromwich Albion – or groups affiliated to the local church – Aston Villa and Everton. As the Victorians began to increase their obsession with the 'healthy body and healthy mind', sporting activity took an increasing grip on all sections of the population and organised games became the order of the day.

None of this detracted from the way in which ordinary people threw themselves into their game of choice – association football. Once it had returned to the fore, there was no stopping its growth for the conditions it required were all in place. Industrial workers had finally secured free Saturday afternoons in the 1850s, the railways meant that people had a new mobility which encouraged football teams to play their counterparts elsewhere, while the authorities were finally making ground available for recreation.

This was a pattern which was repeated all over Great Britain, though in Scotland the passion for the game had not ebbed as dramatically as it had in England. Football remained alive; perhaps this is the reason why English football came to rely so heavily on so many great Scottish players through the years, particularly in the period up to the Second World War, and why it was Scotsmen like Shankly, Busby and Stein who redefined the game in the post-war era. Certainly there is strong evidence to suggest that it was the Scots who first realised the importance of team-work in the 1870s.

Viewed logically, it was surely inevitable that the industrial era would give birth to the age of team-work. After all, by applying production-line values in a footballing context, it was the inescapable conclusion. Throughout the working week, men toiled as part of a team in a factory, on the railways, at the docks or in the mines. No one man was expected to be able to do every job demanded by the increasing complexity of the factory system. The watchword for the new economy was specialisation. So it was on the football field for the working man had now taken over the reins from the middle classes, all the more so as football became a professional sport. There was no financial incentive for educated men to waste their time on a poorly paid game. There was real money to be made in clerical, administrative or even entrepreneurial circles while the footballers were limited by the maximum wage. For a factory worker, even these restrictions failed to make a career in football anything but an attractive escape.

The loss of the amateur influence was central to the way football began to change. As Dr. Walvin points out in his book, amateurs wanted the chance to show off their skills in games and saw sport as a means of individual expression, hence their love of the dribbling game which required a degree of selfishness that would drive today's managers and supporters to apoplexy; it's worth remembering that prior to the seismic changes of the 1880s, teams took the field with seven or eight forwards and just a couple of backs. Men of substance did not want to be troubled with the utilitarian tasks of defending and tackling when at their leisure. As tactics began to gain in importance, the less disciplined amateurs left to play rugby and cricket. The parallel with cricket is striking for the amateur/professional divide often saw the working man doing the donkey work as a fast bowler while his part-time colleague tended to be the dashing, attacking stroke-maker. Cricket, as a series of individual battles, allowed the amateurs the freedom they no longer had in football. It was the advance of tactical thought, the intellectualisation of the sport, that was to finally root it in the working class.

Although the work experience did help to mould a new view, team play did evolve from a Scottish outlook. It was drawn from the wider experience they had of the game and their greater passion for it. While English football was going through its renaissance, the Scots were achieving a new maturity as tactical awareness was grafted on to a game that had previously been something of a free for all. The dribbling game was soon to be consigned to the past, though the Scottish fondness for ball players and exciting wing play persists.

Crucially, though, the Scots were first to uncover the basic truth by which Bill Shankly would live his professional life. It was nice to play the game, important to play it in the right way, essential to win. You could only enjoy it to the full if you gave of your best and came out on top for anything else would leave disappointment in its wake. A football club could only be at the heart of a community if it was successful; failure would mean that the locals would quickly lose interest, a truism that still holds good.

Just why Scotland had this harder, some might say more honest, attitude is a matter of conjecture. In England, football had been run by the ruling classes who played for the sake of playing. Though Scotland too had its gentry, they took a far less prominent role in national life and consequently a smaller part in the national game. Scottish football remained the preserve of ordinary people for whom the game was a release. These people worked hard and played hard; they saw little of value in the Corinthian spirit. If you were going to play the game, play it to win. If you just wanted the exercise, you could run round in circles. The mentality was simple – if you had a talent for football, why not exploit it to the full? The Scots were quicker to realise the potential of the game than their English counterparts and had the local infrastructure to implement their ideas. Scottish footballers also benefited from the fact that it was the only team sport of significance that survived. England's other great game, cricket, found it hard to get a foothold in Scotland for the space and facilities were not there, the game was far more expensive to mount while the harsher climate militated against it. Football was played the whole year round.

Junior football was to have a great impact on the Shankly family as a whole. Its introduction was instrumental in setting up the conveyor belt of talent that rolled on into the senior game and then, very often, into England. Here too, incidentally, the Scots had an enormous effect on the English leagues for it was the availability of talented Scotsmen that forced the introduction of professionalism in England and closed the final chapter on the game's amateur days. Despite its name, junior football in Scotland is a game for men, not boys. It is a tough, hard school that has educated countless Scots in the game before passing them on to the senior ranks. Naturally enough, the junior leagues were formed to give some sort of order to the local matches that were being played between villages and towns across Scotland, though given the Celtic determination to win, such games could hardly be termed 'friendlies'. Indeed junior games were, and still are, played with such intensity that even those schooled in the Old Firm derbies blench at the ferocity of the tackling. Off the field, Glenbuck itself saw sporadic outbreaks of violence in the early days of its club when, according to the Reverend M.H. Faulds' history of football in the village, 'it was not unusual for visiting teams to be pelted with stones ... though perhaps it was the referee after all who had the roughest time, especially if a pond was conveniently near.' Passions clearly ran high and while such behaviour, even if apparently intended partly in jest, could not be condoned it gives a clue as to the origins of Bill Shankly's own enthusiasm for the game. If you didn't know your football, you were out on a limb, Jean Roberts recalling that 'the whole village was centred around football. The girls would play too, we just grew up with it.'

Junior football set out its stall very early on, with the *Scottish Junior Football Annual* of 1886/87 attacking the 'selfish players' of the past and arguing that 'we now see a whole team com-

bining together ... for real scientific dribbling and passing,
football has now reached a platform it never previously occu-
pied', a comment that was only just beginning to be true of
English play. The intensity of league competition added a new
dimension, for each side was keen to win the various trophies
on offer. With so many teams throughout the county, Ayrshire's junior association was founded in 1880, perhaps the
earliest in the country, but true to its self-sufficient, rather
insular bent, it was slow to take its place at the national table.
The Junior Cup was first instigated in 1886/87 for example, but
Ayrshire's first representatives did not take part until 1889/90.

The towns and villages of that county were quite happy to
compete among themselves with the football team forming
the focal point of the village's recreation. In Glenbuck for
instance, *ad hoc* teams were formed to represent the different
mines where the players worked but in the late 1870s, the
time had come to form a village team which at first went
under the name Glenbuck Athletic. The team had to weather
considerable adversity in its early years. With space at a
premium in a village given over to mines and housing, they
had to pitch goals wherever they could. Their first ground was
soon lost when a pit shaft was sunk. Such were their problems,
the second field was literally on a hillside and it was some
little time before Athletic settled in their final home, Burnside
Park, so named because of the burn that ran along one side of
the pitch. To the other was the main road through the village
from where most spectators watched the games.

In its early days through into the 1890s, the side established
an extremely formidable reputation. Based on hard work,
strong tackling and neat incisive passing movements, Athletic
were able to win the Ayrshire Junior Cup in each of its first
three years from 1889/90 to 1891/92, taking the inaugural
Cup by beating Tarbolton 9-2. Among the players were Robert
Blyth, Shankly's uncle, and Alex Tait who was in the Tottenham Hotspur team that won the F.A. Cup for the first time
in 1901. The fact that he was joined in that team by another
Glenbuck alumnus, Alex Brown, speaks volumes for the early

impact this little hamlet had on professional football. In recognition, the authorities allowed Brown and Tait to take the
Cup, albeit briefly, to Glenbuck.

With such links to the professional game, inspiration for up
and coming youngsters was never in short supply. Allied to
that was the village fanaticism for Glasgow Rangers, their
team of choice. Naturally, this had its roots in the religious
sectarianism that is still a part of Glasgow derbies – Glenbuck
was a largely Protestant village and committed to the Rangers
cause. As an adult, Bill was to frown on such prejudice having
a say in the selection of your team, but by then he had already
grown up a Rangers man and could do nothing about his
allegiance. Visits to Ibrox, or, occasionally, Celtic Park, were a
highlight of his young life, all the more so since they were so
infrequent owing to cost: 'When we had the money, we used
to pay 1s 6d return fare on the train to Glasgow and I would
come away fired with the idea of playing like Davie Meiklejohn
of Rangers or Charlie Napier of Celtic for I was always a wing
half.'

Glenbuck somehow regularly mustered a team that could
almost have held its own in the senior game, yet it drew solely
upon the men who lived and worked in the village. Given
that the side was continually weakened by the exodus of
players going off to make their mark in the senior game, the
achievement is even more impressive. There was a terrific pride
attached to their exploits and this was enhanced by the fact
that the team became almost a family affair with the Shanklys,
Menzies and Taits dominating the club, positions in the side
being passed down the clan like some prized heirloom. It was
not only on the playing side that the locals got involved, but
also in the administration of the club, the supervision of
practice games and the collection of the players' weekly contribution of a shilling to cover the upkeep of the ground. Bill's
father John was a great stalwart of the club. Initially he played
for Glenbuck Athletic having previously turned out for his
home team in Douglas; his role later on was as a committee
man helping to arrange fixtures and so on. As a noted athlete,

his views on preparation and general fitness would have been well respected by the players and it appears likely that it was in this capacity that he made the greatest impact. It might be said that John was the first of the family to go into football management!

It can only be a matter of conjecture as to his exact role at the club for no records exist, but whoever was in charge of Glenbuck Athletic was clearly well versed in the niceties of the game. Right from the off, they played the then innovative formation of two full-backs, three half-backs and five forwards. As the Scots had impressed their desire to win on the game, they had tightened up defensively and the eight forward line-up was now a thing of the past. Physically of course, many of the miners who formed the majority of the team were ideal for defensive play – like Bill, they were powerful, thick-set men who were uncompromising in the tackle. It was left to the smaller fellows to take up positions at inside and outside forward. The junior leagues were still seen as the home of good football as the *Junior Annual* for 1894/95 made clear: 'Senior football is not improving in quality. Since professionalism has crept in, the old scientific game ... has been abandoned in favour of the forcible bashing game, which experience shows pays best in the struggle for cups and League Championships.' Clearly Wimbledon did not invent the long ball after all. The Junior game however 'is far more attractive to the spectator ... juniors are rising higher in public estimation.' The annual noted that a few senior teams still played enjoyable football, making special mention of Preston North End. It was no accident that Glenbuck provided seven players for the Deep-dale club, comprehensively schooled as they had been at home.

Perhaps because the 1890s brought no further trophies to Burnside Park, Athletic, seeking improved luck, changed their name to the more picturesque Cherrypickers, which had long since been the club's nickname. The change of name provided the change of fortune and the new century saw the Cherry-pickers become a real force in the local game once more. This period saw Glenbuck celebrated across the country – and even internationally – as a hotbed for the game. It united a village that was slowly winding down towards eventual oblivion but yet more important it convinced the locals that they could make a life for themselves as footballers, such were their skills. The older Shankly brothers made their early appearances and trophies once again came to the village – a treble in 1906 with the Cumnock Cup, Ayrshire Charity Cup and Mauchline Cup, while the Cumnock Cup was also won in 1901, 1903, 1904, 1905 and the Ayrshire Charity Cup again in 1910. Glenbuck was established as a football town with all that that implied. By the time Bill himself was born, the groundwork had been laid for any young lad who might fancy himself as a player.

By the time he was able to take a real interest in the game, the Cherrypickers had already provided around three dozen players to the senior ranks including some of his own brothers. Scottish and English clubs would often send scouts to watch them play and young Willie could rest secure in the knowledge that one day his chance would come. Later on he confirmed that 'when I got a chance to play for a junior team when I was just a boy . . . that's all I wanted, to get the jersey on and play.' It was a conviction that never wavered and helped him endure the years in the mines or drawing dole, when he was too young to play football at the highest level.

Having three much older brothers who were professional footballers is all the encouragement that any boy should require but if more were needed, Glenbuck provided it. In a powerfully nationalistic village, the fact that some of its sons had gone on to represent their country, and against the Auld Enemy at that, was cause for enormous pride. Alex Brown had been first to a Scotland cap playing twice against England in 1902 and 1904 and he had been followed by several others including John Crosbie who by then – the 1920s – was playing his football for Birmingham City. Like so many of the men who had left Glenbuck, Crosbie returned home for the summer, as Jean Roberts remembers. 'He was famous in the village for all that he had achieved but when he came back, there was nothing different about him. He knew that the boys looked up to him and he'd spend the summer playing football with them which was a great thing for them of course. I'm sure it encouraged them and inspired them to follow his lead.' Although football was the Shankly family business, he was suitably impressed by this great international who came from his own little town. This made it seem that while you had strength in your body, anything truly was possible. Yet the inspiration to be had from townsfolk does not account alone for the stream of players who found their way from Glenbuck to professional football. Just what was it about the village that created so many top quality players?

Without doubt, football was the greatest passion among the miners. Jean Roberts remembers that 'the older men played quoits but it was the football that kept the men going. It was a great therapy for them I think, away from the terrible work they did in the mines.' For all the reasons outlined earlier, football was the game of the workers, but Bill admitted later that there were more reasons than those. 'It's a cheap game to follow for those of us who hadn't much money to spend when we were off duty. Once you had a ball, there was nothing left to pay for countless hours of exciting sport.'

Where so many of Glenbuck's players scored over rivals was the spirit of team-work which existed within the village. The air of mutual co-operation which permeated every aspect of village life meant that on the field, players would instinctively combine with one another, would share the responsibility for play and would not indulge in any selfish ball playing. With football's increasing dependence on tactical acumen, the village was blessed with many men who would talk little else but football both at work and play. They were also fortunate in having men like John Shankly available, men who understood not just football but the general run of athletic disciplines and so could help organise effective and efficient training. The early pioneers from the town such as the Blyths started a snowball effect too – tales of their success away from home fired the ambitions of the next generation of players and so on. On their return, the likes of the Blyths and John Crosbie were generous enough to pool their experience with the rest of the town, helping youngsters improve their game. The traditions of the village team also helped maintain the impetus to succeed. Glenbuck lived under the threat of closure as the mining operations slowly began to wind down. Possibly for the men of the town the desire to make a career in professional football was rendered more urgent by the likelihood that if they failed there, they could also find themselves without work at the mines.

It can't be emphasised too strongly just what a transformation football could bring about in the life of a young miner. The danger and deprivations that they had to endure in the pits are almost impossible to imagine today but back in the 1920s and 1930s a young lad leaving school would be confronted with the prospect of fifty years of back-breaking work underground – yet living in the shadow of the ever present threat of unemployment, even this was a bonus. If you could postpone the inevitability of such work, perhaps dispel it for ever by playing football, that was a dream.

The ethics of the village were central to the philosophy of the many footballers who came out of it and particularly that of Bill Shankly. Whatever the religious persuasion of the village, the Protestant work ethic was their guiding light, whatever the nature of their business. The girls were renowned as great workers in the houses where they were in service; the miners worked long hours and achieved excellent levels of production; the women left at home maintained spotless houses, budgeted tightly and turned out clean, tidy children. If the people of the village had a single principle by which they lived, it was that they should give their all to the job in hand.

The greatest worry in the lives of the miners was the lack of job security. Many mine owners, like factory owners in other parts of the country, were quite deliberate and unashamed in their policy of keeping their workforce in line with the constant threat of unemployment. While the organisation of unions had helped secure a few basic rights for workers, they were still largely at the mercy of their employers. In the days before the welfare state came into being, loss of income could be even more ruinous than it is currently. Secure in that knowledge, there was never any lack of application at work; where today the term 'professional' simply means getting paid for a job, fifty years ago it implied a certain quality, standards of performance and level of dedication. Whatever your job, in order to keep your self-respect, you should do it as well as you could. If that job was with a football club, then it was simple common sense to make every effort required to avoid getting the return ticket to the coal face.

Certainly the enforced confinement that the miners had to endure day after day when cutting coal in dark, dirty conditions helped sharpen their appetites for the game and their determination to break out if the chance ever presented itself. Later, in the short-lived *Cumberland Sports Weekly*, Bill reflected on those times. 'We felt so full of life coming out into the daylight after a hard day in the mine, those impromptu games that we had were fought out at a terrific pace. Knocks were numerous but no-one bothered as we were as fit as fiddles.' The competitive nature of matches held on a good surface literally a stone's throw from the mine workings could only have helped the men come to terms with the stiffer competition they would face elsewhere. They would never face tackling harder than that at Burnside Park. Bill knew the importance of these innocent days. 'That was my apprenticeship in football, spent on coal-blackened fields near the pit-head.'

One of the most significant stepping stones towards winning the future he dreamed of came during the summer months. Always looking for something to do away from work, the miners in Glenbuck played football the whole year round. However, as a concession to the warmer weather, full-scale games were dispensed with and the time given over to playing five-a-side matches instead. Within this faster, more physical and highly compact game, close control had to be good, passing accurate and tackling precise, all attributes that were central to his game. Competitions were held in five-a-sides too for the game was far more popular in Scotland than England where the summer would be given over to cricket. According to the Reverend Faulds, 'it was not infrequent for the five-a-side competitions to continue through the whole day, many of the teams playing literally for hours on end. On one occasion at Lanark they went on throughout Saturday and were completed on Monday morning.' For the irrepressible Willie Shankly, the chance to play football at such length was the greatest pleasure of his life. With his ability to run all day, he was a great asset. The way the abridged format helped to improve skills stuck firmly in his mind and most of the training that he instituted in later life was based around five-a-sides.

Perhaps the greatest lesson to be learned from Glenbuck though is that talent is just one component in the make-up of a successful professional. In such a small village over such a short period of time, the production of 50 professionals is unbelievable. Unless there was something in the local water supply, it's naive to think that the level of natural ability was any greater here than in any other town or village. What the young men of Glenbuck seem to have over those from other locations was a ferocious passion for the game and a burning desire to break into the full-time ranks. The game that would have provided enjoyment for them as boys came to be their whole lives as they grew up. The matches would have taken on greater significance and become more keenly fought as the boys got older. The long hours of practice would have brought rewards. Bill was fond of saying later on that 'we as managers or coaches don't make players. Their fathers and mothers make them. But we help. If they have it in them, we can bring it out.' With the vast store of footballing wisdom on tap in Glenbuck, the tenacity that the boys themselves showed in pursuit of their goal was the vital ingredient that was perhaps missing elsewhere.

All who knew Bill Shankly were quick to point out that they knew of no-one else who was driven in quite the same way that he was, obsessed with the sport and with his fitness to play it to the best of his ability. Here of course, he had a great advantage over many of his contemporaries. Although determination can take you a long way, you can go further still if you are properly equipped for the job. The Shanklys were hardy folk, their mother keeping them well fed by means of her excellent management of the family budget. Thanks to her, Willie always had plenty of energy which he worked off on the football field. At school, the headmaster gave the boys all the encouragement they needed to play the game and since Burnside Park was conveniently situated opposite the school itself, they were able to start a game immediately school was finished for the day. There was never anything in life to rival the hold that football had on him, except life itself. Ness Shankly, who became Bill's wife in 1944, remembers his mother being asked ' "Do you never go on holiday?" Her reply was "No, every day when you awake, get up and can do your work, that's a holiday." And she really did mean that.' Taught by his parents to appreciate life, he wasn't the sort of boy or man to take anything for granted. He contented himself by giving back every bit as much as he took.

Helped by this attitude and by the skills that ran down the ancestral line, Willie quickly began to show promise. From a very early age, he was regularly picking up useful pieces of advice from his brothers who knew from personal experience just how a player should train and look after himself. Throughout his life, physical fitness was something of an obsession as John Roberts explained. 'He once told me that his ambition was to die a healthy man! I think he had a fear of being bed ridden in later life and he worked very hard to keep himself fit even in retirement.'

He was fortunate that he was just one of many good players round about. This enabled him to work at his game without the weight of expectations that can hamper talented boys playing in towns where the seam of footballing talent is not so rich. By the time he left school to go into the pits in 1927, Willie Shankly was already a talent in the making yet he was

never able to play for the Cherrypickers. The first year when
that would have been possible, 1930/31, he was not considered
good enough. The Cherrypickers cherished their hard won
reputation and were a side filled with hard nosed players,
ready to play in a difficult league. There was no place for
sentiment. Though a strong lad, Willie Shankly was just that,
a lad, not a man. Though he impressed during a trial game,
he couldn't break through.

That in itself was no disgrace for in what turned out to be
their valedictory season, Glenbuck Cherrypickers captured the
Ayrshire Junior Challenge Cup. The whole village turned out
to see the team bring the Cup back home. This was some small
comfort to the village for just prior to the win, the final pit
had closed and Glenbuck was on the brink of extinction.
The Cherrypickers disbanded as the men were forced to look
elsewhere for work and, within a matter of weeks, Burnside
Park itself was no more, for as Jean remembers 'once the
mining was stopped, it caused the pitch to flood'.

Willie stayed in Glenbuck with the family and village life
continued in a somewhat reduced fashion as people continued
to leave; the loss of the football club also made a big impact
on the morale of the local people who remained. When the
next football season began, he was an eighteen year old, ready
to take part in the junior game. Sadly he was now without a
team. But by the Christmas of 1931, he had found himself a
berth at right half, playing for Cronberry Eglinton, even
though his decision to have a trial there had been 'at the
suggestion of a pal who thought we should join a proper
side'. Cronberry was a small village around eight miles from
Glenbuck, another that was dependent on the mines for work.
Though not as celebrated as the Cherrypickers, Cronberry had
a good reputation themselves and had won the Ayrshire Cup
the year before Glenbuck's triumph.

Quick to make an impact on the game, in his autobiography
he recalled just what a hard school junior football was but
concluded that it had toughened him up and left him ready
for the professional game. In the junior leagues no quarter

was asked or given which in part accounts for its success in grooming players for higher things. For young Willie Shankly, those 'higher things' were just around the corner.

chapter three

THE LONG MARCH

The real test of a sportsman's ability comes when he has to acquit himself at a higher level of competition. Character counts for every bit as much as talent. Without a certain level of ability it's impossible to make the grade but there are countless examples of individuals who, through sheer hard work, application to their craft and a fierce determination to succeed, have achieved greater glories than more naturally talented contemporaries. Kevin Keegan might have lacked the astonishing array of skills that Alan Hudson or Stan Bowles possessed for instance, but the record books show who had the better career.

As a youngster, Bill Shankly recognised his limitations but more importantly, appreciated his strengths. In what was to become a core philosophy in his management days, he did not dwell on his failings for fear that it would encourage an inferiority complex. His assets were a powerful physique, strength in the tackle, an ability to shake off challenges, hold the ball and pass it sensibly and accurately to the ball players. He had an impressive knowledge of the game which enabled him to anticipate the play in attack and defence. The non-stop round of games that took place at Burnside Park also left him well schooled in all the niceties of the game. Finally, his enthusiasm for the game and general physical fitness meant that he didn't flag throughout a full ninety minutes and his innate resolve meant that he would not accept defeat until the final whistle, and not always then. With this impressive list of attributes, it was clear that Willie's future lay in the half back line, breaking down opponents' attacking play and prompting aggressive movements for his own side.

Through the 1920s, he had had plenty of opportunity to

test himself against his peers in the village but though these games were always furiously fought, they were seldom properly organised. Players had the freedom to play wherever and however they liked, so these after-work kick-abouts left little room for any real pattern of play to emerge. While the young Shankly was learning the basics of his trade in these impromptu games, football in general was entering another phase of its development in Britain. This was largely engineered by Herbert Chapman who took Huddersfield Town to a hat-trick of League Championships in 1923/24, 1924/25 and 1925/26, though he actually left the town in 1925 to take over at Arsenal and build that club into one of the greatest powers in the land. Chapman stressed the virtues of methodical planning, a sensible tactical framework but, most vigorously of all, team-work. At Huddersfield, all eleven players were involved in the fortunes of the team. Each had a definite role to play and if all did their particular job, success would inevitably follow.

His work at Arsenal was rather different because of the changing rules of the game. Unfairly perhaps, he did as much to saddle Arsenal with the tag 'boring' as any of Don Howe's tinkering with the offside trap; ironically it was a change in the offside rule that was central to Chapman's success. As he was taking up his post at Highbury the law was changed, requiring just two, rather than three, opposing players to keep an attacker onside. In the midst of a goal rush, Chapman was quickest to adapt and introduced the stopper centre-half with purely destructive responsibilities. Chapman was deemed the most culpable, throwing light on the way people saw football – a game dedicated to goalscoring. Arsenal quickly established themselves at the forefront of the game by virtue of the tightest defence. With that secure, Chapman was then able to unshackle his imagination and proved most adept at devising strategies to cope with the defensive numbers employed by opponents.

If Chapman had been lauded at Huddersfield, at Arsenal he was recognised as a tactical genius. His assessment of players was immaculate, bringing in fresh faces that would fit into his side with the minimum of fuss. His insistence on team play gave his Arsenal side an air of invincibility, a marauding force that was united and, therefore, indivisible. He continually preached that the player on the ball should always be given alternatives, two or three options for his next pass. His meticulous attention to detail extended to matters off the field too. Players had to take care of themselves, eat correctly and train hard so that they could do themselves justice on the pitch. Training was enjoyable and involved lots of ball-work with head tennis a favourite. Chapman also understood that although the side was built on team-work, each member was an individual and he treated them as such.

If there was a blueprint for Bill Shankly's construction of Liverpool, it was the way in which Herbert Chapman created Arsenal. Bill was taking careful note of the Arsenal style for their most celebrated player was Alex James, a Scottish wizard for whom he had a particular soft spot, understandably so since veteran Kopite Billy O'Donnell, a Liverpool fan for more than seventy years, acknowledges that James was 'as good as George Best'. Though he was still just a novice in footballing terms, Bill was careful to accumulate knowledge that would make him a successful manager, watching the way that mercurial individual talents could be harnessed for the good of the team. Though the Gunners took on the trappings of wealth and aristocracy with the marble halls of Highbury, Chapman's Arsenal was the club that moved English football into the era of uncompromising professionalism. Proof of his success came when they continued to pick up trophies after his premature death in 1934, the result, many felt, of his absolute devotion to the game and a refusal to spare himself any effort in producing the best team in the land. There are echoes of Chapman in Shankly's life and untimely death. On the field, just as Liverpool were to maintain their dominance after Bill's retirement, the 1930s with and without Chapman, was Arsenal's decade; they won the League five times and the F.A. Cup twice.

These were features of the game that Bill Shankly would

come to know at first hand, regularly playing against Arsenal throughout the decade and sometimes turning out for them during the War as a guest player. Yet professional attitudes were nothing new to the Scots who had long since taken their football very seriously indeed, even at junior level; in particular, Bill was quick to implement Chapman's philosophy on building from solid foundations. He strived to reach the peak of physical and mental health prior to every game. Wherever possible he ate the right food – not always easy given the poverty the people of Glenbuck had to endure – and certainly never indulged in drinking or smoking, nor did he 'gallivant with women'. All his energies were given over to football, the game which would take him away from a dying village and a lifetime's work at the coal face. John Roberts felt that he had looked into the abyss and was the stronger for it: 'As a youngster, I'm sure that there were times when he thought that he would be a miner all his life and that coloured his views. You don't lose that sense of how hard life can be, that inherent fear of disaster, you never forget it. When you see a way out, you're all the more likely to take your opportunity.'

Such diligent preparation was crucial for Bill was well aware that he was entering a man's arena where victory was a prerequisite. Fancy footwork that might have impressed your pals after school or work was all very well, but results were what counted. Fitting into position at right half, Bill was quick to assimilate the importance of team play, something that had been drummed into him as a youngster but which was all the more important in the wake of Chapman's triumphs at Huddersfield. Though he found himself regularly pitched up against men several years his senior, some of them ex-professionals, he held his own and performed the job that he was asked to do by the Cronberry side. Bill was a hard man, defiant, resolute. He was as fit as he could be, built up by the meat that his mother somehow always found for him and by the physical work he'd done down the pit. In the prime of his young life, Willie was ready for any challenge that the game of football could offer. As he admitted later, his attitude was one of 'when you've got the jersey on, blame nobody but yourself if you fail'. All his young life he'd been waiting to get the chance and then 'I did the rest. Somebody in the crowd picked me out and from there I went on to play for a professional team.'

Given that his older brothers had all played football at professional level and that his uncles, the Blyths, were still involved in the senior game, it's sometimes been assumed that Bill breezed through from amateur status into the professional ranks, but that's far from being the full story. He had to take his place in the junior game just like the others before him and prove himself as a player of quality. His inherent advantage was not one based on family but on geographic location. So successful had Glenbuck been in providing top quality footballers, you could rest assured that scouts would always be on hand.

Such was his determination to make a mark that by the time he'd made a bare handful of appearances, Bill Shankly's name was on the minds of numerous scouts. Peter Carruthers, who had done some reporting for Carlisle United, was always keen to see the young man play. A local man from Kirkconnell, he found it easy to catch Cronberry's games and liked what he saw, continuing to follow his development over the course of half a season until the summer of 1932. Cronberry had had a reasonably successful year and had reached the semi-final of one of the local cup competitions. Their opponents were Kello Rangers and the tie was played on neutral territory at the home of Nithsdale Wanderers at Sanquhar in Dumfriesshire. Once again, Peter Carruthers watched from the touch-line, though this time he was joined by Bobby Crawford, a representative from Preston North End. By this stage, Bill was well aware of the interest in him and was naturally keen to put on a show. Unfortunately, the day was ruined when Kello Rangers hammered Cronberry 6-0, though in mitigation Cronberry were able to point to the fact that they were missing a number of first choice players who had had to go to work that day.

Feeling that, temporarily at least, his chance might have

gone, he consoled himself with the thought that he had had a good game and was man of the match in the eyes of many. Despite the famed Shankly self-confidence he was genuinely surprised when Peter Carruthers approached him following the game to offer a month's trial at Carlisle. Bobby Crawford offered similar terms on behalf of Preston. Bill later wrote in the *Cumberland Sports Weekly* that 'I couldn't get back home to Glenbuck fast enough to tell father, mother and brother Alec the good news. The family having had similar experiences with my elder brothers were pleased with the situation but heard the news in a less excited manner than I did. Approaches by representatives of football clubs was becoming a habit to the Shankly family'. Possibly others in the family were a little blasé, recognising that Bill had as much ability as his siblings and that his chance would inevitably come. For Bill, it was the end of a worrying period; however sure he was of himself and his own ability, until recognition came from outside there could be no guarantees that football would become his life. Now, with his foot in the door at the tender age of eighteen, Bill knew that he was in charge of his own destiny.

The first decision he had to make was which club to go with. Carlisle United offered a number of attractions. Geographically closer, there were strong family ties with the club, his uncle, Billy Blyth, being on the board of directors. Billy had long been an established member of the club and community; he joined the club after seeing an advert that Carlisle had placed in the Ayrshire press back in 1905 asking for players to come forward! He owned a pub in the town, the Bowling Green Inn, and provided a link with the family back in Glenbuck. He could also cast a watchful eye over the young man, putting his mother's mind at ease. Bill conceded later that 'assisted by the family I decided to go to Uncle Willie's team', but even at seventeen, he was sufficiently strong-willed to do what he wanted. He was willing to listen to advice if he thought it worthwhile, but he wouldn't have gone to Carlisle just to keep the family happy. There were sound footballing reasons for the decision.

Preston were undeniably appealing. They were a Second
Division side with a proud history, offering him a higher
standard of football right away as well as the potential to get
into the First Division. On further reflection though, this was
a mixed blessing. A higher level meant better players and Bill
was realistic enough to accept that that might mean a lengthy
spell in the reserves should he progress past the trial stage.
Preston was also a good deal further south than Carlisle and
for a young lad who had yet to live away from home, that in
itself was pretty daunting. All these factors tended to sway
him towards accepting a trial at Brunton Park but perhaps the
clinching factor was the interest that Peter Carruthers had
shown in him as a player. Carruthers had seen him far more
often than the Preston scout and his comments following the
Kello drubbing had raised Bill's morale; he saw that Bill had a
very good chance of securing a first team berth for himself
within a very short time at Carlisle and told him so. With that
tempting prospect, Bill was finally sold on Carlisle.

There were to be several long months through the summer
before he could make the two-hour journey south to play his
trial games at the club. Fully committed to making the grade,
the summer months saw no let up in the punishing schedule
that Bill put himself through. He continued to play in the
round of five-a-side games that took place locally and he
maintained his general fitness with some running. By the time
the call came from Brunton Park in August 1932, he was at his
fittest. He travelled down to the ground with his brother Alec,
who was to become something of a mentor through his early
years in the game. As enthusiastic as ever, Bill looked forward
to this opportunity to take on professional players but he
confessed in his autobiography that the uncertainty of a one-
game trial 'wasn't very satisfactory because if I hadn't played
well I'd have been thrown on the scrap-heap'. Writing in
the *Cumberland Sports Weekly* in September 1954 he recalled
himself as 'being nervous and shy on my debut' and that he
received an enormous stroke of good fortune for that game.

Carlisle, a struggling club in the lower reaches of the league, weren't flush with resources and operated a skeleton playing staff. Injuries prior to the trial game – first team versus reserves, or Blues versus Stripes as they were known locally – forced the club to field trainer Tommy Curry at centre-half for the second team. Taking up his position alongside young Bill, 'Tommy gave me the confidence I needed for such an occasion'. With the steadying influence of this senior figure at his side, Bill turned in a quietly competent performance that justified Carruthers' faith. A brief discussion ensued between Curry and Carlisle's manager Billy Hampson and Curry convinced his manager that Shankly was the genuine article. Hampson agreed to sign him on as a full-time professional there and then without recourse to the remainder of the month's trial. At the princely wage of £4 a week, Bill Shankly had achieved his principal ambition in life and become a professional footballer.

chapter four

THE FUN'S FINISHED

It's difficult to imagine the emotion that must have gripped Bill Shankly when he finally realised his ambition and signed professional forms for Carlisle United. As he remembered later on, 'I felt ever so important as I walked through the club's gates.' It can't be stressed too strongly just how delighted Bill was to make that move; that sense of gratitude, mingled with relief and vindication for his self-belief, never left him throughout his life and it was a vital element in the formidable energy and enthusiasm for the game that became his trademark. 'Soccer is a life of variety with a capital V. Even at that stage, football had accomplished something important for me by providing the only means of escape from the mines. In Glenbuck you had one choice – you went down the pits or you played football.' Life for Bill Shankly now offered many opportunities and choices. He never forgot those men that he left behind at the pit, never forgot those he had stood shoulder to shoulder with at Ibrox. He knew that that was their only true recreation from a very harsh world, understood how lucky he was to be outside it and vowed to give full value to those who paid his wages at the turnstiles. These were the real people of football.

As far as his wages were concerned, Carlisle were generous given their impoverished status. He signed on the dotted line for the princely sum of £4 a week, rising to £4 10s when he got into the first team, a great improvement on the 2s 6d a day he'd originally earned in Glenbuck, though he had eventually achieved a daily rate of five shillings as he took on more demanding work at the pit. Nevertheless, this was a significant rise. It was characteristic then that, recalling the sacrifices made by his brother Jimmy, Bill 'wanted to help out' according to Jean Roberts. 'When he got to Carlisle, he tried to send his mother some money but she wouldn't take it. She thought he'd need it himself.'

His mother was right for he now had to fend for himself, pay his own rent, buy his own food. Even in the 1930s, a wage of £4 a week meant you had to be careful with the pennies. Bill was happy to live by his mother's motto however: 'She used to say "if I have enough I have plenty and I don't want any more".' This humble approach to his status as a footballer and consequently a figure of some importance in his local community was something which remained with him. He was happy to do his job and live an unaffected, unostentatious life; whether this was merely a reflection of his own simple tastes or a specific decision based on a desire not to alienate himself from his own working class roots and the base of his support is a matter of opinion. The evidence supports the former – Bill was a footballing man who had little use for any other comforts. He enjoyed his visits to the cinema, liked smart clothes but was never one for flights of fancy. His public persona was a very honest representation of his own values.

He joined Carlisle United at a very interesting stage in their history. Still a young club, not yet thirty years old, they were formed just a couple of years before their advertisement for players in the Ayrshire newspapers led to the recruitment of Billy Blyth. The club set about working its way through the Northern leagues and finally, on 4 June, the club gained election to the Football League proper, replacing Durham in the Third Division North for 1928/29.

These early seasons were inevitably ones of considerable struggle as the club attempted to come to terms with the new level of competition. Their first season was a reasonable success when, carried along on a wave of euphoria, they came in eighth in the 22-team league. Almost inevitably form dipped once the honeymoon was over and the second season saw the club flirting with the lower reaches of the League and when the pattern was repeated over the next two seasons – eighth and then eighteenth – questions were raised about Carlisle's ability to compete. Off the field, the strain of professional football was beginning to tell too. Early in 1932, the club was on the verge of bankruptcy.

Under these great financial pressures, the club were forced to reassess their position. Their preparation for the 1932/33 season, Bill's first, was far from ideal. In order to balance the books, the club released many of their stalwarts from the pioneer years in League football and brought in fourteen new players, a mixture of youth and experience. One of the newcomers was Bob Bradley, an experienced professional who became club captain. A chance meeting at Carlisle station on the day that Bill signed forms for the club was a piece of good fortune for the young Shankly. Bradley was the right-back and played behind Bill in an ideal position to help and advise the youngster. Though he'd never made it as a regular at the highest grade, he had gathered experience in spells with Bishop Auckland, Newcastle and Fulham.

The two got on well together and shared digs along with Johnny Kelly, the club goalkeeper and a fellow Scot who was about to embark on his final season as a player. The influence of these two made a great impact on the impressionable lad and he was lucky to have two such good role models on whom to draw. They enjoyed their time away from the ground, having a regular 'singsong round a piano' as Bill recalled later. To have the company of such good friends must have been a great comfort, particularly in his early days at the club, for though Carlisle were struggling, Bill could not break into the side until New Year's Eve, 1932.

Those early months were difficult for he felt that he was worthy of a place in the team. His ambition, a form of impatience as he called it, made it hard for him to accept second-team football. Not that that prevented him giving every game his all for to have the chance to play football, and get paid for it too, remained a wonderful luxury. As he candidly admitted, in these first weeks, there was nothing for him in Carlisle but the football ground and training. Though there was never any chance of him going off the rails, such was his dedication to the game and to his own health, he was lucky to be surrounded by the stabilising influence of Bradley and Kelly as well as his Uncle Billy. In addition, with Glenbuck a few hours and twelve shillings away on the train, he was able to return home at regular intervals to see his family.

His spirits remained good for he thoroughly enjoyed the intensely competitive nature of reserve team football. In matches where all eleven men are desperately striving to make their personal mark and gain elevation to the first team, reserve football often lacks any coherent pattern but the Carlisle stiffs performed well after an inauspicious start in the North Eastern League. Bill's first outing came against Middlesbrough Reserves, where he was on the wrong end of a 6-0 hiding. Things gradually improved over the season though and they eventually went on to win the North Eastern League Cup, defeating Newcastle United Reserves in the final.

Bill was showing distinct signs of promise and Tommy Curry was keeping a very close eye on his progress. Having enjoyed playing alongside him in the trial game prior to the season, Curry knew that Carruthers had unearthed a real winner. Shankly had all the natural instincts of a good footballer but he also had that little bit of devil that distinguishes those who really want to succeed from the journeymen. Having played a mere handful of games for Cronberry, he was still a raw youth and there were many rough edges to his game, but the promise was there. Curry was delighted to find that Bill had a tremendous appetite for the game, a willingness to learn and to listen. Anything that Curry could teach him, Bill was keen to know. He wanted to become a craftsman.

This was exactly the attitude Carlisle needed, for manager Hampson had based his strategy on gradually blooding youngsters alongside the senior pros. Forced into self-sufficiency by the club's parlous finances, Hampson had little choice but to look to the future and set great store in developing his own home-grown players. Tommy Curry, though first-team trainer, spent a good deal of time with the reserves trying to spot those that could make a contribution. Curry was renowned in the game as a good judge of players and went on to be a highly respected figure at Manchester United, a career that was only ended by the Munich disaster.

It does seem likely that Shankly was marked down as a first-team player from the outset. Given four months to build his confidence in the reserves, to settle down in the town and in the club and to learn all about the demands of playing for a living, it was always probable that he would get a chance around the hectic Christmas period. By the end of 1932, Carlisle had played nineteen league games, winning just five and losing ten. Flirting with the prospect of having to apply for re-election to the League and having already gone out of the F.A.Cup, Hampson chose to bring in fresh blood in the hope of injecting some enthusiasm into the side. So it was that Bill got the call to make his senior debut in the home fixture with fellow strugglers Rochdale on New Year's Eve 1932, a game which ended 2-2. Hogmanay was especially memorable for one Scot that year.

Curry had recognised Bill's serious approach to the game and felt he would do well. Bill's attitude was 'the fun's finished ... you're playing for a living now', a lesson that he would preach to every player that came under his management. Lining up at right half with his friend Bob Bradley covering for him at right back, Shankly did all that could be asked of him. Playing well in a poor side is always difficult for confidence is low, passes go astray, movement off the ball is sometimes ponderous yet Shankly gave evidence that he was the all-action type of player that Carruthers had recommended. Such was his attitude, Bill managed to play in sixteen of the remaining twenty-three fixtures that year.

He was handled especially sensitively by Hampson, who had no desire to destroy the morale of such a promising player. Mindful of his own side's numerous shortcomings and of the reverses the team would suffer in the remainder of the year, he gave a lot of thought to the games in which Shankly should play; he was acutely aware of how badly the team travelled, eventually losing sixteen out of twenty-one away from home that season, and consequently Bill was spared many of the more arduous and dispiriting journeys. He picked and chose his games very carefully, Bill remembering that 'he'd take me to one side and say "we're playing away to Rotherham. That's not for you."' By the time the season had ended, Carlisle had mustered a further eight wins to go with another twelve defeats; with thirty-three points, they were just two points away from seeking re-election.

Always a team man, Bill was naturally very disappointed with the lack of improvement at first-team level but there were good things to come out of the year too. There was a great deal of consolation to be gained from the way the reserves had handled themselves through the season, culminating in that Cup win over Newcastle. He himself had taken an import-ant step up the ladder and had established himself as a first-team player, an impression reinforced when the club released Edward Cawley, the senior right-half. Bill had high hopes that by the next season he might well become an ever-present in the Carlisle line-up. The close season sparked a mass exodus from the club. Just a handful of players were retained, includ-ing the pairing of Bradley and Shankly. These were the men chosen as the cornerstones of a new Carlisle United.

chapter five

GOING UP

Bill Shankly's performances in the 1932/33 season had won the praise of many on the terraces, people who loved to see their lads putting everything into their game. The local press had even begun to hail a home grown hero who might help Carlisle towards a brighter future. For his part, Bill kept his feet firmly on the ground, realising that he'd accomplished very little. An exuberant player, he communicated his enjoyment to the crowd and covered the whole pitch throughout a gruelling ninety minutes with no difficulty, such was his astounding level of fitness. This enthusiasm, while a great gift, was also a mixed blessing at this early stage in his career. Revelling in the chance to play the game, Bill wanted to take the throw-ins, make the tackles, play the passes, take the corners and make the tea at half-time. His desire to be involved in the game at all times meant that he could be caught out of position, putting additional pressure on his defence.

This was natural enough. Inexperienced players are bound to make errors of judgment; such is their urge to run around and see as much of the ball as possible, the tactical side of the game is given little thought. To his credit, Bill was quick to realise his mistakes and learn from them, though with typical Shankly logic he revealed: 'I don't call them mistakes. No, no. If you think they're mistakes you can get depressed so I use psychology. I call them happenings. Things happened, it wasn't my mistake.' In conversation with Hampson and Curry at the ground and Bradley at their digs, he did his best to iron out these 'happenings', though it would be many years before he became the complete half-back. Shankly's appetite for the game was as voracious as ever and the conversations between him, Bradley and Kelly would go on and on. Football was the central topic for Bill would rarely waste words on any other matter.

News travels quickly on the footballing grapevine and there were plenty who soon knew about Bill Shankly and the single-minded strength of purpose which he lavished on his craft. Having missed out on his signature a year earlier, Preston North End were still keen on the young man. They continued to monitor his progress in the reserves, stepping up their attention once he graduated to the full side. Since relegation to the Second Division in 1924/25, Preston had never threatened to win promotion and were going through a stage of rebuilding. They saw Bill as an important component of their future, a player who might help take them back into the top flight.

Back home in Glenbuck for the summer, Bill was blissfully unaware of Preston's renewed interest. It was typical that he chose to go home, partly for sound financial reasons, but largely because he felt the most comfortable with his family. With the boys spread across the country with their various teams, summer had long since been the only time they could all be together. The communal spirit still burned strong within him even if it could sometimes boil over as he wrote later. 'We got arguing one morning. I knew Bob was egging me on but I always used to swallow the bait. It finished when Bob threw me off my feet and my head bashed against the sideboard, splitting one side of it from top to bottom. My mother left it like that as a lesson to us.'

He spent the close season training hard and, inevitably, playing cards with the miners and football with the men and boys who remained in the village. When there was no-one available for a game, he evolved his own training methods. Keen to master the long throw-in which could be such an effective attacking weapon, he'd spend hour after hour throwing the ball over a row of houses, wait for a small boy to retrieve it for him and then throw it over the top again. This attention to detail was a hallmark of his approach to the game.

While at home, word got back to Glenbuck from Billy Blyth

that Carlisle United were suffering yet more trying times. For financial reasons, Billy Hampson had been asked to take on the position of Secretary Manager rather than simple team Manager and take a cut in wages for his pains. Unsurprisingly, Hampson decided to leave. So poor were Carlisle that Club Secretary Bill Clarke had to take over the managerial duties in spite of the fact that he would have been asked to go if Hampson had agreed to the change in his own responsibilities. Bill Shankly was naturally upset at these new developments for Hampson had been a source of staunch support and advice during his first year in the game. Nevertheless, since he was under contract to Carlisle United, he was in no position to question the decisions of the board of directors, all the more so since his uncle was one of them.

Never one for inactivity, the lack of football was beginning to wear on his nerves so the arrival of a telegram in June broke things up nicely. The mere arrival of a telegram was cause for consternation in the tiny hamlet, but its contents were sensational. Sent from Brunton Park, it read 'Report Carlisle to discuss transfer to Preston North End'. Bill was naturally pleased with this new development for it was the recognition he felt he deserved for a good season's work. It also offered evidence that he was working on the right lines for if Preston had maintained their interest after seeing him play as a professional, he must have been doing something right.

Virtually bald, having been scalped the previous day by brother Bob when attempting to cut his hair, Bill made the necessary arrangements and the following day he and brother Alec, acting as his adviser, made the journey down to Carlisle. Their conversation en route was confined to generalities rather than the Preston transfer specifically. Bill had his own views on the matter and did not want his judgment clouding prior to meeting the Preston officials. Thinking about the move overnight, he had come to similar conclusions to those drawn the previous year; while the idea of playing for Preston was appealing, he felt that a move there would mean he would have to go back to reserve team football in the Central League.

Although this was a generally higher standard of football than that played by Carlisle reserves, it was still reserve team football. Having made the breakthrough at Carlisle, he was looking forward to a season in the first team and forty-two league games. He was of the opinion that a season of that kind of competition, games where the club might be fighting for its very survival, would give him a better grounding in the game than reserve football where, very often, little was at stake. Another good season there, he reasoned, and he would be ready to walk straight into the first team at a top club. After all, Preston had been struggling in the Second Division – another poor season and they might be in the basement alongside Carlisle. So it was that when he arrived at Blyth's Bowling Green pub to meet them, he was not overawed. Again, his own natural grasp of psychology and self-delusion had put him in the right frame of mind.

Preston were represented by Bill Scott, their trainer. Scott approached the meeting confident that he would secure the services of young Shankly, certain that Preston's excellent reputation in Scotland for the type and quality of football that they played would prove irresistible to the ambitious wing-half. The fact that both Blyth brothers had played for the club seemed equally promising. Shankly chose to meet Scott on his own while Alec waited with his uncle. The discussion went on for some time and Bill was impressed with the way Scott spoke about football and about the plans that were being laid at Preston's home ground, Deepdale, for the coming season. If Bill was edging towards making the move, the sticking point came when terms were discussed. He already knew from his uncle that he would receive a signing on fee of forty or fifty pounds, but this made little impact. After all, he could win or lose that much on a game of cards, an indication that he still allowed himself one vice! When Scott revealed that his weekly wage would only increase by ten shillings to £5 a week, Bill was adamant that he couldn't leave Carlisle.

Showing the typical naivety of one raised in such a back-woods environment as Glenbuck, Bill admitted later that he 'imagined Preston as a big city where digs would cost me more than 25 shillings a week as in Carlisle and the train fare home would be so much bigger'. While Preston was an important north-western town, it was scarcely the steaming metropolis that Bill seemed to expect and so his fears were all but groundless. No matter, for however hard he tried, Scott could not convince Bill of his error. Showing the stubbornness that was such a vital part of his game, he could not be moved and finally, Scott bowed to the inevitable.

It's interesting that it was a financial as much as a footballing decision that tied Bill to Brunton Park. Having tried to send money home to his mother the previous year, it's clear that he was not indulging in any sort of riotous lifestyle, nor that he would be desperately short of money. If he was never going to become rich as a professional footballer in the days of the maximum wage, he was still very comfortable compared with the miners he'd left behind in Scotland. On top of that, Bill always maintained that he was in football for the game, not the cash. Was money the real issue here or was it simply a manifestation of some deeper insecurity that he couldn't reveal even to himself? As a player whose whole game and a man whose whole persona was built around an air of invincibility, Bill would never be able to admit to any doubts over his ability. However, his upbringing in a mining community where you could lose your job at the whim of the mine-owner left a scar. Although football was a very different field, Bill still felt very keenly the class barriers in the game and had little time for directors in general, even if his uncle was one. The lack of job security that was a part of everyday life for working people remained with him throughout his life in some degree. John Roberts notes that 'he liked Robert Burns because he attacked what Bill called "the big people". He had a natural antagonism towards them, seeing how well they lived while others were struggling through the deprivations of the depression or the way he'd had to live in poverty in Glenbuck.'

Quite simply, Bill feared the loss of his job. By speaking out of turn, by going through a temporary loss of form or by suffering an injury, he worried that his livelihood could be taken from him. Footballers were still little more than peasants, owned body and soul by their club. At Carlisle he felt at home, was popular with the crowd, felt sure that the people at the club, including his uncle Billy, would see him through any time of trouble. Would that be the case at Preston if there was a problem in his first months? Would it not be better to build a stronger reputation for himself in Carlisle, a reputation that would render him immune from such worries when he made a move perhaps eighteen months hence? Remember, he was a reserved boy and he admitted that he was quiet and shy on his arrival in Carlisle for the trial. Bill was clearly a more sensitive individual than his later public persona would suggest.

One of the more revealing comments that Bill made about himself as a player came when discussing his dedication to the trade. Explaining away his punishing training schedule, he remarked 'the idea was always in the back of my mind that if I was a failure, I could never go back home and face the family'. While this does account for his commitment to physical fitness and hard work, it also exposes the fears to which every athlete must fall prey, that circumstances might conspire to bring about personal failure. As a mere nineteen year old, Bill could be excused such natural anxiety. It was perfectly understandable that he did not yet want to stray too far from home, wanted to test his talents further in a familiar environment, only making the final move away when he was totally confident of his ability to succeed. Perhaps the arguments over money were a useful method of postponing the day of reckoning.

If that was the case, others had greater faith in Bill than he did himself. When he came out of his meeting with Scott, Alec was expecting to hear that he was now a Preston player for Alec knew that he was good enough to play for Preston already. When he heard that Bill had turned Scott down and why, he exploded. With his own experience to draw on, he drummed it into Bill that money was no reason to pass up such a great opportunity to move to a club with history, good crowds, an excellent reputation and masses of potential for the future. It's also likely that he made it very clear that Bill had little say in his own future. Carlisle United were in dire financial trouble and had already been forced to sell players to balance the books. Had that not been the case, it's unlikely that they would have entertained Preston's interest in Shankly, the kind of young player that was essential to the club if they wanted to build. Billy Blyth had almost certainly pointed out to Alec that if Bill didn't go to Preston, it wouldn't be long before he'd be required to move elsewhere. Being handled like a possession did little to mollify his own contempt for the moral standards of the powers that be.

Nothing if not a realist and with Alec's advice ringing in his ears, Bill changed his mind and decided to put his future in Bill Scott's hands. By this stage Scott had left the Bowling Green on his way to the station. The brothers ran to catch up with him but his train was just beginning its journey as they made it on to the platform. Legend has it that seeing them, Scott helped haul them on to the train as it was pulling out. Preston signed Bill Shankly, one of their greatest stalwarts, in a railway carriage somewhere outside Haltwhistle. The fee for his transfer from Carlisle to Preston was £500; forty years later, Bill was to make the appropriate, if slightly exaggerated statement that 'it'd cost you that in rail fares now!'

He picked up the first £10 of his signing-on fee from Scott and then got off the train at Haltwhistle, the first stop. The pair were fortunate that the station-master was a football supporter. Not only did he turn a blind eye to their lack of tickets, he gave them warrants for the return journey to Carlisle. Back in Glenbuck, his family and friends were delighted that one of their number had managed to move up in the world, but everything remained low-key. Not that he was the sort of man to take them, but he wasn't allowed any airs and graces simply because he was now in the Second Division. Glenbuck had produced internationals don't forget! Bill saw out the rest of the summer by staying fit and running what his brother Bob jokingly called the 'Bill Shankly Soccer Sunday School'. Bob saw his brother's future career as a manager panning out for him there and then for he later commented that 'Bill really enjoyed that and he was at his best when helping a bunch of youngsters.'

Pre-season work began at Deepdale in the middle of July. Bill reported early so that he could sort out new accommodation. Preston had fixed him up with a local landlady, Mrs. Hannah Usher, who looked after numerous Preston players. Bill was to stay there for around nine years, including the times he spent in Preston during the War, and became one of the family, so much so that prior to getting married, he took Nessie to meet her so that he could get her approval. Typically, Mrs. Usher told him that 'she's too good for you'. This down to earth attitude made the Ushers a home from home, a haven for straight talking and decent living. He couldn't have found better digs.

Settling in quickly, he soon found the training at Preston very much to his liking. Having been uncertain about the move, there were lingering doubts in his mind. Paramount among these was the fact that Bill Scott was not actually the manager. Preston North End was run on a committee basis by the directors and it was they who picked the team that would go out on a Saturday. By no means an unusual arrangement, with his innate suspicion of directors, Bill wondered how this would work out for him. Scott was the head trainer, working with the players on a daily basis alongside his assistant Jimmy Metcalfe. Chairman James Taylor ruled the roost however and his was the loudest voice when it came to team selection. At other clubs, Bill would have been quite within his rights to be wary but Taylor knew his football and did a super job at Deepdale, taking plenty of advice from the professionals along the way. Areas of responsibility were clearly defined and Taylor's ubiquitous presence left no-one in any doubt as to where they stood. Bill was content to settle down to matters on the field, sure that if he played well, Scott and Metcalfe would make sure that Mr. Taylor knew all about it.

Very early on, Bill was able to note that 'it was obvious that the training system arranged by Bill Scott and Jim Metcalfe was very, very clever. They knew what they were doing and talking about . . . they were dying to win.' The 1933/34 season that stretched ahead of them was vitally important. Out of the top flight for almost a decade, the club and its support were itching to get back to what they regarded as their rightful place. Taylor had brought in a number of experienced players who still had plenty to offer, such as former England goalkeeper Harry Holdcroft from Everton. Bill was especially taken with Bob Kelly, another ex-England man who by then was forty-two. Incredibly fit, he was still capable of playing a good game in attack. 'I have never seen anybody so quick over twenty yards at his age,' Bill wrote in 1976. Kelly was an inspiration, still performing in a footballer's dotage. Shankly looked forward to doing the same.

Preston had always been a good footballing side and Taylor went along with the supporters in demanding that those traditions be upheld. Though he wasn't to join the club until a few years later, Tom Finney remembered that 'we were taught to play the Scottish game, short passes. We were never a physical side and in the forward line we were all five foot six or seven. Good players like it played on the deck and Bill loved that style.' Bill took to Preston like a duck to water, slotting into their play with ease. Like all good players, he wasn't discomfited by the move up in class; he found that playing with good players made the game easier. Hurling himself into the pre-season rituals, he made himself known to everyone at the club with the minimum of fuss but in the shortest possible time.

Jimmy Metcalfe was especially pleased with the club's latest purchase and was a great admirer of Shankly's attitude. While other players might have a quiet moan about returning after the summer break, Bill couldn't wait to train or to play in practice games. Metcalfe recalled later that 'he would try anything. If you told Bill that running backwards up the terraces would make him a better player, he would do it.'

Such hard labour was seldom used though for Scott and Metcalfe had their own training methods, methods that were far removed from those employed elsewhere, but which persisted at Preston for many years. Tommy Docherty signed for the club as a direct replacement for Shankly some sixteen years later and even then, the regime was the same: 'We did very little running. It was all done with the ball. Five-a-side, three-a-side, every day. Even on a Friday before we travelled to an away game, we'd have an hour or so playing six-a-side, passing the ball around.' This attention to ball playing rather than endless running was like manna from heaven to the Scot who had spent his summers in Glenbuck playing in five-a-side competitions. 'Cross-country running is a soul-destroying business,' he revealed later, a business that he wanted little to do with. It was fine to attain a general level of fitness, but he was a footballer not a marathon runner. The best training would use the ball.

In spite of the good impression he was making on Scott and Metcalfe, Bill did not expect to start the season in the first team. Sure enough, his first representative fixture for Preston North End came in the Central League victory over Blackpool at Deepdale. The game provided a vivid example of the precarious career that Bill had embarked upon. Joe Brain, who had already become a good friend in his short time at the club, broke his leg in a tackle; according to Bill 'he was never the same player afterwards'. Still, one thing that Bill Shankly could never be accused of was having a faint heart, and he certainly never shirked a challenge in the wake of his colleague's injury. He put all his doubts behind him and immersed himself wholeheartedly in the fortunes of the club, turning in some enthusiastic performances. Just as in his debut year at Carlisle, by the Christmas of his first season with North End he was knocking on the door, looking for a first-team place.

chapter six

PERPETUAL MOTION

Fittingly, Deepdale, the ground that Bill Shankly was to grace for so many years, was the venue for his first full game for the Lilywhites. Bill Scott was deliberate about his introduction to the Preston team. The call came on 9 December, 1933 for the home match against Hull City. Hull were newly promoted to the Second Division, having been Third Division North champions the previous year, and were not regarded as being among the sterner opposition that Preston would face. Bill had already played against Hull the previous season as a member of the Carlisle side that went down 6-1 at Hull's Anlaby Road home. If that was an inauspicious occasion, his Preston debut would provide the chance to expunge that painful memory. Playing against a team that had been in his own division the previous year meant Bill would suffer little anxiety over the quality of the opposition. Though Scott and Metcalfe would not have expected Shankly to offer them any insight into Hull, it was he who produced the tactical masterstroke that turned the game.

Despite the success of Herbert Chapman's Arsenal and their deployment of the frustrating offside trap, few other clubs chose to use this exclusively defensive tactic; very few supporters would allow their teams to get away with it. Hull City however had used it to good effect in their promotion campaign and had no intention of changing their pattern. The offside trap still had novelty value and Hull were able to surprise many opponents by the adept way they sprung it. Shankly had learned from his exposure to the tactic the previous year; once he had got the pace of the game, he looked to crack Hull's defence. The local press reported that 'City's offside tactics had spoiled a number of North End attacks and

Shankly rose to the occasion. He just bamboozled the Hull defence beautifully, cut between the backs and presented Fitton with a sitter. This boy has great attacking power and quick intelligence. A born footballer.' Forced to go in search of a goal of their own, Hull's game plan was in tatters. Preston won 5-0.

After such an impressive start, Bill became a regular at right half. As he grew in stature, his natural ebullience shone through. The Deepdale faithful took to him quickly and he remained a perennial favourite until he eventually left a decade and a half later. Few were in any doubt that his introduction to the team was timely. Playing some fine football, Preston secured promotion at the end of the season, pipping their close rivals Bolton Wanderers to the runners-up slot by just one point. On a personal note, promotion and a regular place in the side meant that Bill's wage shot up to £8 a week, the maximum permissible.

Bill Shankly above all others would point out that one man does not make a team and that everyone at a football club had to pull in the same direction to generate his success. He'd demonstrated his credentials as a team player in that debut game by setting up Fitton when he could just as easily have scored himself. However, the introduction of one player can often prove to be the catalyst that transforms a side; Cantona's arrival at Manchester United is one example. He added a new dimension to strong outfits as a player but equally important, the power of his personality brought others out of their shell. If Bill Shankly didn't have the same ability on the ball as him, he certainly possessed that strength of character. His enthusiasm was infectious and his apparent lack of any nerves was a steadying influence in the dressing room in the closing weeks of the season. Jimmy Metcalfe explained that 'although he took everything on the field very seriously, he was quite a clown in the dressing room. I remember him skylarking about before a match wearing a false moustache but once on the field there were no half measures with Bill. He was bound to succeed.' Pleased with his contribution, Bill contented himself by making a wry aside in his autobiography. 'Maybe I should make no comment, but the season I went to Preston they were promoted to the First Division and when I left, in 1949, they were relegated.'

If further proof were required that yet another Shankly brother had arrived on the football scene, it came at the end of the season. Portsmouth, who had just lost out to Manchester City in the 1934 F.A. Cup Final and who could boast Bill's uncle Robert Blyth as Chairman, made a bid for his services. They were joined in the market by Arsenal. Their manager, George Allison, was especially keen on bringing Bill to Highbury to strengthen his squad of players. This would have been a tempting prospect since the Gunners had just registered a second successive League Championship victory and were the strongest side in the country.

Bill was never given the opportunity to decide on whether or not he wanted to leave Preston. Where Carlisle had only been too happy to sell him to ease their financial plight, Preston were in no such need. Back in 1934, if your club wanted to keep you, there was nothing you could do about it. They held your registration and without that, you couldn't play. The idea of Bill playing for a club in the south seems incongruous, yet it's hard to believe that he would have turned down Arsenal. Alec certainly wouldn't have allowed that!

Bill was happy to stay with Preston. After all, he was about to embark on his first season at the summit of the English game. For such a devotee of the sport, there could be no more exciting prospect and by this time he was a Preston man through and through, with many friends in the town. Things were progressing very positively. Chairman Taylor had no intention of making up the numbers in the First Division. In keeping with the proud history of the club, he was intent on making a mark and challenging for honours. With promotion won, he embarked on a policy of experimentation coupled with investment in a highly productive youth policy, one which was to lead to the development of the great Tom Finney in due course. Even as a twenty-year-old, Bill always took a great interest in the youth team, as Finney explains. 'He was always looking to watch the youngsters play, to give them advice and help them along; part of it was that he was such a nutter about football that he'd watch any sort of game, but he knew how important encouragement was to young players. We would regard people in the first team like Bill with awe, tremendous respect. It was a great occasion just to get in the dressing room with them and if they spoke to you, it was a bonus. Bill was so obsessed with the youth team that he'd always come and have a word, say you'd done something well.'

The consummate club man, Shankly recognised early on the obvious truth that still escapes so many. A strong youth policy secures the future of the club. He was happy to do anything he could to help Preston North End and the boys affiliated to it. He saw it as a very enjoyable duty, the chance to guide youngsters into the wonderful career offered by professional football. Provided you gave your all, you had a friend in Bill, but woe betide you if you let your standards slip as Finney remembers: 'He never thought that just being able to play was enough. You had to do the work too. He didn't have any time for people who didn't look after themselves properly.'

Imposing himself on a club where he was still the new boy gave an early indication that he was something out of the ordinary. When one newspaper produced a profile of Preston prior to their first season back in Division One, the pen picture composed for Bill read: 'While we were at Deepdale we were told – and we can quite credit it – that Shankly, the "baby" of the team, takes dynamite with his milk.' The challenge now was to fill in a few of the blanks that existed around him. Jimmy Dougal was brought in from Falkirk midway through the promotion run and performed well as an inside forward. He was to be a pivotal figure in a different position later on in his career when he was given a free role at centre-forward, part of the flowing passing game to which Tom Finney has alluded.

The next two seasons were ones of consolidation for Preston, as they looked to confirm their status at football's top table.

1934/35 had them comfortably ensconced in the middle of
the division, though an exciting Cup run took them through
to the Sixth Round where they were despatched by West
Bromwich Albion, 1-0 at the Hawthorns. The following season
saw further steady progress and the gradual evolution of a
side that looked ready to become a powerful force in English
football over the next decade. Jimmy Milne and Andy Beattie
were emerging players and the accent which the managerial
triumvirate placed on team-work was starting to get results;
the arrival of Beattie in 1935 saw the beginning of a lifelong
friendship with Shankly that was to have important reper-
cussions for both. Bill himself was gathering plaudits wherever
he went and by the end of that 1935/36 season he was regarded
as one of the finest half backs in the land. One report called
the twenty-two year old 'perpetual motion with a capital "P".
I have never known a player quite like the Glenbuck boy.' It
was not too far-fetched to begin to wonder if Bill might actually
achieve his boyhood dream and pull on a Scotland shirt.

These were things for the future for Bill was still learning
the game. He had grown in stature and confidence throughout
these early seasons in Division One and had worked hard to
eradicate the impetuosity that had dogged him at Carlisle.
Always a fiercely passionate man when it came to football, he
could still occasionally be caught out, yet by 1936 he was
being roundly praised for his 'uncanny positional sense'. Tom
Finney was still a young boy at this stage but he was a regular
at Deepdale, soaking up the atmosphere and learning from
the professionals. Training with the club as a boy, he had the
chance to observe the first team at close quarters and was
among the first to note Bill's absolute belief in himself. 'He
was a very good player, fit and enthusiastic, used the ball well.
The whole thing about Bill was that he was just intent on
being a great player. It never worried him who he was playing
against, whether it was someone like Peter Doherty, Wilf
Mannion, Raich Carter, all great players. He just went out with
the attitude that he was every bit as good as they were and
he'd show them.'

One of his great virtues was his consistency, rarely having a poor game; in that regard, it's easy to see why he was so fond of Ian Callaghan at Liverpool, another player who turned in a good performance week in, week out. Everyone has a bad game now and again, however talented and committed they may be, but for Bill that was no excuse. If he was having a stinker, he'd still be looking for the ball, trying to get his tackles in. If his timing was off, he'd simplify his distribution and make the easier passes. In short, Bill Shankly wouldn't hide but would keep trying, a characteristic that is prized above all others by managers and coaches. The press tagged him 'Preston North End's most popular player because of his love of the game and his level-headedness.' The affection for him covered players, press and public alike as further tributes illustrated, one commentator noting that he was 'a powerful defender, a brainy, cultured attacker and a whole-hearted ninety minutes player of the finest type'. To Tom Finney, 'in terms of his influence on the pitch, the way he could get other people to play, a fair comparison would be with Bryan Robson'. Given that Bryan Robson at his peak would now command a fee in the region of £9,000,000, it's clear that Bill Shankly could play a bit.

Ironically, it was in their first disappointing season in Division One, 1936/37, when they finished fourteenth, that Preston came close to winning a trophy. The side they had was starting to show signs of wear and tear. Off the field, Tommy Muirhead was brought in to take over as team manager, a one-year experiment that was quickly dispensed with when James Taylor returned to the helm late in 1937. Even so, Preston performed impressively in the Cup, realising that it might represent a last chance of glory for some of their number. Having overcome Tottenham in the Sixth Round, they were drawn against West Bromwich Albion for the Semi-Final. Given their poor record against Albion over many years, few gave them much hope but Shankly was typically defiant. 'I think we are on a good thing if our nerves do not fail us, and why should they? We played at Tottenham in the last round as if we were at Deepdale and you cannot expect a bigger crowd at Highbury.' Shankly's confidence must have rubbed off on his team mates for Preston won handsomely, 4-1, and took their place at Wembley where they would face Sunderland.

Again Shankly expressed no doubts about the outcome – 'I do not think there is any doubt about the result. We have a good team' – but this time his bravado masked a deeper concern. Sunderland were a very powerful outfit and had taken the League title in convincing fashion the previous year; Bill said in his book that 'that team was so good that it was a frightening experience to go to Roker Park'. Just as he drew from Arsenal's approach in later years, his Liverpool teams also owed much to the free running style of the Rokermen and the intimidating atmosphere which they and their supporters could create. With dynamic forwards such as Patsy Gallacher and Raich Carter, it was always likely that the Preston defence would face a testing afternoon and so it proved. Preston froze and despite taking the lead through Frank O'Donnell, the Sunderland attack overran them in the second half to run out 3-1 winners. Shankly was, according to the reports, 'one of the few Preston men to enhance his reputation'.

Unfortunate to be missing goalkeeper Holdcroft through injury, Preston had been outclassed. Like the other members of the team, Bill was bitterly disappointed by their failure but was encouraged by the words of the Chairman. 'He stood up and said we'd be back again. He was crying, shedding big tears of disappointment.' Though the circumstances were desperately discouraging, Bill could at least draw comfort from the fighting spirit shown by Taylor and was pleased to see that he was among people who felt as strongly about the game as he did.

With the pain of their Wembley defeat in mind, Preston set about the new season with renewed vigour. George Mutch joined the club from Manchester United for £5,000 and quickly formed a potent partnership with Jimmy Dougal who was given increasing licence to roam. The addition of ball-juggling inside forward Bobby Beattie, bought from Kilmarnock in October 1937 for £2,250, was the final piece in the jigsaw, with Watmough and Hugh O'Donnell on the wings. Frank O'Donnell, though a Scottish international, was apparently considered too much of an individualist and was often left out of the team, eventually leaving in November; this left Preston with the diminutive forward line that Tom Finney described, players who liked the ball in to feet rather than having to fight for hopeful long balls.

Taylor was now looking for Preston to refine their closely-knit team-work still further and was building a side that played in a similar style to that of Sunderland; fearing that their pattern of play had been too predictable, Taylor encouraged a constant interchange of positions among the forwards, often using Dougal as the leader of the line. Once again, these were important lessons that Shankly picked up on and this fluidity of movement came to be a hallmark of his own teams later on. At the back, Gallimore and Andy Beattie were forging a strong partnership, Beattie having moved back there after playing earlier games at half back and on the wing. His conversion in February 1937 was a springboard to an impressive career for he quickly established himself as Scotland's first choice left-back. Andy's success helped convince Bill that a player's position was not set in stone; the important thing was whether a man could play or not. Liverpool learned that lesson well when changing Ray Kennedy, Bill's last buy, from a forward to one of the finest midfielders in the country. Alec Lindsay was another who benefited from this open-minded approach, moving from midfield to left-back and winning England honours in the process.

Defensively solid and with an enterprising group of forwards, the half-back line was the crucial engine room of the side. Milne and Shankly were well set on either flank but club skipper Bill Tremelling was coming to the end of a long career at centre-half. He was replaced by another Scottish international, Tom Smith, bought for £2,850 from Kilmarnock midway through the 1936/37 season, though it wasn't until after the Wembley defeat that he broke through into the side and took over as captain. Every bit as keen as Bill, he completed one of the most powerful half-back formations in the country, allowing the club to approach the new season in a confident frame of mind. He also increased the Scottish complement which now included Hugh O'Donnell, Andy and Bobby Beattie, Milne, Dougal, Smith, Mutch, Maxwell and Bill Shankly.

The side in place, they made sedate progress through the League that year and were seldom far from the top of the table. One of the biggest reasons for Preston's success was their preparation. Little was left to chance. The club would often get away from Preston for a few days to train, keeping the players together. This fostered an excellent team spirit and also allowed the management to ensure that their men were eating the right food, exercising properly and looking after themselves. Bill 'had my own ideas about diet. Whenever we stayed at a hotel, I would be able to order my favourite dish – huge chops boiled in barley or poached eggs by the dozen ... I always say that if you train like Jack Dempsey, you must feel like Jack Dempsey.' For Bill, his favourite boxers like Dempsey or Joe Louis were the fittest men on earth. If they ate steak, then he'd eat steak. The right food was always central to Shanklyism. Fitness was a prerequisite for a man who 'played on my toes all the time like a ballet dancer. That gave me strength in my calves.' That strength drove him on through game after game.

Preston always travelled to away fixtures early on the Friday so they would be fresh for the following day and sometimes even stayed in hotels overnight prior to a particularly import- ant home game. This was another policy that impressed Bill tremendously. Preston's willingness to channel resources into the right areas – good players and excellent training facilities – became a staple of his managerial philosophy. When he finally arrived at a club with the resources to match his ambition, Liverpool, 'we started to go away for every match, home games too, on a Friday night. That's when the preparation starts, it's tremendously important. We'd get a hotel at ten, have some toast and honey and go to bed. Have a little meal the next day, but it's very important to make sure players don't overeat. Go away for every single match. That way the players stay together, they get to know one another, they play like they're on speaking terms.'

Preston now proved the equal of every side in the country. Their inventive play was a joy and again Bill received plenty of praise in the local and national papers. After a comfortable 3-1 win over Leeds United, Vulcan wrote that 'Shankly and Mutch towered head and shoulders above all the others for sheer genius.' Another reporter at the same match suggested that 'Shankly was inexhaustible.' One further column made the comment that must have pleased him above all others: 'Shankly is the best team man in football.' Living for the game, day after day, Bill had been able to accumulate the experience that helped him channel his instinctive natural ability in the best fashion; he was the beating heart of the Preston side. A veteran of around 200 League games by the season's end, he was coming into his own as a player of the very highest class.

The whole team was much stronger than the previous year and that essential blend of youth and experience was coming into its own. Throughout the season, Preston were always there or thereabouts in the title race. So dominant were they, Bill even had the opportunity to register his first goal in League football in a 2-2 draw against Liverpool at Anfield. Following the hectic Easter period they readied themselves for the challenge of Arsenal at Deepdale, having gone joint top with the Londoners. Having put Arsenal out of the F.A. Cup with an epic victory at Highbury, hopes were high that Preston would take the points at home, and with them the title. Sadly, Jimmy Milne was seriously injured early on in the game, sustaining a broken collar bone that put him out for the rest of the term. Hard though they fought, the ten men were no match for Arsenal who won 3-1. An understandable end of season slump saw Preston finally finish third, three points behind Arsenal.

That slump had its roots in another competition for another

F.A. Cup Final was on the horizon. With all realistic hopes of the League now gone, Preston saved themselves for Wembley and the chance to exorcise the ghosts of the previous year. The club had opened the 1937/38 season desperate above all else to return to Wembley and avenge their defeat of the previous year. Their passage through the early stages of the competition was serene enough, a George Mutch hat-trick disposing of West Ham early on, Preston then going to Highbury and beating League leaders Arsenal in a tense tie. In the Semi-Final, they came up against Aston Villa, where the winning goal was created by a long throw from Bill Shankly. All those long summer days in Glenbuck throwing balls over the houses were made worthwhile in that one moment and Preston were back in the Final again.

Certainly they could have faced fiercer opponents than Huddersfield who ended the season in the lower reaches of the First Division and the team were able to make light of the loss of Jimmy Milne. Having been guilty of over-confidence the year before, this time Preston set about their task in workmanlike fashion. The first Cup Final to be televised live was a disappointment for though Preston had the better of the play, neither side could score. A dour spectacle ensued, Shankly barking instructions alongside Smith, marshalling operations for his side. Contemporary reports suggest that 'Shankly was effective and inspiring . . . he played Huddersfield's Barclay out of the game and still gave fine service to his wing in front.' Indeed, Bill came closest to breaking the deadlock with five minutes of extra-time remaining, forcing an acrobatic save from a long shot.

With the game entering the final minute, Mutch darted into the penalty area and was brought down to give Preston a penalty. Thrown down against the bone-hard ground, Mutch wrote later 'I was dazed. I did not even understand that a penalty had been awarded. They handed me the ball. I placed it automatically.' Given that Bill always said that a professional footballer should never miss a penalty – he scored eight in his career at Preston – it was possibly a little surprising that he didn't take the responsibility from his injured team-mate. Mutch certainly thought so. 'I wondered hazily why none of them seemed anxious to take the kick . . . I took that kick more casually than I would at morning practice.' The kick rattled against the centre of the crossbar and rolled down the back of the net to give Preston the trophy. There was scarcely time to kick-off again.

For Bill this was the greatest moment of his playing career. 'When the whistle blows at Wembley and you've played in a Final and you've won, that's the greatest thrill of your life . . . No doubt about that. I thanked God for that. The feeling is unbelievable.' 1937/38 had been his greatest season and it ended with a European tour, a reward for their hugely successful year. The club played in France, Czechoslovakia and Romania and took in much of central Europe in what was a real eye-opener for the young men, most of whom had never left Great Britain before. 'We went all the way along the Danube. In Munich, we missed Hitler by a day. He'd just left. In Oberammergau they were all wearing beards. I was ignorant, I didn't understand why. It was the Passion Play . . . In Budapest, the people were wonderful. In Romania, a man offered Harry Holdcroft, our goalkeeper, his sister in exchange for a ticket for the match!' Further oddities were around the corner for Preston, for as Cup holders they had to play Arsenal at Highbury for the Charity Shield in September. The evening game attracted just 7,233 fans and was, for some reason, played in total darkness, the Arsenal authorities failing to switch on the floodlights. As soon as the game ended in a 2-1 win for Arsenal the players trooped off the pitch. Just then, the lights came on!

At the end of the 1937/38 season, Bill Shankly could consider himself to be a half-back at the top of his profession. He believed that he was coming to his peak, achieving the perfect balance of experience and physical fitness. Perseus wrote of him in the local press that 'a more whole-souled footballer or finer club servant I have not known and none has earned his preeminence more fully.' James Taylor felt the same for after the Final, he approached the Football League and secured their permission to pay Bill the then maximum benefit of £650, as a token of the club's esteem. However, it appears that that payment was never made, the first of many disappointments Bill was to suffer at the hands of the game's administrators.

Few professionals were more highly regarded than Bill Shankly. Proof had come with the realisation of another long cherished ambition prior to the Cup Final. In April 1938, Bill was invited to make his international debut for Scotland against England at Wembley Stadium.

chapter seven

SCOTLAND THE BRAVE

With Preston set to face Huddersfield Town in the F.A. Cup Final at Wembley in May 1938, those fans that were left in Glenbuck got their money together to buy tickets through their local association. After the disappointment of a year before, they were determined to see their boy pick up a winner's medal. With Cup Final tickets at a premium, the only way they could afford them was to sell those they had for the England-Scotland game at Wembley a month earlier. A few days after they'd sold them, the team was announced with Bill Shankly filling the number four shirt. So it was that Bill took the stage at Wembley without any of his townsfolk in the crowd. This was a pity for he was as pleased for them as for himself; honours meant little if they could not be shared and he described his international debut as 'the greatest day of my father's life'. In an attempt to show that his roots were still of vital importance, he addressed the children at the village school prizegiving in June, showing them his Cup winner's medal and Scotland shirt.

Given their impressive play and the high proportion of Scots in the side, it was no surprise to see Preston providing Scotland with four men – Shankly, Mutch, Smith and Andy Beattie; the *Daily Despatch* termed the game 'England versus Preston'. For Bill, this was excellent for it helped him fit in right away. For Preston it provided problems. In those days, internationals were often played on the same day as ordinary League games. The national sides had first call on the players so Preston had to play Derby without four regulars. It was testament to their quality that they won 4-1.

Determined as he was to help Preston in their quest to take the League and Cup double for the second time, all thoughts of that flew out of the window once Bill got his call up papers, for he really did treat it as if he was going to War: 'Steeped in the history of Robert the Bruce and William Wallace, we were Scottish to the core. The wee lion on your dark blue shirt roared out "Get out and kill them" and your heart swelled twice the size.' Jack Mindel remembers that 'he was a very nationalistic Scotsman, the Scots could do no wrong. His idea of a good evening was to talk about Scotland and listen to Kenneth McKellar singing.' McKellar was one of his choices when he went on *Desert Island Discs*, singing the Burns composition 'My Love Is like A Red, Red Rose'.

Those at the club were delighted for him since they knew how much he wanted to play for his country. Such recognition was just reward for his sterling efforts at club level. Thinking back to his years as a child in a mining village, Bill remembered just how important it was that they should put one over on England, revenge for all the indignities the bigger country had heaped upon them and for the economic deprivation that always seemed worse in his homeland than down south. With all this in mind, he readied himself for battle. The England team was a powerful one with Hapgood, Cullis, Copping, Matthews and Bastin, but with the backbone of the Preston contingent, Scotland were a cohesive unit too.

Bobby Reid played for Scotland that day and later wrote that 'Bill was an honest, hard-working player and ran until he dropped. The lion on his shirt was always tearing out for victory. That was how he played the game.' Bill received a painful introduction to international football when Wilf Copping met him in a tackle that 'burst my stocking – the shin-pad was out – and cut my leg ... he was older than me and had a reputation. He had no fear at all. But while we were fighting for Scotland that day, we didn't go round trying to cripple people.' Shankly had the last laugh though when Tommy Walker scored the only goal of the game for the Scots, a fierce drive from fully thirty yards out.

Bill's pleasure in victory was heightened the following day when he saw the newspapers. He was always happy to remind people later on that his 'boyhood idol Davie Meiklejohn praised me in a report on the match', a moment as thrilling as playing in the game itself. Though he had to miss out on Scotland's next game in Amsterdam, along with his other Preston colleagues, Bill was a fixture in the Scottish side and went on to play in their remaining four internationals before the War. His second game, against Ireland in Belfast in October 1938, saw the Scots win 2-0. Waverley described him as 'a master of defence and forceful in construction. The Glenbuck boy simply lives for football and is of such a temperament that I doubt if he could play a bad game if he tried.'

A month later the Welsh were beaten 3-2 at Edinburgh's Tynecastle in his best game for his country. Certainly Meiklejohn singled him out for praise again with comments that must have warmed his heart: 'If I ever served my country as well as big-hearted Bill Shankly – well, I would feel proud. What a gallant worker he was, anywhere was his territory. More, since the last time I saw him, he has improved on the feeding of his forwards.' Tam O'Shanter wrote that 'Shankly was the star, a worker on behalf of everyone and brilliant in his passing.' Waverley added that Bill Shankly 'is our number one right-half without a doubt'. Another of his heroes, Alex James, noted that 'Shankly has practically made the half-back position his own. He is a real Scotland player who will fight until he drops.' Perhaps this was the most significant comment. Playing before his home supporters for the first time Bill was desperately keen to do well. Together with Tommy Walker and Jimmy Delaney, he formed an intelligent combination on the right flank that created many problems for the opposition. On a mud-heap, his immense physical strength was the perfect antidote to the dreadful conditions for he was able to keep running long after the cloying ground had sapped the strength of others. It was this willingness to run all day for the cause that so endeared him to his native supporters.

International games still mean a great deal to fans, though perhaps rather less than they did fifty or sixty years ago. As club football has grown in importance, the role of the national side has diminished. Yet it still plays a crucial role among those deeply committed to the game in their country. When an international is being played, supporters can turn a blind eye to the property developer or porn-merchant that runs their club and delude themselves for a few brief hours that football is the people's game once more, unsullied by high-finance and the need to generate revenue. Fans can remember how they once felt about the game before they were forced to take refuge in cynicism, when they thought football was all about glory. Those lads running out in the country's colours represent the fans, supporters are united behind them. Everyone knows that the establishment is run by the footballing equivalent of the living dead, that men so far out of touch with the game pick and choose managers, but with an effort, it's possible to ignore it. They don't take the supporters' money and abuse it every week, just four or five times a year. Everyone can live with that if they have to. When the national side takes the field, they are the people's team. They don't belong to Walker, Sullivan, Hayward, Hall, Littlewoods, Coca-Cola or anybody else. They are ours. They are doing what everyone dreamt of as a child, pulling on their country's shirt. They should appreciate the honour, not by the histrionic kissing of the badge in celebration of a goal, but by carrying themselves with pride and with dignity.

Despite the views of certain commentators, football supporters are not stupid and never have been. They recognise a player who gives everything and quickly differentiate between him and the cheat, who will go missing when his team needs him. Fans will forgive a lot if they can see that a player is giving of his best. Bill played the game the way they would have played it if they'd been good enough to pull on that blue shirt. Shankly wore his Scottish jersey like the great privilege it was and they loved him for it. A devoted club man at Preston, these games for Scotland were special. He was playing for all the little people that were abused by the 'big men' in mining villages, in shipyards and in factories all over Scotland.

They needed an excuse to unite and to forget their worries. As their representative on the field, he would do his damnedest to give them what they deserved. He resented the committee men who selected the team from ignorance rather than knowledge but, just like the crowd, he submerged this resentment beneath his pride in his country.

Two further games for Scotland followed, a 3-1 win over Hungary at Ibrox and finally, at Hampden Park in April 1939, a game against England. With victories over Ireland and Wales in the bag, a win over England would take the Home International Championship and the triple-crown. It's a game that he recalled vividly. In pouring rain, Scotland were a goal up through Jimmy Dougal with just twenty minutes left when Pat Beasley of Huddersfield equalised. Then, Matthews went past two players and Bill approached. Halfway across, Matthews lifted the ball over him towards Tommy Lawton. 'As the ball went home like a bullet,' Bill recalled forty years on, 'the swish and ripple of the soaking net made a sound that frightened me. "Pick that one out" said Lawton, and it was like a knife going through me ... That moment was like doomsday.' That was how much playing for Scotland meant. The game lost, there was some consolation: 'Lawton, a great centre-forward. And Matthews. So we weren't beaten by nobodies, we were beaten by players.'

Although the political situation in April 1939 was deeply worrying, no-one realised that England and Scotland would not line up against one another in a full international for another eight years. Bill Shankly's full representative career was over at twenty-five. Bigger battles were about to be fought.

chapter eight

LIFE DURING WARTIME

At the outbreak of the First World War, the Establishment had sought to quash all organised games, fearing that they were preventing young men from joining up and diverting those in reserved occupations from their patriotic duty on the home front. By the outbreak of World War Two, the Government realised that sport had a role to play in maintaining morale. While the Football League was suspended for the duration, the authorities wasted little time in inaugurating regional tournaments.

In spite of the wartime conditions, Bill continued to look after himself and played regularly for Preston in the Northern League. For the first time he lined up with Tom Finney, who was to become his favourite, 'the greatest player I ever saw. Good in the air, close control was unbelievable, he could attack you and run past you, face you and deceive you. He was crafty, kept the ball away from you. Great awareness to deal with an opponent the way that man should be dealt with. He was quick, elusive, all the attributes. When he had the ball, it was his, he was composed, didn't have to do anything in a hurry.'

Bill always had a Finney anecdote to tell. John Roberts remembers that when they were putting together *Shankly*, 'whatever part of his life we were talking about, it would invariably trigger a story about Tommy Finney'. Tommy had all the skills that Bill would have loved. Bill knew the game and had more than enough ability to play it well, but Tommy was special. Working with him at Preston, Bill knew everything that Finney was capable of and was favourably disposed towards him but he didn't pick too many poor players in his time. His opinion of Tom Finney commands respect.

Just as important, Bill commanded respect from Tom Finney.

As a youth team player, the encouragement he and the other lads received from Shankly was central to their development but once they were in the same team they were colleagues. Bill was never one to pull rank or demand favours as the senior pro. Instead 'he was a great character in the dressing room. He was never one to be worried,' explains Tom. 'He'd be keyed up, but he helped relax players who were nervous, he'd make jokes or put on some long johns and pretend to be an old-time boxer.'

In the face of war's real casualties, to describe the loss of a footballing career as tragic is dubious to say the least. In a sporting context however, the Preston supporters were denied perhaps the finest team that even that town with its proud history had ever produced. The Cup winners were still young and the Beatties, Shankly, Dougal and Mutch would have been in their pomp through the war. With the addition of Tom Finney, the Preston trophy cabinet would have been well stocked. Instead, they had to make do with regional games and a constantly changing side. Although the level of competition was weaker, Bill played it hard but fair. According to Tom 'there was no difference to Bill between wartime games and what had gone before. He was just as keen.'

North End proved just what the country was missing when they became champions of the North in 1941. After two penalties from Bill had disposed of Newcastle, they went on to play Arsenal in the wartime Cup Final, Tom Finney's first big game. 'Bill was behind me at right-half. We played at Wembley and got a 1-1 draw and then won the replay at Blackburn 2-1. It was a great occasion for me as an eighteen year old but playing with players like Bill made it easier; he was never quiet during a game. If you can come into an experienced side, you've a much better chance of improving your own game.'

Even Bill's war wasn't given over to football. Having been a coal-miner he could have returned to the pits, a reserved occupation. Instead, he went to work as soon as war was declared on 3 September. Tom Finney recalls him going 'to a local firm, Thomas Crofts. He was shovelling sand and I know from people there that he attacked that job in exactly the same spirit as he did his football.' Bill reckoned later that he shifted 'a Sahara's worth of sand' over several months. However much he moved, he would never have got rich doing it for the pay was an hourly rate of one shilling, tuppence three farthings. He had a spell as a riveter working on Hampden Bombers, though the factory stifled him and every evening he went for long walks to get his necessary quota of fresh air. It was no surprise then that, on 18 June 1940, the day after Winston Churchill made his famous 'finest hour' speech, he enlisted in the Royal Air Force.

His initial posting was Padgate, near Warrington, which offered him the chance to continue playing for Preston when his duties allowed. Early on, he was sent to RAF Cosford for training. Among the intake was Ellis Robinson who had played first-class cricket for Yorkshire prior to the war. 'We were on a PTI (Physical Training Instructor's) Course and a nicer man you couldn't wish to meet. The "bull" when you first join up is a terrible bind but Bill took it in his stride; I think he saw it as useful discipline and a way to keep fit and keep busy. He even undertook the chores of some of his colleagues, most of whom were fellow sportsmen. He'd do more than his share of window cleaning, stove polishing and so on.'

Though committed to the war effort and a passionate opponent of fascism, Tom Finney felt that 'his main ambition in the RAF was to get out and start playing again!' He threw himself into his work at Cosford, where the generous side of his nature came through time and again. Ellis Robinson remembers that 'each lunch-time, we went to the NAAFI where we met up with some elderly soldiers, members of the Pioneer Corps, who worked on the station with the anti-aircraft guns. Bill would always buy a drink for them every day.' This was just a part of his lifelong identification with men who had done their job and done it well. He felt that working people should receive recognition for their efforts in the service of their country, in whatever capacity they had done it. This gesture was one of solidarity with the older men.

It was typical of him that he spent time with the ordinary soldiers rather than kowtowing to the top brass. At Cosford he received another unpleasant reminder that those in charge held all the cards and weren't afraid to play them against the lower ranks. A natural PT instructor in many respects – he was adept at getting men fit when he became a manager – he was taken off the course quickly. According to Ellis, 'the powers that be thought that his broad Scottish brogue would not be understood on the parade ground'. Though he thought little of service life, this would have been a painful blow to his ego, an example of the way ordinary people were discriminated against.

After his spell at Cosford, Bill was trained for duty in a barrage balloon unit. This saw him moving around the country from station to station. After a brief period in St. Athans, his next posting was to Manchester in December 1940. Since this was close to his adopted home of Preston and offered excellent sporting facilities, his days there were amongst the best he had during these war years. At Manchester he rekindled his interest in boxing, turning out for the camp on occasion at middle-weight. He won a trophy as the camp team were winners of the Duke of Portland Cup. Not restricting himself to boxing of course, he played football for the Balloon Barrage Depot (Bury) in the Manchester & District RAF League. The level of commitment to these minor games was never in doubt. Phil Townsend, a left-back who proved good enough to play as the only amateur in a station team full of professionals under the captaincy of England international Jack Crayston, came up against Shankly in a game for RAF Hanforth in the 1941/42 season. His son John recalls that 'my father said it was like tackling a brick wall. They engaged in several fierce but fair tackles, but Shankly was very terse and single-minded, interested only in winning, saying very little throughout.'

While at Manchester he suffered the only serious injury of his career in a Cup game for Preston at Halifax in November 1941. He wrote in his autobiography that 'I came from Halifax to Manchester on a bus over the moors and my leg was a terrible size. I went to Crumpsall Hospital and ... they thought at first I had a broken knee-cap ... When I got back to the camp in Manchester, the old MO said "I don't think you will play again."' Eventually, the problem was diagnosed as cartilage trouble and was rectified later in the War. Even so, Bill continued to play with the injury for two years.

Service life was very hard, designed as it was to bring men to a high level of fitness. Bill's greatest problem though was in finding food. John Roberts notes that 'I know he enjoyed his boxing but I think he got so involved with that to make sure he got extra food!' Given the views he had on diet and his intense desire to keep himself in the best condition he could, this view is entirely credible. With meat rationed, Bill would always be on the look-out for a good steak. He enjoyed boxing but recalled later on that 'I fought one fella, and he was a professional. Candidly, from the start I knew he was in a different class. We fought three two-minute rounds and I spent all the time wrestling with him! He won, but at least he didn't land a punch!'

Great emphasis was placed on maintaining 'normal' sporting activity and a host of representative games were arranged. Bill played in his fair share of these fixtures, turning out for an RAF team that also included Hardwick, Hapgood, Joy, Matthews, Carter and Doherty and playing for a Scottish XI and even Army sides at times. International fixtures were played and Bill amassed seven caps through the War, once captaining Scotland in a 3-1 defeat against England in front of 78,000 at Hampden in May 1941. The following year, Bill gained his revenge, scoring in a 5-4 triumph over England at Hampden, with the press reporting that 'Shankly and Busby were the architects of the win'. Though Dodds and Lawton both scored hat-tricks, it was Shankly's goal that stayed in the memory. Billy Liddell wrote later: 'Shanks shot from thirty yards and as England keeper George Marks came out, the ball bounced over his head and into the net.' Jimmy Carabine was right-back that day and remembered 'although I was captain,

Bill shouted instructions the whole game'. Rex painted a vivid picture of this dogged warrior: 'Shankly was a great fellow all the time, shoulders braced, the blood of The Bruce in his veins and the skill of the football ace in his feet.'

One feature of the War was the number of 'aid' games staged where the proceeds would be used to fund war-work. One such match was staged at Wembley in January 1942 while Bill was in Manchester, an England-Scotland 'Aid To Russia' benefit. Things were so bad on the home front, the entire Scottish side had to be kitted out in jerseys worn by Tommy Walker over the course of his own representative career; there were insufficient clothing coupons available to get new Scottish shirts.

It was during the War that Bill's international career came to an end. The hierarchy were worried about the knee injury, despite the fact that he'd completed many games, including internationals, successfully. As Willie Waddell wrote later, the committee insisted that he undergo a fitness test prior to the Wembley international in February 1944. 'There was no doubt about Bill being fit to play. Our trainer took him to Stamford Bridge and asked him to kick the post with the injured leg. Bill didn't waste time and told him he wouldn't do it with his other foot either. He was withdrawn from the team.' He was never recalled, an example of the petty behaviour that he despised in the authorities.

Disappointed when he had to leave Manchester in August 1942, he took solace in the fact that he was being posted back to his native Scotland, to an NCO course in Arbroath. There for six weeks, he took advantage of the relaxed registration rulings that were effective throughout the War. This meant that a player who was in the services could turn out for the local side depending on where he was stationed; he'd already had a number of games for Cardiff City during his stay at St. Athans and for Liverpool and Bolton Wanderers from his Manchester base. When in Arbroath, he managed to play five games for East Fife, which included a 2-1 victory over Glasgow Rangers and a 3-2 win at Hibernian, despite the fact that he somehow contrived to miss a penalty, the cardinal sin.

From Arbroath, he was sent to Great Yarmouth for a month in January 1943 prior to yet another posting. He still had time to fit in three games for nearby Norwich City at Carrow Road though. In spite of the way in which football was held up as an ideal recreation throughout the war, certain Commanding Officers weren't always keen on releasing their charges. Keen to get a game, many would slope out of the camps anyway and play under an assumed name. With Norwich happy to use him, he played for them under the name Rod Newman. This provides an indication of the difference between the position players hold today compared with fifty years ago; would a top Premiership player and regular international be able to play league matches under an alias without anyone recognising him today? Back in the 1930s, players might occasionally have their blurred photo in the paper or be sufficiently well known to take their place on a cigarette card. Though the name Shankly was well known to football supporters throughout England, few outside Preston, and certainly outside the First Division clubs, would know what he looked like. One of his colleagues in two of these games was Ginger Johnson, one of Norwich's own players. When I informed him of Shankly's participation in the game, he thanked me 'for answering the mystery of Rod Newman's appearance at Carrow Road. All these years, I have been unaware that Newman and Bill Shankly were one and the same.' Whether the increased celebrity that players have today is an entirely positive development is a difficult question to answer, but there must be times when Paul Gascoigne would enjoy the anonymity that Bill had in those days.

From the Great Yarmouth recruiting depot, Bill moved on to Henlow, just north of Luton, in February 1943. It was here that he encountered Jack Mindel and struck up a lifelong friendship. 'I was a PT instructor in the RAF and I was on duty when I saw this figure approaching. I recognised him and I was surprised to see him because he'd only recently played for Scotland at Wembley. I went over to him and said "Bill Shankly! What are you doing here?" He was thrilled that I knew about him,' presumably all the more so after his experience at Norwich. Unlike his experience of PT instructors elsewhere, Bill took to Jack straight away and enjoyed his company, finding him free from the 'bull' that many employed to keep the lower ranks in check. A keen sportsman, Jack's father had been a successful boxer and this common feeling for the sport brought them closer.

'I was organising boxing shows at the camp and I invited him to the gym. I knew the game, I'd been busy in boxing, arranging exhibitions and so on. Bill put the gloves on and we started sparring. Although he hadn't a lot of experience, he was a natural. His physique, his balance, his sense of timing was as good as most professional boxers.' The way Bill had kept in shape during the war impressed him too. 'He loved to train in whatever form, whether it was boxing, kicking a ball around, running. He was just mad on physical fitness.'

Bill worked as hard as any man could to keep in shape. While at Henlow, he had the call to go up to Hampden Park and play for Scotland against England, in front of 105,000. The game ended in a 4-0 win for England, Raich Carter notching a brace. The result wasn't the only source of disappointment for Bill. Throughout the war, he could occasionally be drawn off the subject of football and on to wider topics. At Henlow, he would talk about politics with Jack Mindel who quickly saw that 'he was a Labour man, with politics shaped by poverty. He would always give his opinions to Tories or Labour supporters just the same and if they didn't like it, it was too bad because he was an ardent socialist. As a player, particularly at the internationals, he met officials who were far removed from the game and that upset him. He felt they knew nothing about football, these people could select a team without even knowing who the players were, without recognising them. He didn't like it because he was a proud man. He didn't like to be treated as a nobody by people who were nothing except for the fact they had money. He resented it very deeply and would stand up for his rights. He did feel that class distinction very badly and that only made him all the more a Labour man.'

The distinction was especially marked for games in Scotland. 'They had to meet up at King's Cross station,' Jack explains. 'A few of the players were talking and one of the selectors came over and addressed him and got his name wrong. Bill was angry about that and that while the players who would have to go out and play for their country all travelled third class, the officials were in first class. The selectors had a buffet and yet the players had to bring their own sandwiches.' Disgust at the way officials placed themselves above the most important people in the game – players and supporters – was an emotion that was to dog Bill throughout his career. Petty rules of any sort that came between him and his football were wholly unacceptable. Jim MacLaren, who was at Carlisle when Bill was manager, remembers his wartime tales: 'On Tuesdays, they had a drill where they had to wear gas masks for an hour but Bill wouldn't have it. Some junior NCO came up to him and told him to put it on. "Do you not realise who ye're talking to? Bill Shankly, right-half for Scotland next week. I need the fresh air."'. Certainly over his career at Preston and then at international level, the realisation that he was in the upper echelons of the professional game had helped him to conquer the shyness that had afflicted him early on. He now had that swagger that became famous later, a bottomless pit of self-confidence and a certain dogmatic arrogance that was somehow endearing. Bill maintained a boyish air over his obsessions such that it was hard to be upset with his assured behaviour.

As Jack Mindel stresses, 'At Henlow he made life very interesting for all the kids. He was a big name so everyone was interested in what he had to say. He'd hold sessions in the evenings, little lectures. He got hold of a blackboard and he'd explain tactics and how a manager would do things. The kids were thrilled with him.' His status could only increase every time he took the field for he was still a very impressive player, enjoying what he later thought were his best years in the game. With no intention of wasting them, he was pleased to be able to play for Arsenal while at

Henlow, though this caused some controversy. There were letters in the local press that suggested he should play for his nearest club, Luton Town, rather than travel down to London in such straitened times. However, he was given permission to play for the Gunners and took full advantage of the opportunity that offered.

His very short stay at Arsenal, through the final months of the 1942/43 season, was pivotal to his later career. Arsenal had been the dominant club in English football right through the 1930s. They had good players and good coaching staff, but so did other clubs and they had failed to achieve the same results. Shankly looked into the way the club did things and was impressed with what he saw. Their facilities were first-class, on and off the field, no expense was spared to give the players the best and, more importantly, to make them feel that they were the best. The palatial atmosphere of the ground made the players feel like kings.

There were disappointments in store at Arsenal. 'He used to tell me,' says Jack Mindel, 'that he couldn't ease off in those games the way the others did. Even if we were having a game at Henlow with the kids, he had to give 100%. He couldn't do anything else. When he saw some of the Arsenal players weren't trying, he used to go crazy, he couldn't understand them holding back. He was strong as anything, a tough player, his whole demeanour was very forthright, he lived a very straight life.'

He gave many excellent performances for Arsenal, helping them to the Football League South title. He was particularly impressive during their League South Cup run which took them all the way to the Final against Charlton, missing just one game. With Wembley beckoning, Bill was looking forward to another wartime medal. However, when they got there 'they wanted to get all the Arsenal players in the team,' Jack Mindel explains. 'Most of them were out of London which is why they had players like Bill guesting for them, but they called them all back to give them a game in the Final.' Typical of the non-controversial press coverage of the day, one paper reported that 'it was characteristic of a great club that although Bill played for them in every match through the League and wartime F.A. Cup ties, in the actual Cup Final at Wembley, they drew in their own players from far and near. Drake for example was brought from Reading and Crayston, hitherto kept out of the right-half position by Bill, was now loyally preferred to him. Bill Shankly himself had not the slightest grouse. No team ranks higher in his estimation.' The truth was a little different according to Jack: 'You can imagine what he thought of it! Ever after, if you spoke about Arsenal he got very upset, he just fell out with them. He was straight and he wanted everyone else to be. If they weren't he was upset. If you didn't do things right, he didn't like it, wouldn't tolerate it.'

Arsenal offered him tickets for the game along with some money but he threw it back with contempt. 'I wasn't playing for that. I played to keep my place in the team and now sentiment has come into it and you are playing your own players,' he told them. It was difficult to know which crime was worse – that they had dropped him from the side or that they hadn't understood that he was playing for the sake of it. Recalling Bill's indignation, Jack notes that 'he always stressed the importance of integrity, honesty. There was so much sleaziness going on around then, either side of the War. He told me of many instances where he'd been offered money for certain things but he refused it. He didn't agree with it and he didn't want anyone to be able to point the finger at him. He was very protective of his own reputation. When Arsenal had behaved badly towards him as he saw it and then offered him money, he was finished with them. He wouldn't play for them any longer and he went to Luton.'

Luton Town were taken with Bill's attitude and after the War they were keen to take him on as a player and then as a manager, but the timing was never right. Like so many other clubs, there were Shankly links there, brother John having played there. Bill was happy to turn out but it was a short-lived alliance. In September 1943, another posting came through, to

Bishopbriggs in Glasgow, though this time he had requested the move. A compassionate posting, he was allowed to go to Glasgow to be nearer his dying father. With Glenbuck around thirty miles away, this was the closest station he could find. His early days there were spent trying to engineer opportunities to visit the family, but there was no shortage of football. As he got off the train in Glasgow, he was greeted by directors from Partick Thistle who wanted him to play for them. Partick had a number of youngsters and they were keen to bring in an experienced pro like Bill to help them along. If Bill had had his eye on a Rangers shirt, the Scottish FA put a stop to that, ordering him to play for Partick, the closest team to the Bishopbriggs camp. It was an ideal combination, for the Partick supporters took to Bill, nicknaming him General Willie, and he remained with the club through the rest of the war. Alex Douglas, a lifelong Thistle fan, recalls Bill's days at Firhill very fondly and was told that 'Bill used to tell his young Thistle mates that if they happened to have the ball at their feet and were not sure what to do with it, they should just stick it in behind the opposing goalie and it would be safe enough there!' Though in his first game, on 2 October 1943, Thistle lost 6-2 at home to Dumbarton, the results through the rest of his stay were much more impressive.

Partick were good to Bill, paying the £150 necessary for him to go into a nursing home and have his cartilage removed. The knee had continued to bother him, but he refused to let it interfere with his appetite for the game. On that Partick debut, he took a further knock and had to succumb to the surgeon's knife. A piece of displaced cartilage, which should have been diagnosed in Manchester years previously, was taken out and Bill was soon playing again. Had it been treated at the time, he would not have been required to take the Stamford Bridge fitness test which ended his days at international level.

During his convalescence, he came to the attention of a young teleprinter operator on the station. Day after day, Bill would go out running alongside champion heavyweight Jock

Porter in a determined effort to regain his strength. Whatever the weather, the two of them could be seen pounding the lanes around Kirkintilloch, winding their way back to camp. Agnes Fisher, or Ness as she was soon to be known, 'was in the Signals hut right opposite the Guard Room. I'd see this couple running around, they weren't even stopping to salute the officers! I wondered who they were, these crazy men, so I asked someone. When they told me it was Bill Shankly, it didn't mean a thing because I didn't know a thing about football, didn't know that he was a professional, he was just another airman. I thought he was a nutcase!'

Word must have got back to Bill that an attractive young WAAF had been asking about him, for he quickly introduced himself. His initial welcome was less than rapturous because 'I couldn't stand him at first! But time passed and he'd come into Signals, which wasn't allowed, he'd bring toasted cheese over and ask me to go out with him. I wouldn't but he gradually wore me down!' The two discovered quickly that they were united in adversity. Ness' posting to Bishopbriggs was a compassionate one too for her mother was very ill at the time. Pretty soon they were arranging to take their leave together and he was trying to introduce Ness to football, an indication of the seriousness of his intentions.

'In the end, it was my father who said "Well, he's a nice boy, just please him and go to a match." He wore me down again and we went. They were playing against Celtic and I was petrified. I thought they were going to kill each other. I'd never been to a game before and I thought "he's not going to get killed in the war, he's going to get killed on the field!"' Bill's memory of the occasion was a little different. 'Half-time came and afterwards the teams came out again like at the beginning and Ness said "This is where we came in!"' Ness went to a few more games around then, though Bill's selection of fixtures might have been better: 'We were playing Rangers at Ibrox. It was cutting up rough. We'd gone to the game in a taxi, and the driver was a rabid Rangers fan, which is quite something. I had a fracas with Scott Symon so after the game the taxi driver just went and left me and Ness at Ibrox. We had to find our own way back!'

Bill's greatest success during the War came when he finally persuaded Ness to marry him. He'd taken her to meet his family. 'Glenbuck to me was the back of beyond,' she admits. 'He suggested we go down there to meet his parents. I was an only child and he'd been to see mum and dad already so I agreed. Little did I know it was a gathering of the clans! He hadn't even told me he had brothers and sisters so it was a shock! They were all very nice to me because in the village especially, they didn't really like Glasgow people, but I soon overcame that. His mother was a lovely lady, she never had a bad word to say, but she was strict, kept them in order.'

On 29 June 1944, Bill and Ness were married in Glasgow, carefully planning the date to make sure it didn't coincide with the football season. 'We married in church in Glasgow and then we went to Glenbuck for a little celebration there, but then it was back to work at the unit,' Ness recalls. For Bill, it was also back to the football. His performances for Partick were generally excellent, the more so after his knee operation when he wanted to pay them back for their generosity. In sixty-nine games, he notched twelve goals, seven from the penalty spot, and helped Thistle win the Summer Cup in June 1945, when they beat Hibernian 2-0. One game that stuck out in his mind came against Rangers, another 3-3 draw. Alex Douglas was there and the game remains as vivid in his mind as it was in Bill's. 'It was Easter Monday and Firhill was packed. Bill took a free kick 35 or 40 yards out and he hit it with such force that it went over the goalkeeper, Jerry Dawson's shoulder and stuck up high in the net. Dawson had to pull it out and he was shaking his fist at Bill as he did, though he was smiling too because they were team-mates in the Scotland side.' Jack Mindel remembers that years later, long after the war was over, 'he showed me a cutting that he always carried from this Partick game. He'd made the headlines by scoring from 35 yards.'

This goal was the icing on the cake as far as Bill's time at

Thistle was concerned, for he and the crowd ran a mutual appreciation society. When the time came for him to return to England after the war, he was given a rousing send off. Alex Douglas was on the committee of the Supporters Club at the time: 'It was my job to fix up a hall in which to hold a presentation. At that time there were so many events taking place it was difficult but I finally got hold of the old Grove Boxing Stadium. It was packed to the seams because he was going to be sorely missed. He gave his all in every game.' More than 1,000 people turned up to see Bill and his young wife accept a canteen of cutlery and a silver cake stand. Gifts such as these meant everything to him for they came from his own kind, people who perhaps couldn't afford to make a donation to the cause but did so anyway because they appreciated what he'd done.

As the War came to its close, the Shanklys began to plan for the future. Although they were staying with Ness' parents in Glasgow for the duration of Bill's service at Bishopbriggs, there was no doubt that Bill would be returning to Preston to resume his playing career. Time constraints meant that it was impossible to run the Football League for the 1945/46 season which gave everyone a breathing space to reorganise, the local leagues continuing in their stead. Bill remained in the RAF until January 1946 when he was demobbed. Much had changed in his life by then for not only was he now a married man, but a father too. The Shanklys' first child, Barbara, was born in Glasgow just before he was released from active service, to his great joy as Ness remembers well: 'He loved Barbara, he was delighted to be a father and he was devoted to her.' The new post-war world was going to be one filled with new realities for Bill Shankly.

chapter nine

THE BITTER END

Just as in the country at large, football clubs were undergoing a period of rebuilding, some structural, some in terms of personnel. Some placed their faith in the older men returning from the War, feeling that they would help players in their mid-twenties who had yet to amass any real experience while simultaneously recognising the contributions they'd made to the clubs and to the country's war effort. Others took a more youthful route, though there were problems here too as those lads were often called away to do their National Service. Tom Finney explains: 'We lost six years of our careers to the War. Bill was very unfortunate because he was that bit older and missed out on probably his best years,' a view with which Bill concurred, suggesting later that his peak had been from twenty-eight to thirty-three, or 1941-46. 'He was thirty-two when he was demobbed,' Finney continues, 'and he'd not have that long left. Some felt that it would probably be harder for the older men to pick up where they'd left off but Bill had kept himself so fit and strong that there didn't seem to be a problem.'

There were reservations among the Preston directors. With Bill the head of a new family who were still in Glasgow, foolish questions were asked as to his commitment to the club. Given that league football would not start until August 1946 when Bill would be approaching thirty-three, he was allowed a release to return to Glasgow. Preston had it in mind that Bill would be too slow for first-team play and might do better to find himself a new club in Scotland. Strangely, no-one came in for him, though how hard he tried to elicit any interest is questionable; Bill felt he was good enough to play on and would have been keen to prove the point. Turning out again in Football League North fixtures, he convinced James Taylor that he would still be a useful man to have on the team and a late approach from St. Mirren was rebuffed. Bill left digs in Preston and brought his family down 'to a club house in Deepdale Road,' as Ness recalls. 'It was a lovely little terraced place and our first real home.'

The wisdom of Preston's decision was illustrated when the Football League started again in August 1946. He was one of the few pre-war players left, alongside Bobby Beattie and Andy Beattie who soon moved on to become Barrow's manager. Results were poor – Tom Finney made an early Deepdale appearance in a 4-0 defeat against Bolton Wanderers. His abiding memory of that match is that 'Bill never knew what defeat meant, he enjoyed every minute and he was constantly telling us that we could still get back into the game with just a couple of minutes left.'

Despite these early reverses, Preston went on to have a solid season. They finished seventh, ten points behind Liverpool. Bill proved an inspiration the following season where he fought to fulfil one last ambition – to captain Preston in a Cup Final. That dream was dashed in the sixth round by Manchester United. He was unwilling to retire too early though and felt he was giving a good account of himself. Through that second full season after the war, he continued to draw plaudits. The Glasgow press suggested that 'the most amazing man in British football [is] Willie Shankly. But it would be putting back the clock to choose him [for Scotland],' a sentiment that was doing the rounds at club level too. He took pleasure in such praise and in the knowledge that he had become even more of a hero to the Preston faithful who applauded his every move as the club repeated their league form of the previous year. Tom Finney saw their affection at close quarters. 'He had an excellent rapport with the supporters. They held him in the highest esteem. Of course, he'd been part of the team that won the Cup which helps make you popular. Bill had been an up and coming player before the War, a real star of the future and I think people felt a little sorry that he had missed out on those years. Even now, the Preston people still have a great deal of time for him.'

His pugnacious tackling and workaholic running was a feature of his game even in his mid-thirties. He also 'acted as a minder in a sense' Tom admits. 'If I played against a full-back who had a go at me early on, he'd come up to me and say "Leave him to me, I'll sort him out" and he would. He was a fatherly figure.' The full-blooded approach was, in a strange way, his downfall. Like other players down the years, Bill's all action attitude and hard approach to the game disguised subtle skills that could light up an afternoon and unlock a defence; Tommy Smith at Liverpool is an example, an iron man whose ability on the ball was overlooked. Some jumped to the con-clusion that once Bill started to age he would no longer be as effective, ignoring the quality of his distribution and the way he could spot an opening to set Finney off on one of his dazzling runs.

With Bill on the verge of his thirty-fifth birthday, the club committee felt that he had outlived his useful life as a first-team player. James Taylor wanted to use him in the reserves to bring them on. To sugar the pill, they also made him the offer of a three-year contract. Bill was interested but chose never to accept it. At this stage, he still wanted to play and thought he might get a berth elsewhere. At the same time, while he was looking to the future and wanted to 'stay in the game at all costs', he felt he would be better suited to a managerial rather than a mere coaching post. He wanted to run a club from top to bottom, doing things his way. He worried that a three-year deal would leave him tied to Preston but unable to influence affairs as he would like.

He accepted his demotion at first and looked forward to his new responsibilities: 'I'll try to see that no-one's heart is broken by the disappointments that come to all players. I'll try to make them feel at home at Deepdale and show them all I know.' Good as his word, when Paddy Waters arrived at the club from Glentoran, 'he wanted to see me. He invited me to his house and he just talked non-stop about football. If there's a word bigger than fanatic, that was Bill. He made you feel welcome, happy to be at the club.' He had been preparing assiduously for this day and had taken a masseur's diploma by correspondence course. This meticulous side to his nature was at odds with the impetuous irrationality that could afflict him at other times, yet together they provided an efficacious cocktail – while others needed assistants to complete the picture, Brian Clough and Peter Taylor or Matt Busby and Jimmy Murphy, Bill embodied everything that was necessary in management. He was to draw on others and use their expertise but was never reliant on their personalities in the way that others might have been.

The massage course provided him with excellent background on how the human body operates, information that helped him produce teams that were incredibly fit. Even so, he wasn't given much time to put his newly acquired skills into practice, for by 23 October, he had earned a recall to the first team. A dreadful start to the season had seen North End win only two of twelve games, including five straight defeats away from home. With just six points, the fixture at fellow strugglers Huddersfield was crucial. Bill still hated the fact that he couldn't get in the first team. In those early weeks as results went against the side, he became increasingly frustrated. Tommy Bogan was inside-forward at the time and wrote that 'the team sheet went up at 12 every Wednesday and Bill would be first out of the bath and down the corridor. We'd see him peering at the list and hear him talking to himself. He'd say "Look at that, bloody juveniles keeping Bill Shankly out of the side." This went on for weeks, then we heard him shout "A bloody good side".' Looking for the steadying influence of experience, Preston had chosen Bill.

Preston won 2-0, Bill turning in a good performance. It was on the coach going to the game that he made his mark though, initially by geeing up players depressed at their lack of form. However, he had to spring into more decisive action when the coach caught fire; he extinguished the flames, his fire fighting training in the RAF coming to his aid. Perhaps now things were going his way and he would reclaim his position in the side. Ness was certainly hoping so for 'he wasn't really happy in Preston during that time. He could never settle because he wasn't in the team and that upset him.'

The next game was Manchester United. Tommy Bogan remembered the team-talk: 'United had a good side. Delaney, Morris, Rowley, Pearson, Aston, Carey but Bill criticised the lot and said no-one was a good player.' Early on the tactic worked for Preston took the lead and Bill went round the team saying 'Told you they're easy'. There was no fairytale conclusion this time as United ran riot and won 6-1. Bogan again: 'The following Wednesday, Bill recoiled from the team sheet, uttering "What a bloody side!" He was the only one dropped!'

That Bill was singled out for demotion was highly significant; Taylor was making it clear that he no longer had a future as a player at Deepdale. Tom Finney still believes that this decision was precipitant: 'Like most sides at that time, we were building again and they wanted to use younger players. We struggled badly that year and I think the loss of Bill had a lot to do with it. His experience was worth a lot because not only could he still play to a good standard but he brought the others on. Fellows like Bill are rare, they're a tremendous asset because they're inspirational. In training he was still very enthusiastic, especially in five-a-sides, and that radiated through to the rest of the players. My own feelings were that he could have gone on for another two or three years. The policy of the club, which was common in the game, was that once a player got to thirty, he was on the wane. It was a lot of nonsense because actually you were in your prime. You were using your knowledge to make you a better footballer.'

As the season wore on, relations between Bill and the club began to sour and communications broke down between him and the directors. This situation wasn't eased by the prolonged absence of James Taylor. Illness meant that he was rarely at Deepdale. Given Bill's respect for him, it's possible that matters might have been resolved more amicably. Things came to a head early in 1949 when Preston made it clear that they wouldn't be retaining him, obviously irked by his refusal to take up the three-year contract. Perhaps they were trying to force his hand and make him reconsider. Without a contract, the future was suddenly precarious. After all, he lived in a club house and had a wife and child to feed.

This was typical of the way clubs used their power over players. The system in those days was weighted heavily in favour of the clubs, players little more than wage slaves. Clubs held a player's registration, without which he wasn't eligible to play. At the end of a season, the player was retained for the next year or put on the transfer list. Once on the list, his wages were stopped on 30 June. In the face of that, he still couldn't play for anyone else until a transfer acceptable to his former club was arranged because they kept his registration. This was the situation that Bill faced, as Tom Finney knew only too well: 'It was a mistake to let him go but in those days the management was so strong they could do anything they liked. Consideration for the player was nil and there was nothing you could do about it. If they said you were out, that was it. He was very upset that Preston could just dispense with his services so easily. It was such a waste because I was certain that he'd stay in the game in some capacity. I couldn't imagine him doing anything else. It was sad that that ability couldn't be used at Preston.' Bill knew that Preston did not want to lose him and so might be awkward when arranging terms with another club. In the end, it boiled down to buckling to Preston and staying on the staff or retiring as a player, freeing himself from the registration problems. That would mean giving up playing the game he loved so much. There could be no bigger step for him to take.

For several weeks, Bill wrestled with his dilemma. Ness recalls that 'I knew he was hurt and disappointed by what was going on there but I kept out of it. It was his job and he had to come to his own decision. I looked after the house and made sure we were fed but I knew there was something wrong.

He didn't bring the football worries home with him but I could tell there were problems by the way he wouldn't talk and would want to do something about the house to take his mind off things.'

In the end, Bill felt he was being harshly treated. He had given yeoman service to Preston's cause and was being forced into a corner. He felt that Preston's behaviour in blackmailing him into staying was unworthy of decent men and that he could no longer work with them. This was yet another episode in his life when the 'big men' had conspired to destroy the livelihood of those without adequate representation. His own troubles were just the latest incident to turn him against the directors as Tom Finney admits. 'I picked up a lot of injuries in 1948/49 and Bill was disappointed by that because the injuries were made worse by the club. Because we were struggling, they'd stick a needle in me and send me back out and then you'd make the injury worse and be out for a month instead of a fortnight. He didn't agree with that at all. He always felt that you were the only one who knew if you were fit. He was angry that I wasn't given the chance to decide.' Irritated by this injustice, his own trials and tribulations came as no shock, but he couldn't help but feel resentful. Yet worse was to come.

Nursing a resentment over the way the War had cheated him of his finest years as a player, it was heartbreaking to find that now his club were casting him aside while he still had plenty to offer. In February 1949, Carlisle United approached Bill with the offer of the manager's job. Their youthful player-manager, Ivor Broadis, had just been transferred to Sunderland for the then exorbitant fee of £18,000 and the club were seeking a replacement. With Billy Blyth still on the scene, they were well aware that Bill was unsettled and might be willing to move. Taylor's absence left the Preston board exposed; realising, late in the day, that Bill still had something to offer the side, they wanted him to see out the season and help in the fight against relegation.

Bill was initially unsure whether or not he should make

the move and Taylor's presence might have made all the difference. Bill and Ness were settled in their Deepdale Road home and had many friends in the town and a strong residual allegiance to the club. It would be a wrench to leave. Carlisle persisted with their advances throughout February however and wore him down, a case of the biter bit. The final sticking point was Bill's benefit, vitally important to a player of his age. As a player, the maximum wage, while comfortable compared with other working class jobs, was not likely to allow a man to save much for his retirement, while men of Bill's vintage had had to endure six years on service pay too. For that reason, the benefit system had been introduced as Tom Finney explains: 'We were all on twelve-month contracts. If you were five years with the same club, you were entitled – that's all, entitled – to a benefit of £150 per year, which made £750 in total, quite a bit of money in those days. Most first teamers would get it automatically, but we made sure that we asked for it all the same! If you got transferred after three years, you were still entitled to some money, but few got it.'

Bill had been at Preston for almost sixteen years and was set for a full benefit payout. Preston used that as a final lever to keep him at the club – if he left, he wouldn't get his money. To make matters worse, they even offered him a benefit game if he agreed to stay, a match that would be similar to the testimonial games held now. Bill was enraged by their hypocrisy. Had he not earned the match by playing more than 300 League and Cup games for the club? Were they simply awarding it for the work he had yet to do between then and the end of the season? What guarantee was there that he'd get the game anyway? 'I felt that the people who were running Preston at the time had cheated me out of my benefit match and that was the biggest let-down of my life in football,' he wrote in his autobiography. Tom Finney remembers that 'he was very bitter about that and he was absolutely right but it was the way things were. It wouldn't be tolerated today. He was due his money but he wasn't the only one to be swindled out of it. He was furious. He felt, rightly, that he'd given good service and that he wasn't properly rewarded, that he'd been fiddled out of his due.'

This was the final straw and in March he accepted the Carlisle job, though he did pull out of the running briefly when he couldn't agree terms with the club. He finally signed for the same money he was getting at Preston, £14 per week. Preston kept him on until 19 March when he played his last game for the club in a 3-1 defeat at home to Sunderland. Preston then refused to transfer his registration. This finally ended his career as a footballer. His dedication to his own physical fitness was rendered invalid by the small-minded behaviour of a board of amateurs who, he felt, knew nothing about the game. It's likely that he allowed himself a wry smile in May 1949 when Preston were relegated.

Unlike the club, the supporters realised they had lost someone special and instituted a testimonial fund. A few weeks later, Bill returned to the town to receive a cheque for £169 5s 7d. Fund Chairman, Mr. T. Davies, said that he would have liked the cheque to have been five times that given but Bill was gracious in acceptance. Telling the assembled throng that he would have returned for 5 shillings so touched was he by their gesture, he made it abundantly clear that they were the people that mattered to a football club, not the directors. 'Supporters go on for ever, but directors can be gone in a month' was his view. Such recognition from the people he considered his peers was priceless for it showed that he had served them well. That burning sense of pride in his work and achievements was sometimes his downfall, yet it was a virtue too. It drove him on past exhaustion to accomplish goals that others thought impossible.

Many tributes were offered when it was clear that he had played his final game. Peter Doherty called him 'the finest ever wing-half', a much appreciated comment for Bill felt that Doherty had been his most awkward opponent. The most eloquent eulogy came from Bill's great friend and long-time opponent Joe Mercer in a letter sent in April. He wrote 'I feel I must write you a few lines of congratulation and good wishes on your recent appointment. I hope most sincerely that your career as a manager will be even more successful than that as a player. In my humble opinion, no player ever gave as much to his club, country and football as you. It was always a great pleasure to play against you (and we've had some grand tussles haven't we?). The game will be much poorer without you Bill and though I glory in your appointment I regret the passing of a great player.'

A great player. He'd have settled for that tribute when he was kicking a ball around in Glenbuck. Now it was time to become a great manager.

chapter ten

UNCOMPLICATED

Management is a very specialised craft. Wisely, Bill chose to serve an apprenticeship. In March 1949, there was no question in Bill's mind that he could become the best manager in the country: 'I went to Carlisle to learn a new job feeling that I was going to make a success of it.' He'd been lucky in that most of his career had been spent at the highest level at a progressive club like Preston. He'd also had the chance to look at other clubs through the war; Arsenal were particularly impressive he felt, run on the grandest scale. Bill had kept his eyes and ears open over seventeen years in professional football and knew the game inside out. Just as important were his humble origins in Scotland because those days had taught him how to deal with ordinary people. He understood the value of hard work and relished the life that he had carved out for himself. Refusing to take advantage of the game's generosity, he maintained a boyish enthusiasm for the sport that was perhaps his strongest managerial weapon. Dealing with hard-bitten, often cynical pros who had seen and done it all, his evangelical zeal transformed attitudes. Shankly was able to turn 32 year olds into boys of twelve. Football really was the glory game as far as he was concerned and the glory of victory was all that he desired. He made his players feel the same way.

With Carlisle United his first port of call, initial concerns were off the field. With the club safe from relegation and a mere handful of games remaining, he used the final fixtures to assess the strength of his team. Living in a club house at Preston, he was required to vacate that once he had moved on. Ness 'moved back to Glasgow with Barbara while Bill sorted out a house for us in Carlisle and that was a struggle for

a while. Once we settled, I loved it there because it was closer
to home and I'd been a bit homesick in Preston.' At Brunton
Park, the season went out with a whimper. In the seven games
that saw Bill in command, the club drew four and won only
one to finish in fifteenth position in the Third Division North.
He was unconcerned, concentrating purely on the forthcoming season where he would be able to stamp his authority
on the side.

In these early post-war years, football was going through a
boom. Though the War had been over for four years by the
time Bill got to Carlisle, Britain was in the grip of austerity
with rationing still necessarily imposed. Sport was the popular
escape. Through the 1940s and into the 1950s, football had
yet to discover the phenomenon of the 'away' supporter. Few
owned cars or had the time and money to use public transport
to go to matches not in their immediate vicinity. Consequently, the local football club assumed enormous importance
within a community, surpassing even that of the troubled
1930s. A manager of the local side could become an enor-
mously important and influential figure.

Attendances rocketed, the greatest concentration coming at
the larger clubs. For their smaller counterparts such as Carlisle,
crowds were healthy if unspectacular. From his previous
experience of life at Brunton Park, Bill knew that the club
suffered a number of inherent disadvantages that he had to
overcome. His central idea had an inevitability to it; Carlisle
United would become the epicentre of a new community that
he would try to create. In Glenbuck, life was lived within a
moral framework of helping your neighbour, looking after one
another, taking an interest in your locale. Carlisle United
would become a village where all those virtues were practised.
The club would become the focus of the city, bringing it to
life, giving it a source of pride, a virtuous spiral that would
benefit club and city. He wanted to put them on the map.

In footballing terms, Carlisle was still an outpost. Their
entire League history – fourteen seasons as Bill took over – had
been spent in the Third Division North and they had yet to

better the eighth place they achieved in their first and third seasons. The board had taken the ambitious step of appointing Ivor Broadis as player-manager just after the War, giving the club a boost, but it was always likely to be a short-term measure. Broadis, just twenty-three when he took over, was a top quality player and it was inevitable that he would have to move on. The final parting of the ways came as the result of a disagreement between Broadis and Billy Blyth, Bill's uncle and still an active member of the board. As Ivor admits, 'We didn't get on. I was a young man and he was sixty-five. I bought a player in for £350 and he gave me hell over it so one of us had to go.' It was Broadis' departure for Sunderland in February 1949 that created the vacancy. The side Bill inherited had some useful players and the three League seasons since the resumption saw encouraging signs; much of the credit for any improvement went to Broadis the player rather than manager, for he contributed fifty-two goals in ninety-one League games for the club. Bill saw very quickly that there was much work to be done if he was going to transform Carlisle into a side to threaten promotion.

He attacked his job on several fronts. His first concern was to raise morale around the club and the city and capitalise on the increased profile that Ivor Broadis had given them. Carlisle's geographic location was problematic not simply because there was a relatively small population and catchment area but because it made it hard to attract players from the south. Away games were that bit harder since the team had to embark on some horrendously long treks across country. Bill turned this perceived disadvantage on its head; if it was tough for Carlisle when going away, just think how difficult it would be for clubs coming to Brunton Park. Home games should become a formality, they were playing teams of exhausted men. Similarly, Carlisle should take on a siege mentality. They were cut off from the rest of the country, so football matches should be approached as the perfect opportunity to show the rest of England just what the place could do. Carlisle should unite behind the team and use them as a badge of civic pride.

Shankly was painfully aware of the fact that the club had little history. Events have shown that ailing clubs with a successful past can weather the storm of failure and return – Bolton were sustained by memories of golden days long since gone while in the lower divisions. Without such a history to cling to, there is often little hope for a club rooted to the lower divisions. Bill had to fill that void by instilling a sense of purpose. He knew of course that there were many like-minded football fanatics there – they had to be fanatical to sustain their interest in such adverse circumstances. With that in mind, he knew he had a nucleus of support with which to work. Ignite that base and the flame of their enthusiasm would sweep through Carlisle.

If Bill had a blind spot, it was that he couldn't understand that there might just be a few people who didn't share his passion for the game or his vision for Carlisle. United's goal-keeper Jim MacLaren remembers going to Tranmere for a game: 'We were near the ground. Bill got off the coach to ask for directions but the person he asked couldn't help. He got back on shaking his head. "Can you believe that? Imagine not knowing where the football field is!".' So consumed was he by football that he tended to ride roughshod over anyone holding differing opinions and was storing up unrest at boardroom level even in his earliest days.

He was quick to realise just how important an ally the press could be. In April, in the middle of his first month at Brunton Park, he spoke to the *Cumberland News*. Their reporter, The Rover, wrote 'to be in his company is to be in football. He oozes with football and the most striking feature of his conversation about the game is the determined manner in which he empha-sizes the points he wants to put over.' At about the same time, Bill diplomatically referred to Preston's decision to release him as 'magnificent' and promised there would be no panic buying. Jim MacLaren agrees that 'he put us on the map nationally. Anyone wanted a story, he'd give them one. He'd tell the press that his boys were the best and wouldn't let them argue with him.'

With the £18,000 brought in from Broadis' transfer, supporters expected new signings, but Bill bided his time until the close season. His most significant piece of expenditure came when he bought new strips for the team. A small but symbolically important step, it represented a break with Carlisle's shambolic past. Jim MacLaren recalls: 'When Bill got here, the place was a mess. My goalkeeping sweater was so bad that I used what I'd had in the army. I think the strips the forwards used were slightly different to those the backs had. Bill burned the lot of them and the training kit too and bought us new ones.' If you treated your players as if they were the cream, they might start to believe it and play like it. Jack Lindsay played centre-forward for the club and well remembers Bill's fastidious approach to the kit. 'He had a cupboard full of new strips. You'd get ready to go out and he'd come and have a look, pull a bit of loose thread off your shirt. He wanted us to look right, always said "If you don't look well, you won't play well." It was all part of his desire to instil an overwhelming pride in his players, showing them it was both a privilege and a responsibility to turn out for the club. He also arranged for the club to buy a house and convert it into flats to help players with accommodation in the midst of the post-war housing shortage. He also had an on-going argument with the board over the purchase of a coach for away travel. Initially sanctioned in August 1949, it was regularly deferred and the players were forced to use hired coaches. Six months into his job, he was already becoming frustrated at the club's lack of vision.

Right away, he had the players on his side according to MacLaren. 'We were excited about Shanks, he was a big name. Ivor hadn't mixed with the players because he was the same age as the rest of us and was trying to establish some authority. Bill was the best thing to happen to the club. He turned it round. There was no side to him, he'd help clean the terraces and the dressing rooms, it was football twenty-four hours a day.' Ivor Broadis agrees that Shankly's arrival was timely. 'He came as that post-war boom was beginning to fade. It needed someone like him to pick it all up again.'

Though he made few team changes early on, the new Shankly broom swept through the club. One of his greatest innovations was to broadcast to the crowd over the tannoy before the game, something that he organised with an old friend from his previous spell in the city, Bill Forster. Forster had played in Carlisle's wartime side on occasion but was now working in a solicitor's office. 'Bill came to see me and asked if I was still interested in football. "You've got to be," he told me. He wanted to talk to the crowd, tell them about team changes, how they'd played the week before, any new signings he'd made. He asked me if I'd help him put his talks together and of course, I was pleased. We'd get together a day or two before a match and decide what he was going to say and I'd write it all out for him. The first week, he came on with "Good afternoon ladies and gentlemen. This is your new manager Willie Shankly speaking now. I've put forward a team and I want you to get behind these boys and cheer them on. They're going to give their best, there are some local boys in the team remember, so encourage them."' At a time when only the managers of the biggest clubs ever spoke publicly and then only in stilted radio or newsreel interviews, Shankly's direct appeal to the paying public was revolutionary. His idea was 'to have a frank and friendly talk to the supporters. It is not an appeal for support – we are getting ample support. I just want to take the crowd into the club's confidence and let them know what is happening.' As Bill Forster explains, in those first few weeks 'he lit the place up. He was such a great character that people got to the ground early just to hear him talk.' Jack Lindsay confirms that, citing an encounter with 'an old fella on the way to the game at one o'clock. I said "You're a wee bit early," and he said "I like to hear Shankly speak".'

Having achieved the first objective, the summer of 1949 was when he got down to the real hard work. He became a familiar face around Carlisle, spreading the footballing gospel. Many of the players were released and he set about constructing his own squad of players prepared to play to his principles. Replacing Ivor Broadis was a particular priority and Shankly pulled off a master stroke in bringing in Billy Hogan from Manchester City. 'He was a wizard, an exceptional player,' according to Geoff Twentyman, then a young centre-half at Carlisle and a man who went on to become chief scout at Liverpool. As the man who uncovered the likes of Steve Heighway and Ian Rush, his opinion is worth something: 'Billy was a real player, he could do anything with the ball. He'd pick it up in his own half and beat three, four, five men, not just once as a fluke but most of the time. We couldn't understand how we got him at Carlisle but apparently he'd been ill with a bad head injury.'

Hogan was to be the cornerstone of Bill's new side and for his benefit he stretched his own rules a little as Twentyman explains. 'Billy was the only player he allowed to travel, everybody else had to live in Carlisle. I think it was because he knew he could trust Billy to live a quiet life!' Hogan was recruited to provide the flair, the attacking ingenuity that would create chances for Lindsay and another new signing, George Dick, a Scot, from West Ham. Bill's reliance on Scots and northern Englishmen betrayed both his own preference and the terrible trouble he had in getting players to sign for the club. Jim MacLaren felt that 'English people thought Carlisle was at the end of the world so it was very hard to get anyone from the south to come. This was in the days before the motorways and we were out on a limb. Newcastle was the nearest place of any size.' Unable to combat that, Bill turned Carlisle into what resembled a Scottish League side that happened to play in England.

With a few new faces recruited, the players reported back for pre-season duty in good heart. Right away, Bill had a surprise for them. 'He changed everything,' Geoff Twentyman concedes. 'It was much more professional. I was a part-timer and within a week, he'd arranged with my boss that I should take two mornings a week off to train with the first team. That carried on into the summer. Most teams come back and do a lot of roadwork to build up stamina but he wouldn't have any of it. "You play on grass so you train on grass" which was far better. I think it stopped a lot of injuries later on.' Rather than a chore which had to be endured, training was now a pleasure to be enjoyed. Ivor Broadis points out that Bill's ideas went completely against the grain: 'He felt football was a simple game. He wasn't a qualified coach but he knew how football should be played and how you should prepare. It wasn't until a few years later when the Hungarians came over that things changed a bit. Until then you never saw a ball in training and Bill had to work against that. I went to Newcastle in 1953, and we weren't even allowed on the pitch in the week! Bill had a lot to overcome.' Broadis saw at first hand how Bill worked, for despite moving to Sunderland he continued to live in Carlisle and sometimes trained with the club. 'He was very good on fitness. He used to say he saved me for England because he made me train harder! He felt that you had to punish yourself and come off shattered and that was a lesson I never forgot. He was very genuine too. Although I'd had a row with his uncle, that never spoiled the relationship between us. As long as you were doing your job and interested in your football, that was all he was concerned about.'

His most important innovation was to make training fun: 'He didn't go in for too much coaching, he let you use your natural ability,' notes Jack Lindsay. Many players find training a bore and so don't reap the benefits. At Carlisle, training was something the players looked forward to every bit as much as playing. They had to master the basic skills of the game which meant using the ball. As early as July, he told the *Cumberland News* that his aim for the 1949/50 season was 'organised football, played properly with the maximum of effort which, in my opinion, is the only way to get results. Producing a good team might take a couple of seasons but judging by the shape they made at the back end of last season, I hope we have a good team this term. If we don't get immediate results, we will eventually get them and these results will come from organised football. I don't want any haphazard football at all.' Ivor

Broadis felt 'his creed was passing to feet. It's called football and you played it on the ground,' precisely the philosophy that Preston had followed so successfully.

In order to impose such disciplines on the side, training sessions were of paramount importance. Thinking back to the summers he spent as a boy in Scotland, the five-a-side games stood out. This was an excellent vehicle for developing every skill in the game. Such games were the staple diet in training, along with head tennis. Ivor Broadis recognised the good that came from the games but felt there were other reasons for his insistence on them. 'He needed to play. He was so competitive. The hardest day for him was when he finished. He couldn't play League football any more, so training games were a run out for him.'

He was delighted to be at the helm at Carlisle United but over the summer of 1949, he began to have twinges of regret over his decision to leave Preston since it had robbed him of his greatest joy, playing on a Saturday. Summers were always tough for Bill simply because there was no football and he would have had time to brood on the fact that August would not provide its traditional release from his frustration. Happy to be in the game, he was starting to realise the enormity of his decision. Convinced that he still had a contribution to make on the field, that made matters worse.

With that in mind, part of the recess was used to investigate the possibility of transferring his registration from Preston to Carlisle. This began a long, drawn out saga. Preston wanted a fee, arguing that they had released him to become a manager, not a player. Bill, still indignant over the benefit fiasco, would not pay one on principle. At the end of 1949/50, twelve months later, his registration was cancelled and he was required to reapply for new registration. The League turned down his new application, finally bringing the curtain down on his hopes of a return, an example of the unsympathetic way players were treated by the authorities.

Two things went against him. On his departure from Preston when his prospects of playing looked slim, he withdrew his money from the provident fund, a scheme that was a cross between a pension and a benefit. Forced into leaving Deepdale without his club benefit, he had little choice but to take that money for he had nothing. Once the money had been drawn, that was effectively the end of a career. Only in very exceptional circumstances were players allowed to return. With this uppermost in their mind, the League took advantage of the fact that as a manager, Bill was being paid £14 per week, more than the maximum wage that was then operating at £12. League rules insisted that he would have to take a pay cut which he accepted, simultaneously agreeing to pay back the money he'd had from the provident fund. The League refused registration on the basis that 'there is a danger that if he or anyone else were allowed to play again, he might be the subject of under-the-counter agreements which will give him more than the £12 maximum.' On hearing this ruling, Shankly was furious. In one paragraph, everything that he hated about the game had been used against him. He had worked to maintain a clean reputation and he felt that the League were insulting his own integrity. Worse still, there was a tacit acceptance in their judgment that such behaviour went on – as everyone knew it did – without any action being taken to clamp down on real examples of it. They were penalising him for an imaginary offence. After twenty years in the professional ranks, he was scarcely surprised by such hypocrisy but it wounded nonetheless. Another black mark against the 'big men'.

There were disappointments still to come, however, as Carlisle embarked on the 1949/50 season, Bill's first full year in charge. As the season opened, the team were ready to go. The Third Division North was a tough league, not simply because of the competition but because just one club of the twenty-two – expanded to twenty-four the following year – achieved promotion. If there happened to be one outstanding side in any one term, you were set for a frustrating spell. As he told the local press, this first year was a transitional one as both he and the players bedded down into their new roles. The players

had to adapt to new tactics and, in some cases, new surroundings. Bill himself, for all his confidence, had to develop
his own style as a manager, learning the ropes as he went. As
Jim MacLaren notes, his first months were not faultless: 'He
made a few mistakes over players. If we played a team and one
of their boys had a good game, he'd want to sign him.' In
mitigation, it was terribly difficult for Shankly to get to see
players in action because of Carlisle's isolation, but in truth,
it was a lesson he learned the hard way. There were any number
of players who had just a handful of appearances for United
under Bill. Possibly by insisting that his boys were the best
players in the country, he had brainwashed himself into believing it – if anyone outplayed them, they had to be brilliant,
which wasn't always the case. Whatever the reasons for this
slight extravagance, he still managed to balance the books
for 1949/50, bringing in £15,000 and spending £14,300 on
transfers.

That first year was something of a mixed bag following an
inspired start. Bill's policy of turning Brunton Park into a
fortress was working well and they didn't lose their first points
at home until the last Saturday in October. Thereafter, excellent results were followed by embarrassing defeats as the new
blend struggled to find consistency. The harsh winter conditions began to bite too making away games a real trial. Jim
MacLaren recalls with a wince that 'driving to a game over
Shap in the winter on the old roads was dreadful. Very
occasionally we might stay overnight, perhaps if we were
playing at Grimsby, but usually it was an eight o'clock start
on Saturday morning.' Travelling a couple of hundred miles
pre-motorways on non-luxury coaches must have been exhausting and it showed in their away results. Between 22 October
and 29 April, they scored just two wins when visiting and one
of those came at Barrow, which passed for a local derby.

Despite these set-backs, Carlisle were starting to look like a
useful side. The Rover could not 'remember any season when
United have provided such a high standard of football as at
present'. Certainly Bill was convinced that things were

heading in the right direction and told anyone who would listen. Every now and then, he'd go back to see his old friends at Preston. They had so missed Shankly's presence on the field that in November they'd been forced into the transfer market to buy a replacement, paying Celtic £4,000 for Tommy Docherty. Pleased to see a fellow Scot installed in his old position, he wrote to say 'Congratulations. You are now the greatest right-half in the world,' adding 'Just put the shirt on and let it run around, it knows where to go.' Tommy remembers 'Bill came into Deepdale to wish me luck but he was full of enthusiasm for Carlisle. He'd come down to the ground every week or two to tell us what a great team they had, what they were going to win.'

With resources scarce, Shankly was always willing to try something new to liven matters up at the ground. In his never-ending drive to instil pride into the team, in October he made representations to the authorities to have the city badge and motto – 'Be just and fear not' – on the team jerseys. He finally got his way fifteen months later! Another experiment came when he took the team away for a short break in Morecambe prior to a Cup tie, though Jack Lindsay's view is that 'he tried to keep us all together so that we wouldn't be going off for a few pints'. Hoping that a change of scenery would help, he remarked that 'the boys will train hard, eat hard and sleep hard'. A week's hard sleep obviously did the trick for they reached the Third Round that season before Leeds United, then in the Second Division, accounted for them.

There was no end to his commitment to the club and he demanded the same from all those connected with it, even his own wife. Ness remembers that 'he got me to wash the team's kit lots of times. There were no facilities at the club, no laundry room or anything so Bill organised a Bendix washing machine for me. It was an enormous thing, it had to be specially piped in.' Jack Lindsay recalls going to see Bill at home, finding the place with 'steam and bubbles all over the place' as Ness fought to get the kit ready in time for the following Saturday! The Bendix posed further problems for Bill when Ness went 'into the nursing home to have our second daughter, Jeanette. He thought he'd do the washing while I was away. You never saw such a mess in your life. Barbara's clothes wouldn't have fitted a doll, he just put everything in the wash together. He'd no idea at all! He thought he was doing a good turn but when I got home I'd an awful mess to put right.' On the domestic front, Bill had little time to help out though there were times when he could be useful as Bill Forster explains. 'I went to see him at home. Ness asked me "Do you think they'll win this week? I hope they get beat." Shanks went mad, "We'll win 2-0" and on and on about how well they'd play. After, I asked Ness why she wanted them to lose. "I want the cooker cleaned and if they get beaten, that's how he puts his time in, cleaning the cooker from top to bottom."'

Jack Lindsay, another of Carlisle's Scots from Cambuslang, hit it off with Bill 'as soon as he came; we had a great rapport between us'. On Thursdays when there were no professional games to be hunted down, 'after training I'd go to see him. Ness would let me in and say "I hope there's no matches on!" I'd tell her there were and she'd call "I thought you were going to watch Barbara" but Bill'd always come back, "Aye, well business comes first Ness." We'd find some local games because he was always after local talent. Bill would be standing there shouting. One game, the ref stopped the match, came up to Bill and told him to stop shouting because he was putting everybody off.' The kids were of particular interest for he instituted a youth policy to try to ensure that a supply of good quality players was always coming into the club. Jim MacLaren remembers sitting in an away dressing room feeling pretty chuffed after a good win and 'Bill came in shouting "Did you hear about the A Team – they won 8-0!" We were all thinking "What about us?" Every side at the club had to do well.'

Shankly began to suffer the withdrawal symptoms that dogged his retirement from the game. Any excuse for a game, he'd take it. Ivor Broadis remembers vividly the 'one-a-side games we had together if I was the only one around. We played on the car park with a chimney pot at each end, you had to knock it over to score.' Even on a Friday, traditionally the lightest day of the week, Bill would manufacture a game. Jim MacLaren explains the ritual: 'We'd go in to do a few sprints or have a massage ready for Saturday. Bill always wanted to play so he'd organise a two-a-side with Freddie Ford, the trainer, whoever was twelfth man and me, because he reckoned the goalkeeper wouldn't get hurt.' Jack Lindsay questions that however: 'In practice matches, you daren't go near Bill, because he'd get stuck in right away. He was still fit and strong, you knew you were playing somebody when you came up against Shanks. Hard as nails. If you got past him once that was it, you couldn't do it again!'

The season petered out with United coming in ninth but the spadework had been done. Bill had created an incredible team spirit. The players got on well and were inspired by Shanklyism. 'He bred enthusiasm,' remarks Jim MacLaren, 'made you feel you couldn't lose.' His belief in his players extended to their welfare too. Paddy Waters, who joined in December 1950, adds 'He was always checking to see if your house was all right, he'd arrange for a plumber or electrician if you needed one, anything he could do he would, because he thought you should be left to concentrate on your game.'

Paddy's signing was a perfect example of Bill's devotion to the cause. Bill Forster recalls that 'Paddy wasn't sure, "Carlisle's a long way." So Bill started off at him: "It's the finest football field in the British League." Paddy said "I'll have to sleep on it" so Bill pointed to a couch and told him to get his head down. Paddy went to sleep and a couple of hours later Bill woke him up. "Well?" "Well, I don't know." "Get back to sleep." So Paddy had another sleep then Bill woke him up. "Well? Come up and see the pitch." So Paddy said "No, it's all right Bill, I'll sign now."' Paddy agrees: 'I wasn't keen to go but I didn't think I could get back in the Preston team. When I got there, Bill made the place for me – I would only have moved there for him.'

Such a relationship was not exceptional. Bill gave the same

level of attention to all though sometimes his enthusiasm would get the better of him. Knowing of Billy Hogan's ill-health, he decided to take him to see a doctor in Scotland. Geoff Twentyman remembers that 'Bill got a taxi in Carlisle and they were going up towards Edinburgh. He told the driver which road to get on, "We'll come to a house on the right somewhere, that's what we're after." They went on for miles and miles and finally, they found this house. Bill got out, knocked on the door. It was the right place, but the doctor had been dead three years! That was typical of the things that could happen to Bill, he'd just get carried away.'

Bill Forster concedes that 'Hogan was a favourite of Bill's, they thought the world of one another. If the team weren't playing well, they'd come in at half time and Bill'd say to Billy "Stand over there." Then he'd turn on the other ten, "You stupid lot of so-and-sos!" There were no rifts in the team and the players continued to warm to his attitude. Unlike many managers, he wasn't above playing the occasional practical joke. Bill Forster remembers one at Jim MacLaren's expense: 'We were at Tranmere and Bill told Jim "The Scottish selectors are here today to watch you, so put on a display." Jim had a great game and at the end he said to Shanks "I hope the selectors enjoyed that." "What bloody selectors? Can you not take a joke man?"' On another occasion, he berated skipper Alex McIntosh for calling wrong at the toss!

Even these moments were forgiven for Shankly would always stand behind his men. No-one could criticise them and he would never do so in public. As interest in the team increased, so too did the idle gossip. Prior to games, they met in the Red Lion hotel, so that Bill could ensure they ate the right things. One week, Jim MacLaren came out a little later than his team-mates and was spotted making his way to the ground. Someone reported him to the manager, accusing him of illicit drinking, and Bill explained in no uncertain terms that five minutes earlier, the whole team had been there. Then he went on the tannoy before a game: 'Don't listen to these stories about Big Jim. Jimmy's a good lad.' With an attitude like that, it's no wonder that according to Paddy Waters 'the players would have done anything for him'. Jim MacLaren agrees, admitting that such was his energy, it was impossible to take offence even if he dropped you: 'He didn't do it from malice.' He could be understanding too as Jack Lindsay testifies. 'I was having a lean time. He called me into the office after a game and I'd missed a couple. He said "Here, sign that, £1 a week extra. There's a pound of steak and half a dozen eggs. Get that into you and you'll get scoring again."'

Beyond the team, he made his mark on the local people too; in readiness for 1950/51, sales of season tickets were a record. Everyone felt the club was on the brink of a new era. Bill refused to spare himself and worked through the summer, looking for players and fighting the fruitless battle for the return of his registration. In training, he preached the principles of good football. Paddy confirms that 'he always had his style of play. At our level, we played in the same way that Liverpool did when he got there.' Jack Lindsay could feel the team growing in confidence: 'He'd show us an idea in training, explain it to us. We'd try it and it'd come off, things we'd never imagined before.' An active footballing brain, he was always looking for new ideas, as Bill Forster illustrates: 'I came home for dinner and found knives, forks, cups, saucers, pepperpots all over the place. My wife said "I've had your pal Bill Shankly here." He'd been talking to her about tactics for an hour and a half using the crockery as players. He went on and on about what had happened and what he was going to do next week and my wife wasn't interested in the game!'

He introduced discipline without being heavy handed. 'He wasn't bossy,' Paddy recalls, 'he just created a good atmosphere.' Geoff Twentyman argues 'He came down hard if anyone stepped out of line, but we knew where we stood. If you were doing anything wrong, he soon let you know about it because he was very straight. He didn't want lads that wouldn't give everything but if you did, there was no problem.' Jim MacLaren's view is 'he got his point across but he wasn't dictatorial. He didn't have to be because we respected his judgment.' Training sessions demanded dedication, nothing was allowed to interfere with the work that was in hand, even injury. 'Geoff Hill got a kick on the end of his chin,' according to Jack Lindsay. 'He was out cold, but we were in the middle of a game. Bill said "Get him off, lay him out on the dressing room table" so a few lads picked him up. "Right! Let's finish this game" and poor Geoff's out to the world!'

All the lessons they'd learned when knitting together the previous year began to bear fruit in 1950. The away form showed little initial improvement but at Brunton Park they were well nigh invincible, scoring eighteen wins and four draws in twenty-three starts. Jim MacLaren felt 'the whole town was buzzing, the excitement he generated got through to everyone'. Shankly became an important local figure, regarded by some as an eccentric since he could only talk football. Roped into judging a beauty contest, Jim remembers him saying 'Candidly, ladies and gentlemen, I'd much rather be off watching a good football match than sitting here.' The talks on the tannoy remained a feature and he was always looking for a telling word or phrase that would make them memorable. 'We were talking about a game,' says Bill Forster, 'and he said "We were brilliant, like the Barrow game," and when I answered him, I used the word retrospective. "What's that? Retrospective? Good word. Make sure we use that next week. Brilliant word, brilliant!" He was quick to seize on anything that intrigued him or was a bit different. It helped make his speeches more lively.' If his speeches to the public were lively, team talks were simple. Rarely touching on the opposition, they were masterpieces in motivation, invariably ending in the command 'Now get out there and keel-haul 'em!'

There were signs, however, that Bill was starting to get itchy feet and was looking for a club with more potential. In November 1950, on the day of the First Round F.A. Cup tie against Barrow, the club announced: 'The United board of directors have been informed by their team manager that he has been offered another appointment with a club in a higher sphere of football which offers him advancement and is a more lucrative post than his present one. The board have fully considered the situation and have now come to an amicable agreement with Mr. Shankly whereby his services to Carlisle United will continue.' The offer was a coaching post at Grimsby Town and followed a voluntary wage cut that Bill had taken when Carlisle plunged into debt. Unable to raise his wages to compete with this alternative in the face of their financial plight, United offered Shankly a handsome bonus if they finished in the top three. Though the board's action prevented him leaving, it did not halt continuing speculation which saw him linked with Bolton.

By now, there was a very big match on the horizon to keep Bill busy. Having reached the Third Round of the F.A. Cup, they had the plum tie, a visit to Highbury to play Arsenal. Bill Forster recalls the day of the draw vividly. 'I saw Bill on the other side of the road so I shouted "Bill! Have you heard the draw?" "Aye," he said. "I wish it was just me against Joe Mercer, there'd be no contest!"' Fuelled by resentment following his treatment there in the war, Bill was determined to do everything in his power to stop the Gunners this time around, however long the odds. Carlisle were in the middle of a run that took them towards the top of the table. In five games since the Second Round, they'd won four and drawn the other.

'We were second in the League,' recalls Jack Lindsay. 'A week before we played Arsenal, we'd had to play Barrow at home. The pitch was bad, icy, they wanted to postpone it but Shanks said "No, we'll get two points today and go to Highbury top of the table." We'd been playing ten minutes and we were slipping all over the place. There was a ball through the middle and as I went after it, their centre half, George Forbes, a big lad, sixteen stone, slipped and caught me with his elbow on the jaw as I went past. I could see stars. Actually see them. The trainer gave me a sponge and told me to hold it to my mouth. I'd lost a couple of teeth, bleeding a lot. Half-time, Willie's standing there. Looks at me. "You all right?" and I could hardly speak. The club doctor had a look, told me it wasn't broken. Shanks says "You'll be all right", the blood's still flying out my mouth, but I went out and finished the game.

'At the end, Shanks took me to his house, Ness made me some fish and milk, I ate a bit of it. Then he took me up to a local doctor to get some pills and took me home. He said "I'll pick you up at nine in the morning and take you to Doctor Connell" who was a surgeon. I couldn't sleep, there was blood all over the pillow. We went to the surgeon, he took some X-rays. "How long did you play after the accident?" "The whole match." He shook his head. "You know the jaw's broken here and fractured here, you could have haemorrhaged to death." Willie looked at the pictures and then said "Aye, he'll be right for Saturday though." We just looked at him, it was so painful I couldn't even laugh! "I've played with a broken leg," he said. Give him his due, he looked after me, up every night to see if I needed anything. You couldn't get upset with him. That was his way, the game was everything."

Despite the loss of his main striker, Bill was able to put out a good team for the match at Highbury and had finally managed to get the city badge and motto on the shirts for this big game. Jack Mindel went into the Carlisle dressing room and found him 'bursting to play'. Fired up by a typical Shankly team talk, Carlisle gave a bravura performance to force a 0-0 draw. Reflecting on this success later, he told Workington groundsman Billy Watson 'When I got back to Carlisle, they wanted to make me Lord Mayor! They'd have given me anything!' A slight exaggeration but it did sum up the mood and the excitement that Arsenal's midweek visit was generating. Bill Forster remembers that 'he had the town mad, people talking on the buses, women who weren't normally interested wanting to know the scores'. His goal of unifying the city behind the club had been achieved on a scale beyond even his wildest dreams. In that sense, Carlisle provided the blueprint for what he would do in a real footballing city, Liverpool.

Sadly, the harsh realities of footballing life intruded and in the replay, Arsenal imposed their greater quality on the game and won 4-1. Even so, Carlisle had had a glimpse of the big

time, experienced the excitement that a good football team
could create. For the people, these were unforgettable days
and Paddy Waters makes it clear that 'even when the club got
into the First Division in the 1970s, everyone still talked about
the Shankly era as the best time.'

That Shankly era was drawing to a close. His success caused
many bigger clubs to take notice of him and in February, he
had an interview for the manager's job at Liverpool. He was
convinced that he'd got it until late on when the board informed him that they would be selecting the team. 'What am
I manager of then?' he asked. Even so, he went back to Carlisle
confident, so much so that he told Jack Lindsay ' "I'm off to
Liverpool, but Southport've been after you." I was due a benefit
but he told me "the only way to make sure you get some cash
is to sign for them" and so I went to Southport.' Having been
denied his due at Preston, Bill was always keen to ensure that
his players were properly looked after according to the rules.
When the news came through that Don Welsh had been
appointed at Anfield, Jim MacLaren remembers Bill asking
trainer Freddie Ford 'Is Don a mason?' 'Yes.' 'Aye, that'll be
how he got the job then.'

Despite all these distractions, Bill managed to keep Carlisle
in the hunt for promotion, though the Arsenal defeat did
knock the wind out of their sails, contributing to the only
home defeat of the League season against lowly Wrexham a
fortnight later. Shankly was determined that this was going to
be Carlisle's season. The idea of defeat after nine months of
strenuous work was too much to bear. In common with every
other manager, he had to put up with the disruption caused
by players being called up for National Service, something
which irritated him beyond words. Unlike his colleagues elsewhere, Bill didn't take it philosophically but tried to put things
right. Geoff Twentyman went into the Army in March 1951
as the season was reaching its climax. Stationed in Oswestry,
he was ideally situated for the first game, when Carlisle travelled to Shrewsbury. Other fixtures would not be so convenient
however.

'The following week I got called into the Camp Adjutant's office. "Gunner Twentyman, does the name Shankly mean anything to you? He's been on to the War Office. He's told them that Carlisle United can win the Third Division North provided he can get you off to play. We've decided to let you go, but once you're out of the running, it will stop." Bill thought it was a waste of time, "You're keeping 20,000 Carlisle people happy on a Saturday and you've to do National Service. Terrible waste."' According to the local press, Bill had told the War Office that by releasing Twentyman, productivity in Carlisle's factories would improve because they would win the league! This didn't come to fruition for over Easter, they drew at home and lost away to leaders Rotherham, ending the year nine points adrift in third place.

That third position was significant of course for it meant that Bill had earned his bonus. It was a promise never fulfilled. Whether Carlisle simply could not afford to make the payment or whether they were simply using an opportunity to wreak a little vengeance for two years of having Bill complain about their every move is open to question. It may be that they were disappointed that he applied for the Liverpool vacancy after the bonus agreement was in place. Feeling that he might well be set to move on in any case in the next few months, they probably chose to keep their hands on the money but they broke an agreement. 'He was very disappointed with the directors there, especially as his wages were so low,' says Jack Mindel. Bill felt he deserved better treatment. A proud man, he felt insulted.

When Grimsby Town had offered him a coaching post, it was with a view to taking over as manager. Sure enough, in the summer of 1951, Charles Spencer resigned and Bill accepted the position. Even had the Grimsby job not come about, it's hard to imagine him staying. Bill Forster was on hand when Shankly decided to go. 'He came in to see me. "Bill, I want you to type a letter to the Chairman of Carlisle United. I'm resigning." I was nearly in tears, trying to get him to change his mind but he said he wanted to go to Grimsby.

"This bloody club's no good," which wasn't like him but he'd had this dispute and he wouldn't stay. He was adamant the letter had to go there and then, so I told him "The post won't go 'til eight o'clock." "What's that matter? Let's have it in the box now." "It's only ten to twelve." "Now." So we walked up to the box to post it and that was it.'

Would Bill have left Carlisle anyway? He was starting to lose patience with the lack of funds at the club and the inability of the board to raise more. If he had a vision of Carlisle climbing to the top of the League pyramid, it was an ambition that he alone cherished. The board were happy to struggle along as they had. That was not good enough for a man of Shankly's ability. He wanted a challenge, but one where he did not have both hands tied behind his back. Carlisle could not give him the freedom he required. His players are unanimous in their verdict. Paddy Waters: 'I was shocked when he went but he'd taken things as far as he could. The heart went out of it when he'd gone.' Geoff Twentyman's view is 'he knew what he wanted and it wasn't easy to get because of the money.' Once he'd gone, the local paper was deluged in a flood of letters complaining about the falling standards since Shankly's departure, play which had 'deteriorated beyond recognition'.

Although he left the club in controversial circumstances and never forgave the board for their duplicity, he remained a popular figure with the fans. He had brought the place alive by the force of his personality. Carlisle's people found themselves living by the Shankly book, even those who knew nothing of football. In that drab post-war world, his engagingly idiosyncratic personality, sharp wit and generous nature had added colour to everyday life in an isolated city, a priceless commodity in those days. He saw that as part of his job, to help the people of the community; his contribution in two short years was immense and he is still thought of with great affection. Once he had gone to another club, he had no time to dwell on the past.

chapter eleven

THE FINEST TEAM

Entering the manager's office for the first time at Grimsby Town, Bill knew that he had a very different task on his hands. Grimsby had just suffered relegation to the Third Division North for the first time in a quarter of a century. They had had a number of seasons in Division One, finishing fifth in 1934/35, also reaching the semi-finals of the F.A. Cup in 1936 and 1939 so Bill hoped he might rouse a sleeping giant. Since his interest in the club had persisted from their abortive attempt to sign him up as coach in December 1950, there was clearly something about the club which attracted him.

Once again, Ness had to make the now familiar trek back to Scotland with the girls while Bill found a house for them. Alone in Grimsby, Bill took stock of the squad he had available and was disappointed that good players had been released. Even so, he felt he had a nucleus of players to work with. The club even made some money available to him, something of a surprise since it was widely reported that Bill went to Grimsby for less money than he'd been getting at Carlisle. Les Triggs, Grimsby historian, also records that 'the directors of that time weren't noted for being entirely supportive of managers'.

Bill had learned a great deal at Carlisle and was always looking to maximise his own performance. However, in the field of public relations, he would have found it difficult to improve. Breezing into Blundell Park in June, he was immediately recruiting the help of the local newspapers to whip up interest in the coming season. The previous five years had seen them slip from a secure mid-table berth in the First Division in 1946/47 to relegation to the League's basement. Tom Daley was a young goalkeeper with the Mariners and recalled that 'after we were relegated, that despondent, lethargic attitude spread throughout the club'. That was an attitude that Bill had to dispel. If the players and the supporters weren't raring to go, he could do nothing. Tom Wilkinson, now Life President, but then heavily involved in local football, recognised that 'he had a big job to do here'.

The Grimsby players were lifted out of the doldrums, according to Daley: 'as soon as he opened the doors at Blundell Park. He made himself known to everyone, talking about what he wanted to do, talking football. You couldn't fail to be enthused by him.' The same applied to the wider community. His first pronouncement to the press was that he wanted any local amateurs who felt they were good enough to write to him at the ground and arrange for a trial. A day or two later, he was making a speech at the local Grimsby & District Football League: 'I have come to work for Grimsby Town so I have come to help all classes of football and that includes you.' Pretty soon, he had invited Tom Wilkinson's amateur side to train at the ground and was giving talks to a number of clubs, maintaining a high degree of anticipation throughout the town. At a stroke, every hopeful amateur in the Grimsby area was looking forward to the new season, training harder, ready for the first game at Blundell Park. A week into his new role and Bill was a local celebrity. He went out of his way to help the town and was disappointed if he didn't receive their backing. Wally Freeburn, a full-back at the club, spotted his tunnel vision. 'He used to let the Police side train at the ground once a week with the part-timers so that he could watch. One night, he got pulled up for speeding. He got out of the car and when the policeman saw who it was he said "You were going a bit fast there Mr. Shankly." So Bill told him "You must have been going fast yourself to keep up with me." He got fined and so he stopped them training!'

Though he remained well known, few at Grimsby knew much about him as a manager. They'd been in a higher division as he was making his way at Carlisle and hadn't seen his team play. Few knew what to expect so he made it abundantly clear in the *Grimsby Evening Telegraph*: 'What I am after as much as anything is to get the players happy. When they are in that frame of mind, club spirit is good. The lads play football because they want to and because they enjoy the game. There is nothing so disheartening to the opposition as to be up against a team playing football all the time and playing it in every department.' He provided a breath of fresh air. One new idea was to actually use the playing surface itself for training, a move that had been unthinkable before his arrival when the groundsman jealously protected his patch of earth. Grimsby was a stimulating change for Bill. After the sour political atmosphere that had dogged his final months at Carlisle, he had high hopes that he would be free to manage Grimsby as he saw fit with adequate financial backing. Never one to hide his feelings, he wanted to start afresh and resolved to enjoy himself, approaching Grimsby as a club with potential. Clarry Williams, another of their goalkeepers, notes that 'we were still thought of as a big club, one that should be in the First Division'. If things worked out as Bill hoped, this might be his home for a decade or more. He quickly upset the directors though by chasing them out of the dressing room before games. 'He was incredible in the dressing room,' recalls Tom Daley. 'You had to tie him down, he was pacing around, clapping his hands, king of the heap. Ten minutes before we went out, he'd disappear and then come back in. "Christ boys, they're frightened to death. I've just seen them and they don't want to come out!" By then we were almost kicking the dressing room door down to get at them.' Clarry Williams felt the same way: 'He'd make you think you could beat anybody – they look shattered, they're weak as water, the winger's hopeless. You went out on top of the world.'

As the season approached, the Grimsby players were benefiting from the Shankly regimen. Their hopes were further raised when Bill dipped into the transfer market to bring in Bill Brown for £1,000, Walter Galbraith from New Brighton and Jimmy Hernon from Bolton. In the same mould as Billy Hogan, Hernon was a revelation and with his incredible ball control, he provided an outlet for the rest of the team. If they were under pressure, they could give the ball to Hernon and relax. Again, the Grimsby lads couldn't understand what such a great player was doing in the lower leagues, but his signing was due to Shankly's encyclopedic knowledge. Hernon had suffered a mild case of tuberculosis and his doctor recommended that he should move out to the coast to take advantage of the air. Shankly snapped him up and he recovered well to become the centre-piece of the attack.

Bill's greatest problem was time. The side he had put together leant very heavily on experienced professionals who knew their way around the game. George Tweedy was brought back into goal for much of his reign at the age of thirty-eight, Billy Cairns was thirty-nine, Galbraith thirty-three, skipper Reg Scotson thirty-two, Brown and Duncan MacMillan were fast approaching thirty, with Johnston, Hernon, Jimmy Maddison, Stan Lloyd all in their late twenties. Only Jimmy Bloomer and Alex McCue among the first team regulars were in the early stages of their career. It was obvious that he had one or, at best, two seasons in which to win promotion. If he could take Grimsby up at the first attempt, then he would have both the time and the wherewithal to gradually replace the oldest members of the side, revitalising the side over a three- or four-year period. If he couldn't, a wholesale rebuilding job would be required.

It was important to get the team playing his way as quickly as possible, so pre-season training was intense. Wally Freeburn joined the club that summer and saw that 'he emphasised that we should be playing the right way, that Scottish passing game. You had to win but he felt the two went hand in hand – if you could play, you would win. Bill was more a trainer than a manager in the old fashioned sense. He mixed with the boys which was very different. He played in practice matches and in reserve games to help bring the players on.'

That desire to keep playing came out a lot at Grimsby, to everyone's benefit. Finally resigned to his enforced retirement, he loved the opportunity that minor games provided. Early on, the *Evening Telegraph* reported that in a game against Ashby

Institute 'the biggest lesson to be learned from the Shankly demonstration was that the game should be played according to its name and that means carpet stuff all the time. It is doubtful if any of the Shankly passes left the ground and they were all in front of the man ... he is a great believer in the practical demonstration as against the theoretical.' Bill was returning to the player/coach role he'd been given at Preston. His presence on the field was instructive and formidable, a major factor in getting the team playing to a pattern. Training methods remained the same, but he felt he had an even greater chance of success because he was working with players who had already played at a high level and so could adapt more quickly.

The overall standard of football in the lower leagues in the 1950s was far closer to that played in the top flight than is true today. The gulf between Chelsea and Walsall is currently immense, yet forty years ago a decent Third Division side would not be too far behind a mid-table First Division team. That made the lower division clubs much more attractive, for spectators could turn up knowing they'd see a good standard of play. Local pride did the rest so it was possible to mobilise a useful side even in the backwaters.

Grimsby were far from a backwater team. Importantly, their team had not disintegrated as they dropped down the divisions, again an important distinction between then and now. Nowadays, if a team is relegated, the first problem for the manager to deal with is half his squad wanting to leave. Under the strictures of the maximum wage, there was no legitimate financial advantage to be had by moving on. Clubs found that if players were happy with their surroundings and had settled in the area, they were happy to stay put unless they had an international career to consider. Certainly at Blundell Park, Bill was lucky to find men like Scotson, Johnston, Bloomer and Maddison still in residence and with the addition of Hernon, he felt that he should make a good job of things.

Reg Scotson was captain, a strong running right-half who'd played for Sunderland in the top division. Similar to Shankly in terms of commitment and enthusiasm, he was the ideal choice to lead the side. He acknowledges that 'Bill had a bit of luck because he got a gang of blokes together that hit it off on and off the field.' Even then, with all the experience on show, it took them time to knit together on the field as they went through an horrendous opening to the season, losing their first two games. The first home match with Lincoln City was lost 3-2. Grimsby finished with just nine men on the field, Stan Hayhurst the goalkeeper going off with a broken finger and Alex McCue breaking his leg. In the next game, George Tweedy, second choice 'keeper' picked up an injury which put him out of the return at Lincoln on Wednesday.

'I was the junior 'keeper,' remembers Tom Daley, a seventeen year old at the time. 'When George got injured there was no-one else. We were in on the Sunday but Shanks didn't say a word to me. I didn't know what was happening until twelve o'clock on the day of the game. He 'phoned me at work and said "Tommy son, bring your boots, you're playing at Lincoln tonight." Afterwards he said he didn't want to tell me on Sunday because I'd have been a nervous wreck which was typical psychology.'

Pacing the dressing room, desperate for his men to avenge the nine-man defeat at home a week earlier, Bill paid special attention to his juvenile 'keeper. ' "Don't worry son," he told me. "Be brave. If a forward breaks through, run to the edge of the box with your arms out and shout 'Shoot you bastard! Shoot!' Just like Sam Bartram used to do.' I had a run of about seven weeks and he'd say that to me before every game.' Wally Freeburn agrees that 'we didn't bother with tactics, he was more interested in geeing us up for the game.' Clearly the approach worked for Daley kept a clean sheet.

Though tactics were never especially important, he did develop one particular move which was extremely profitable. 'We did so well from it that Matt Busby brought a camera crew to film it,' recalls Reg Scotson. 'If we won a throw in the middle of the pitch on the left, Paddy Johnston would take it. Everyone ran away from Paddy, Jimmy Hernon, inside left, going towards his own goal and leaving a big space. Jimmy Maddison, outside left, ran down the touch-line, taking the full back. As Paddy threw, Hernon would suddenly change direction and nod the ball back to him. Paddy had time to trap it 'cos no-one was near him and then it'd be a nice ball along the deck into the space to Billy Cairns at inside right. Little flick to Jimmy Bloomer at centre forward and it was a shot on goal. We scored loads of goals from it because we had ball players. Nobody knew how to cope with it, so Shanks chased this crew away because he didn't want to give people the chance to see it!'

Motivation remained the key. Tom Daley remembers him telling Alex McCue, 'Go and run your heart out for Grimsby Town son. If you die of exhaustion, I'll have you buried in the goalmouth. Just think of the honour.' He instilled good habits and kept players on their toes. He was still fanatical about appearance as Reg remembers. 'If your shirt came out during a game, he let you know. He'd be on the touch-line shouting "Get that tucked in. Maybe you can't play but you can at least look like a footballer." He introduced the short pants here. We were embarrassed the first time we went out 'cause the crowd were whistling at us but Bill'd say "What do you want to be running around with bits of cloth flapping around for?"'

In the days before rigid formations came into the game, a team that was psychologically ready was always a threat. All through the week, Bill never stopped making comments to individuals, trying to push them on to a better performance, joking with some, cajoling others. As a game got closer, he got down to work in earnest. If they were off to an away fixture 'he'd check us all on to the bus with a comment – "You want a haircut", "Have you had a shave?" – just a little dig to get you going, and we might be travelling the day before!' says Scotson. '"Sit at the back lads" because the directors were down the front. He'd lean on the arms in the aisle and talk to us. "Did I ever tell you about the Preston-Huddersfield Cup Final?" He'd start from the beginning and go through every pass. By the time we got off and had heard him talking about football and the opposition, we were two inches taller. We'd get off knowing we'd win.'

Bill was determined that his players should enjoy the game and he wasn't above pulling their leg. Tom Daley travelled 'to an "A" team game and it'd been pouring. The ground was soaking and we went to look at the pitch. I came in and told him that the goalmouth was covered in sawdust. "I had that put in specially for you son. You've been playing like a clown. I thought you'd feel at home!"' Gradually the side started to play the kind of football Bill wanted. His speeches over the tannoy were now fairly infrequent because, according to Reg Scotson, 'the folk down here couldn't understand what he was saying because of that thick accent he had!' It wasn't until Christmas that the town really began to see the best of their side however, a resounding 8-1 thrashing of Halifax Town rounding off the festivities nicely. The New Year opened badly though and by the middle of January with twenty-six fixtures completed, Grimsby had just thirty points, nine behind leaders Lincoln City but with a game in hand. What followed was a sequence of performances that were astounding even by Bill's standards, achievements that Liverpool were unable to match.

From the 19 January when they thumped Rochdale 4-0 at home through to the 29 March when Oldham lost 3-1 at Blundell Park, Grimsby pieced together eleven consecutive wins amid mounting hysteria, closing the gap on Lincoln to just five points with two games in hand. After the ninth win, Bill told the local press that 'I think we have the best team in the section and have a wonderful chance of promotion. The success has been due to the harmony which exists within the club with everyone pulling his weight from the Secretary's office to the outside left. No-one could ask for a finer bunch of players. They are giving all they have got.'

In the interests of that harmony, Bill chose not to mention a meeting he'd had with Reg Scotson the previous week. 'I was captain and as we were winning, the crowds were getting bigger. We won the eighth and the lads said "Go in and see Shanks, get us an extra bonus, we're doing marvellous, they're getting the money at the gate." I didn't fancy it 'cos I knew what he was like but I went in. "We're doing well boss and the lads are asking if there's any chance of an extra bonus." We were on £14 a week, £1 a draw, £2 a win. He sat back in his chair amazed, I'll never forget his face. "You want some extra money? I know you're doing very well but d'you mean to tell me that if I give you an extra fiver you'll do better?" I didn't know what to say, he'd floored me. "If you'll try harder for a fiver you can try harder for what you're getting now," which is true. I went green. When I came out, they were all waiting and they could see from my face what had gone on. I don't think anybody'd ever asked him for more money before!'

By sheer determination, Bill had forced the football club into the limelight. Grimsby, a town based around the docks and the holiday industry in Cleethorpes, was suddenly interested solely in football. In some respects, the best times of Bill's football career came there. He conceded in his autobiography 'that Grimsby team was, pound for pound and class for class, the best football team I have seen in England since the war. In the league they were in, they played football nobody else could play. Everything was measured, planned and perfected and you could not wish to see more entertaining football.' Shankly became a cult figure. Attendances frequently topped the 20,000 mark with 'people coming in from Hull, Louth, all the country places roundabout' according to Scotson. Local men were 'coming in on their bikes' says Williams. 'They were straight off the docks and into the match, dumping the bikes in the houses around the ground for tuppence a time. Everybody in the town was behind him.' As word got around that Bill was a regular feature of the reserve team in midweek their crowds shot up, to an incredible 5,000, more than most second and third division sides attract today. Tom Daley often played in the same reserve team as Bill and watched him enjoying himself. 'We were at home to Scunthorpe reserves and the ball went into the stands. Shanks went to take the throw and he started talking to the crowd. He was having a great time taking questions and the referee had to go over and give him a telling off. At half time, he was fuming. "I was just telling 'em about the first team game away last week, trying to get a bit of atmosphere." '

Referees were never Shankly's cup of tea. 'My brother Alec told me what to do when I was a boy. Never argue with referees because you can't win. Fancy being sent off for talking! You won't upset the ref, he just blows a whistle, he doesn't score goals. Side with him. Flannel them and later, when they get to know you, you can get away with things! It's all psychology.' In the heat of battle however, Bill couldn't always promise to behave. One of Tom Daley's earliest games was at Barrow, a midweek match that prefaced an interminable journey home across country. 'The referee was from Scunthorpe,' Tom remembers. 'He'd come on the train and someone arranged that we'd give him a lift back. We lost 3-1 and Shanks insisted two of the goals were offside. When the ref was ready, Shanks just ignored him and we drove off!'

Following the game, Shankly gave an example of his skills as a supreme psychologist and motivator. Tom Daley: 'I thought two of the goals were my fault and I was sitting alone on the bus feeling miserable. Bill came and sat next to me and said, "Those two goals you let in. I saw Frank Swift let seven in like that once," and by the time we were home, he'd convinced me I was five goals better than Swifty.' On the Saturday, Tom kept a clean sheet at Rochdale.

The eleven-game winning streak had to come to an end eventually, and it did so at Hartlepool United. The team recovered their composure and won six of the last eight, completing a final surge for promotion which saw them collect thirty-six points out of a possible forty, an enormous achievement. It wasn't enough for their moderate form early on left them with too great a deficit. Lincoln took the title with sixty-nine points, scoring 121 goals. Failure to gain promotion was a crushing disappointment especially when the team had performed so admirably. He could not have asked for more; they were denied by a system that allowed only one team to go up, a system that was to be changed before the decade was out with the amalgamation of the regional set-up. Bill wrote: 'All those points and nothing to show for them. That was shocking.' It was clear that Bill had an idea that Grimsby had missed the boat for he applied for the job at Middlesbrough in the close season. George Aitken was a Middlesbrough player at the time. 'He was interviewed on the Wednesday and was more or less given the job. Then on the Saturday, they appointed Walter Rowley without telling Bill first.' Again, he was left disillusioned at the behaviour of the directors, a class that he viewed with open hostility. He felt that he could not trust any of them, with good reason, since it's likely that Grimsby's board had gone behind Bill's back to warn Middlesbrough away, again without consulting him first. Bill wrote later that it 'was a terrible disappointment, because I was bubbling with ideas and Middlesbrough had a good ground and a lot of useful players. Before the war, they'd had one of the best footballing teams in Britain. Ayresome Park represented potential.' Thus was football denied the fascinating prospect of Bill Shankly managing a team that featured Brian Clough at centre-forward.

Starting again the next year was a terrible task. Whether he tried to strengthen the side and was unable to find players or funds isn't clear. He may well have felt that the team had done so well in the previous campaign that they deserved another crack. Whatever the case, the 1952/53 season was begun with almost the same side that had completed the last one. As Reg Scotson makes clear 'he loved to get in the dressing room with the lads, get out training and play football'. Tom Daley feels that one of his greatest assets was that 'he was in with the players, first team, juniors, reserves. He'd be in the bath, delighted at winning the five-a-side against the kids. When he was with the kids, he was fourteen, when he was with the first team, he was a senior pro. He was always creating the right atmosphere.'

At training he remained 'a hard taskmaster', according to Clarry Williams. 'If we had a three-a-side in the gym, he'd kick heck out of you if you didn't get stuck in. He was a hard man

and he expected you to play hard.' Wally Freeburn provides
an example of that: 'We played at Chester and their winger
was giving me a chasing. Half-time came and Bill said "Look,
this boy's got bad knees, just crack him one and that'll do it."
A further example of his attention to detail and determination
to reach the top with the team came after a 3-1 win. Reg
Scotson remembers: 'We had our usual meeting in the boardroom on Monday. When we played well, he didn't single
anyone out, but if you'd made a mistake, he was ruthless. He
wasn't happy about the goal we let in. Jimmy Maddison was
a quiet lad and he'd lost the ball to their full back and hadn't
chased far enough back and the full back laid on a goal. Bill
gave him hell, there were tears streaming down his face but
he let him cry. He was hard as nails when he had to be. The
same with injuries – unless you'd broken your leg in two
places, you weren't injured, you could run it off.' Wally Freeburn recalls that 'he asked you to tell him if you weren't fit,
but you didn't dare!'

The extraordinary thing about Bill Shankly though is that
despite incidents like these, no-one ever seemed to take
offence. His innocent compulsion to speak the truth left him
immune like a rough and ready, hyperactive version of the
Peter Sellers role in *Being There*, a simple man with a beguilingly
honest demeanour, a man of unimpeachable integrity. Anyone
who worked with him and was on the wrong end of a tongue-
lashing knew there was no malice involved, but that he was
simply trying to improve the game. In his favour was his
incredible talent as a manager. No-one wanted to miss out
on the opportunity of working with him and so few risked
arguments, while Bill himself rarely bore a grudge once the
shouting was over. His eccentric behaviour also captivated his
charges. Reg Scotson again remembers one particular example:
'He had us playing five-a-side on a full size pitch, exhausting.
Grimsby's second strip was white tops and he got some blue
tops from somewhere. We'd have Scotland versus England
every week, four Scottish lads and him against the four Geor-
dies – me, Cairns, Lloyd, Maddison, plus Paddy Johnston.

We'd get ready to run out and Shanks thinks he's playing at Wembley Stadium in front of 100,000, he's on cloud nine. "Come on boys, let's get these English so and sos." Just before we went out, he called the office so that as we walked on to the pitch, the record of "Scotland The Brave" would come over the tannoy. He walks out, captain of Scotland, his chest thrust out ready to play for his country.'

Bill had to win. Scotson remembers how they first realised it. 'We played a lot of head tennis up at "Wonderland" in Cleethorpes when it was closed for the winter. Bill would always get the ball players on his team to help out. We usually knocked off at twelve but some days we were there at one until we finally tumbled that we didn't stop until Bill's team were winning. If we wanted to pack in, we'd give him a couple of points, then he'd clap his hands. "OK lads, into the bath!".'

He could keep going for as long as it took for he was still a fit man, though now given to playing at inside right on occasion. The *Grimsby News Pictorial* commented on a performance in a floodlit friendly: 'What a pity he is unable to play league football. Here we have a man in the advanced veteran stage as a footballer, playing in a Midland League game on a Monday and then against a Second Division side two days later. He finished as fresh as the youngest man on the field after playing keenly and intelligently for the full ninety minutes.'

The secret of his fitness was his secret of eternal youth. Football rejuvenated him every day. He couldn't get enough of the game. Tom Wilkinson recalls he'd turn up on a Sunday morning to play with the youngsters. 'They were thirteen or fourteen and he'd say to them, "Now kick me, or I'll kick you." I was talking to the physio and he said "What do they do to the Boss? He comes up here at half past four on Sundays and I don't get rid of him until eight. His legs are wrecked, kicked to pieces."' Wally Freeburn remembers watching Shankly on a Saturday before the game. 'You could see it in his face in the dressing room, thinking "roll on tomorrow morning".'

Though Grimsby got off to a sprightly start, winning the first four games, things took a turn for the worse as an ageing side still troubled by the disappointment of the previous year struggled to maintain consistency. Bill needed the help of all his players but again faced the National Service problem in relation to Tom Daley. 'I joined the RAF with a friend. Bill 'phoned Whitehall and got me transferred out of the RAF and into the Army because he thought I'd be stationed nearer to home and be available for games. My friend stayed in the RAF and was posted to a camp six miles up the road for the duration. I got shipped out to Germany!'

A wretched spell through December left them eleven points off the pace and doomed to another season in the Third Division North. The atmosphere at the club changed as did Bill's own attitude. Reg Scotson saw at first hand what the pressures of management did to him. 'He'd been full of fun the previous year but as things went downhill a bit, he started to worry because he couldn't see how to turn it around. In the winter, he wore a black and white scarf and by the end of a game he'd chewed the fringes away at the end. He was beginning to fret, he was drained and worn down. After a match when he stood up, he wasn't as tall because his feet had been scrabbling away at the gravel on the cinder track where he'd been sitting. There were big holes where he'd been trying to kick balls away. There were even a few fag ends – he just lit 'em up and threw 'em away. He was so worked up, he didn't know what to do with himself.'

Without cash, he knew that he could do little; picking up a share of the gate money from away games, they returned from Accrington Stanley with £46. Onlooker, correspondent with the *Grimsby News Pictorial*, wrote some vituperative columns about the club's affairs. In February after a 1-0 home defeat to Stockport he remarked that 'the forward line failed lamentably. There was not a trace of the Shankly plan of attack. Surely a better line than this can be fielded. If not, why not?' Worse was to come in February 1953 when Duncan MacMillan was suspended. Onlooker once more: 'The management errs on the side of generosity.' After the season fizzled out, he added 'there has not been a happy spirit and this has been reflected

Mother, father and the boys (from left: John, Bill, Bob, Jimmy and Alec) (*Shankly Collection*)

Preparing for battle at Preston North End (*Shankly Collection*)

(above) Balloon
Barrage Depot (Bury).
Manchester and
District RAF League
Champions 1941/42.
Shankly is second
right in the back row
(*Shankly Collection*)

(left) Captain of
Scotland, May 1941
(*Shankly Collection*)

(above) Meeting King George VI before the 1938 F. A. Cup Final
(below) The Dads and Lads team at Crosland Road, Huddersfield. Shankly keeps hold of the ball (*Sporting Post, Dundee*)

(left) First day as Manager at Carlisle United, March 1949 (*Billy Watson*)

(facing page) All you need is a ball and the green grass. Bill Shankly at Melwood, ready to make Liverpool great (*Billy Watson*)

(below) Billy Watson and Bill Shankly, Melwood Training Ground (*Billy Watson*)

(above) With daughter
Jeanette at Huddersfield
Town's Leeds Road
Ground, Summer 1956
(*Billy Watson*)

(left) The F. A. Cup in safe
hands, Anfield, May
1974
(*Harry Ormesher*)

With Nessie and the OBE

Bill Shankly in retirement, 1974 (*Daily Express*)

LEST WE FORGET… The Kop's Last Stand, April 1994
(*The Football Archive*)

on the field. Lack of decision and enterprise in the boardroom. Lack of the right kind of disciplinary action in the dressing room and lack of the proper respect and loyalty to the manager by the players are lapses which could have been instrumental in bringing the morale at Blundell Park down to the low ebb which predominated ... the club cannot be allowed to drift along on its present course. There are rocks ahead.' Onlooker may have overplayed his hand and painted a gloomier picture than was the case. Bill maintained a firm grip on his players but the mood of the club was not the same as had existed a year earlier. Bill even used the tannoy to tell the fans 'we have had a disappointing season but we shall profit from the experience'.

It was hard to see just how they could because Shankly was not given the chance to introduce new faces while too many of his team had reached the end of the road and could not be sold on. As Reg Scotson's vivid portrayal of Shankly's mood swing shows, he had reached a point where he was unsure of his next move. For the first time in his career, he was facing a crisis that was seemingly insoluble. He tried to inject life into the team on the training ground and aimed to promote the same spirit that had done them so much good in his first year. He organised group visits to the cinema, though even then, football wasn't far from his mind. 'We had complimentaries to the Ritz,' says Wally Freeburn. 'The interval came along and Bill was right at the front. He turned round to the rest of us and shouted "Lads! If we got the seats out, this'd be grand for five-a-sides!"' Another night out came when he was in action in a benefit game at Doncaster alongside Tom Finney. Freeburn recalls: 'You daren't miss the game. He played the ball in to Tom and started off down the pitch. "Set me away Tommy, set me away!" He ran his heart out to get that ball but he just couldn't reach it. That was Bill, all heart.'

With a team that was largely past its sell-by date, heart was no longer sufficient. Arguments between Bill and the board became more pronounced. Onlooker wrote that 'Mr. Shankly is not on a contract with the club and they would not stand in the way of any contemplated move . . . one can form a very good idea of how things are moving at Blundell Park.' Without the support of his board, Bill knew that there was no use trying to hold the fort. Despite working day and night, he was not given adequate backing. Things were going so badly that he spoke directly to Onlooker, his sternest critic. In an interview that wasn't published until after his departure, Shankly told him that 'he was very concerned about the club's position and told me that he had received offers from other clubs but he felt it would not be fair to consider them while the Town were in such low water. Bill Shankly lives for football. No club possesses a manager who works harder or puts in longer hours.'

Though Onlooker couldn't go into print at the time, there was an immediate change in tone after his frank chat with Bill. 'Who is going to be loyal enough to the club and those who pay to support it and raise a voice in the boardroom like a clap of thunder urging a "Save The Club Campaign"? . . . The lot of a manager in these circumstances is not an enviable one and he should be supported up to the hilt by those who voted him into the managership of the club . . . Reorganisation of the club is well overdue and this goes back to before the War.' Beset by these internal travails, Bill knew when he was beaten. There were no winnable battles left to fight. In December 1953, Bill Stockwood and Billy Webb were invited on to the board but when it was made apparent that they were unable to provide any capital, he accepted that the game was up and tendered his resignation. There could be no clean break for Bill was betrayed once more by the board. Wally Freeburn remembers that 'he didn't just leave. He got us all together in the boardroom and told us that they'd promised him a bonus for getting in the top three in that first season and he had never received it.'

It's probable that this time, the bonus proved less crucial though Bill's anger at his treatment might well have added to the simmering discontent that seemingly existed during the latter stages of his tenure. Having settled well in Grimsby, Bill may well have bitten his tongue over the bonus and tried to get on with his job; if that hadn't been the case, he'd have gone twelve months earlier. When he realised that he was not going to receive the unqualified backing that a manager has to have and that in essence he was not in control of the club, that would be the final straw. A manager has to manage. Without money, you couldn't really control anything. Some twenty-five years later, Bill had this to say. 'Some managers are only interested in keeping their job, sucking up to directors, yes sir, no sir, three bags full sir. They should be drummed out of the game. You've got to be your own man, be in charge of the whole affair. If you don't have the guts to do that, get out.' It was sad that Bill had to admit defeat at Grimsby Town, though his powerful pride would not, could not, accept it as a reflection on himself. His feeling was that he had been betrayed by the board in their failure to match his whole-hearted commitment to the club.

Could Shankly have done more? Is it fair to apportion all the blame to the board? Certainly as a young manager he made errors of judgment. Possibly in that first season he was too carried away as the team made a bee-line for promotion. His attachment to the senior pros, men with enormous experience of the game, was a source of strength and weakness. Their know-how helped see them through that first season, picking up points that should have been beyond them and generating a marvellous atmosphere around the town. Bill always had a soft spot for characters and there's little doubt that men like Scotson, Cairns, Brown, Galbraith and Tweedy were that. He enjoyed their company and was sucked into deriving too much fun from the game and losing sight of his responsibilities. That problem resurfaced in the late '60s at Liverpool.

Prior to that second year at the club, he should have introduced more new faces than he did. Finances clearly limited his hand in the transfer market, but Grimsby had some useful reserves. This was the time for such introductions to be made, but such was Bill's affection for the men who had worked so hard for him and who had been so disappointed by their failure to be crowned champions, he allowed them another

opportunity. Such loyalty is laudable, but it can also be dangerous. Too many players went on for too long and should have
been replaced by players who were inferior only through inex-
perience. Grimsby's decline was largely the fault of an unam-
bitious, short-sighted board of directors but Bill has to take a
share of the blame.

The loss of Shankly was disappointing to the Grimsby supporters even in the light of his few mistakes. He had reawak-
ened their passion for the game and heightened their
expectations after a number of dismal post-war seasons.
Though they were unhappy with the decline in the club's
fortunes in the latter part of his stay, they knew enough about
the game to realise that given appropriate backing, Bill was as
likely to bring back the First Division days as anyone. With
him gone, interest in the club continued to decline and the
Mariners were forced to apply for re-election eighteen months
after his departure. Grimsby supporters are still left to wonder
just what their club might have achieved had Shankly been
given a glimmer of hope by the board. If it was never the
hotbed that Liverpool was, there's little doubt that Grimsby
could have comfortably sustained a First Division side
throughout the 1950s and 1960s. A blinkered board failed to
appreciate the manager they had found, failed to back his
skills with some judicious speculation in the transfer market
and left future generations of directors and supporters to face
the consequences.

Bill had to face the consequences of what the outside world
would consider failure. Having earned a good reputation at
Carlisle and strengthened that considerably in his debut
season at Grimsby, subsequent events left him vulnerable. Had
he simply inherited a team at Grimsby that was too good for
the Third Division and ridden on the back of those established
players? Had he failed to get the best from them after the initial
burst of enthusiasm? Were his transfer dealings questionable?
These were the kinds of questions being asked by those who
were not privy to the internal difficulties that he faced. His
stock in the game took a beating and he was left facing an

uncertain future. Part of his desire to stay with Grimsby when in 'such low water' came from the fierce loyalty he always had to his real employers – the supporters. There must have been a part of him that realised that he could redeem himself in the eyes of the football world by turning the club round, thus giving him the chance of a better move than he could presently expect. Exasperation with the board's tight grasp on the purse strings forced him to leave for he could see no way in which he could make improvements; the only way Grimsby could introduce the new men that were desperately required was from the youth policy and that could take years. He didn't have that long.

He left Grimsby with a heavy heart for he liked the place and the people, commenting 'I am sorry to leave Grimsby and Cleethorpes, as of all the places I have been in, including Preston, these two towns I have found the best. At one time I had visions of staying there for the rest of my life, but that's football. Things change a lot.' In his final speech to the crowd prior to the Stockport County game on 2 January 1954, he thanked the crowd for 'all your support and friendship during my short stay'. He also left a wiser man, for as he said, 'You can learn more from losing than winning.'

Bill's greatest asset had been in galvanising both his players and their town. He'd been able to perform this trick with ease at both Carlisle and Grimsby, where football's grass roots community had warmed to his honest fanaticism. In so doing, he had created a powerful momentum that had all but swept his sides to promotion. Both were a couple of good players short of a winning team and Bill was unable to buy them. As with everything else, some directors are better and richer than others and Bill, who hadn't found the best ones yet, had assimilated the harsh lesson that without money, creating a good team is well nigh impossible. The problem that now faced him was that he found this truth unpalatable. To feel that he could not survive without the goodwill of directors was anathema and it created a dichotomy that he was never to fully resolve. A dogmatic character of supreme self-confidence, he felt that he was the only man to run a club properly and to do so he had to run it on his terms. The stark realisation that he would have to go cap in hand to directors for that money was an unappealing one, all the more so for such a proud man.

Half measures were never remotely good enough. Those very standards made him such a formidable player and manager. Two clubs into that second career, he felt that his efforts were scuppered by meddling and/or insufficiently committed amateurs. Worse yet, at both places he had been deceived by those who had employed him. Bill had an instinctive dislike for those who ran any business. It was as deeply ingrained in his psyche as was his love of football. Some of his behaviour where directors were concerned may have been irrational on the face of it, deliberately provocative or antagonistic where there was no need for him to be. That was the point.

Knowing that loyalty was a one-way street, he made strenuous and deliberate efforts to map out his territory and impose himself on the club. That's why he threw board members out of the dressing room, why he kept his players separate from the board. The players inhabited his private universe where directors had no place. They had no business even talking to his players. He would prepare them, he would train them, he would replace them when necessary and possible. All footballing activities were within his domain. It was precisely because he understood the precarious nature of football management and knew how exposed his position would always be that he had to take these steps. A manager is only as good as his results. If those results aren't good enough, the manager carries the can – as the owners of the club, directors are unlikely to sack themselves. Bill knew all about the demeaning nature of unemployment, being unable to care for your family properly. He'd had first hand experience of all those things in Glenbuck and feared a return to them. John Roberts saw that 'in the '20s and '30s, everyone helped each other but you had to look for charity rather than assistance then which is bound to leave an impression. He always had an us and them attitude. In his youth, the workforce was expendable. His philosophy was that whatever job you do, you do it to the very best of your ability, whether it be scrubbing tables or managing a football club. That's a legacy that people who went through the depression often carry, they have a special dedication to their work, often very meticulous with it.'

There was always that terrible thought lurking in the back of his mind, that one day someone would tap him on the shoulder and say 'OK, you've had a good run. Back to the pit for you.' As John Roberts notes, 'If you knew how easy it was to lose your job and how hard it was to find another, you never lost your concern for doing a good job in order to keep it, nor that fear of losing it without reason.' Bill had to be successful as a manager for only that success could postpone such a painful day of reckoning. Grimsby was part of a long and difficult learning process, and it offered the first inkling that Bill might have to work with directors in future. One perennial problem he had was in disentangling the club from its supporters. He always loved supporters wherever he went for he knew that they were unashamed in their bias towards the club and gave their money gladly, hoping to see good games and a winning side. Their appreciation of the game was naive and joyous. It made it difficult for him to do anything that might harm the club. At Grimsby, he didn't resign his post as early as he should have done because he didn't want to let the crowd down. For his own benefit he should have made his stand earlier, left the club and allowed the directors to sort out the problems that were largely of their own making. As a result of those final dispiriting months, he left the town with one decision very definitely made. Wherever he went, he would stay with a club only to the point at which he had reached the extent of the board's aspirations. If they weren't willing to go further, he wasn't willing to stay – this was made clear at the end of the decade when he was in charge at Huddersfield Town.

The real question was where did he go next? Events at

Grimsby had left him uncertain, not of his own ability nor of his future in football, but of the way he should manage, the sort of club he should work with and the relationship he should have with players, supporters and board. By the end of 1953, he needed time to regroup, to evolve a new strategy. The top clubs were unsure of him and so he was resigned to working in the lower leagues for a little longer. He needed to be reinvigorated, to take on a fresh challenge and win to restore his reputation. Wherever he went, money would be a problem so he needed to get used to that idea; the ideal compromise would come with a club that was not necessarily aiming for the heights and which had a modest but reasonable set of expectations. There was no club in the Football League more in need of a dose of the Shankly magic than Workington and there could have been no club which better suited his current requirements.

chapter twelve

A LONG WAY DOWN

When Bill Shankly went to Workington in January 1954, the Reds could hardly pretend that they were a club of the highest pedigree. Elected to the Football League two years earlier, those first seasons in the Third Division North had seen them finish in the bottom two on both occasions. As Bill took charge, the club were again rooted to the bottom of the table and there were whispers that should they have to apply for re-election for a third successive year they would get the thumbs down. The club had made a few astute signings, bringing in Dennis Stokoe, Rex Dunlop, Hughie Cameron and Norman Mitchell, so all wasn't doom and gloom, but there was still a huge amount to be accomplished in a short space of time.

Expectations were realistic but stark. Bill had to lift Workington out of the bottom two to save the club from returning to non-league football, a heart-breaking prospect for the people of the town who had worked tirelessly to bring the League game to Borough Park. The people in the club from the players to the groundsman to the board had all put in an enormous amount of work while the relatively small crowds were still boisterous, excited by the novelty of hosting the likes of Grimsby, Port Vale and local rivals Barrow and Carlisle. Though Bill knew he'd have little money to spend and little hope of ever taking Workington into the Second Division, he was among football people who cared passionately for the game and shared his enthusiasm. Everything that was happening at Borough Park was a new experience and the people wanted to share in it.

When Shankly arrived, the football fans were naturally excited for he was the biggest thing to happen to the club. Their feelings were reciprocated for he and Ness were happy to be back in the north again, nearer their native Scotland. Bill was also suitably impressed by the quietly determined way everyone at the club went about their work. He was particularly keen on the hard-working Supporters Club which managed to raise desperately needed funds throughout the town. In Workington, Bill had similar problems to those he had encountered in Carlisle – geographic isolation, lack of money, difficulty in bringing players north, lack of tradition. As far as support went, Workington had an even smaller catchment area, with a town population of around 30,000. This time he had one further hurdle to overcome. Workington was most definitely a rugby league town. Workington Town RFC had a fervent following. They were led by the legendary Gus Risman and in the previous year, had done the League and Cup double so their pre-eminence was scarcely surprising. If that wasn't bad enough, they shared Borough Park with the football team.

This was brought home to him when he'd taken the job following a December meeting with directors in a Blackpool hotel. His first day at the club was described in his auto-biography.

> 'I opened the door, put my hand up to the wall and was feeling around. A fellow said to me "What are you doing?"
> "I'm putting on the light."
> "There's gas in here," said the fellow.
> Bloody gas! Next I heard a noise outside and said "What's going on?"
> "That's the Rugby League," he replied.
> "What do you mean it's the Rugby League?" I said. I nearly went mad. I didn't know about that. I went outside and saw Gus Risman.
> "What the hell are you doing?" I said.
> "We're scrumming."'

One man who found the dual use of the ground an even greater trial than Shankly was groundsman Billy Watson. Imagine trying to produce a playing surface suited to the neat, passing football that Shankly demanded when a rugby league side was churning the ground up with a match every other week as well as their regular practice sessions. Watson and Shankly quickly forged a strong friendship that was to endure right until Bill's untimely death in 1981 when Billy was proud to be Workington's representative at his funeral. The two were alike in many ways, possessing the same unquenchable enthusiasm for football, the heroes of the past, so it's little wonder that they combined so well. Yet on first meeting, Billy was unsure about this new arrival. 'When he first came, you'd look at him and you daren't speak. He looked like he'd never smile, a tough fella.'

Bill soon realised that Billy was a genuine football man. Working for Workington, you were never going to get rich. The people that were there weren't involved to take advantage of the game but to contribute to it, to work within the sport that they loved. Between them, clubs such as Liverpool on the one hand and Workington on the other embody everything that has been great – and successful – about the Football League in its first century. That both could co-exist was testimony to the strength of the institution. Those who wish to tamper further with the structure of the game would do well to study the historical importance of the relationship, one facet counter-balancing the other. Without the Workingtons, the clubs like Liverpool would be starved of the talent that feeds them. If towns like Workington are lost to football, football will be the poorer. While Liverpool is a city built on the game, it is in the hundreds of smaller places like Workington, where the footballing flame is fanned by a small but committed band of ardent enthusiasts, that its appeal lies. Shankly, 'a working man who liked working people and who had no time for people who thought they were above them', according to wing-half Jackie Bertolini, fully acknowledged that relationship. Football was a wide community. He knew only too well just how crucial the game could be to the welfare of its most far-flung satellite towns.

Rugby league provided him with some of his earliest difficulties. Faced with the need to get the team playing well to stave off the spectre of re-election, desperate measures were required. Jackie Bertolini recalls that 'it was a low key, struggling club. They'd been through a few managers but no-one could make a success of it. Sharing the ground with the rugby league people was disturbing. The part-timers like myself had to train at the same time as the rugby lads and the ground would be cutting up. They were nice chaps but it just depressed things as far as football was concerned.' Billy Watson has cause to remember 'there was hardly any grass left on it sometimes. At training, we might have eighty people on the ground at one time. The main thing was that I could keep it flat.'

The first lesson Bill had to learn was that he couldn't shift the rugby men because they were paying £800 a year for the privilege of using it. Though £800 a year was a lot of money in those days, Workington Town were still getting it on the cheap bearing in mind their gates of 15,000 and the fact that they used it for training as well as matches. The football club was so hard up they couldn't afford to lose their tenants. Instead, Bill found that he had to turn the town on to football. Jackie Bertolini saw it as 'very much a rugby town and Bill got a mixed reaction. The rugby people were happy with things and they didn't take to him at first, though for the football people he was manna from heaven. Over the first weeks and months, he even got the rugby people interested because he could talk to them so well. He was instrumental in getting things going on the football side.' Billy Watson agrees because 'we'd never seen the big names in football up here. It was a great thing for the town to have someone like Bill. Gus Risman was already a legend so Bill sort of balanced it up.'

Bill and Gus harboured a healthy mutual respect, but it didn't stop each trying to take advantage of the other as Billy Watson testifies: 'They had a terrible row one day. We'd just had a running track put in, so the touch-line was near to that instead of there being a wide fringe of grass to the stands. Bill says "We want width in football, make the pitch as wide as you can." First game of the season was rugby and I'd got the line two feet off the track like Bill wanted. Gus came up and said "Can you not bring it in a bit and then take it out again for football?" so that they wouldn't end up on the track after a rugby tackle. I thought a minute and told him that after a few weeks, you wouldn't be able to rub the lines out because the paint got into the soil and the line stayed there. Gus wanted me to try it so I took the line in. On the Sunday after, I got in early to put it back out before Bill could see it but he soon spied it and I had to tell him what Gus had said. "Tell me when he gets in." I knew there was going to be some fun and I told the lads to come and watch. Gus got in at ten o'clock and I told him Bill wanted a word. Bill started on him right away. "What are you playing at? That touch-line. It's a football field not a rugby pitch. You're getting the ground for nothing. I want that touch-line where I told Billy to put it." They were at it hammer and tongs, but Bill won in the end.'

Similar battles were fought with the directors according to Billy. 'Before we had terracing, we used old railway sleepers and I was building the ground up when Bill saw me up there with a pick and shovel. I told him it was one of the directors who told me to do it, so Bill came out to see him when he got in and laid into him. "Billy's job's on the pitch, not up there." He won again. That was his way, he always said "look after the small things and the rest falls into place". He was so thorough, it rubbed off on all of us.' He also tried to instil his refusal to be beaten into the players, maintaining the familiar pattern of never finishing a session until he was on the winning side. At Workington, the players had to ease off when Billy Watson 'went to the edge of the field to give 'em the signal. They had to come in then 'cos the water was hot for a bath and it wouldn't stay hot too long.'

George Aitken had been signed from Middlesbrough in July 1953 for the sum of £5,000, an enormous amount for a club like Workington. He remembers that 'we were in the doldrums, playing poorly. Bill arrived and he took the place by storm, had a big impact right away. He was bursting with ideas, telling us to play attractive football, full of confidence.' The first test came with a home fixture against Carlisle on 9 January. Bill inspired Workington to a 2-2 draw, continuing the improved run of form that the managerless side had enjoyed since the middle of December when news of his imminent arrival had begun to leak around Borough Park. They picked up five points in four games and lifted themselves out of the bottom three. Derwent wrote in the *Workington Star* that 'they play with skill and precision, neat man to man football. Workington supporters have every right to feel proud of their team these days. Manager Bill Shankly, keen as mustard to get the side as far away from the bottom as possible, is creating a fine atmosphere of confidence and team spirit ... donning track-suit and joining the players in training shows that he means to make a go of things ... he also wants co-operation from the supporters.'

Jackie Bertolini is in no doubt of Shankly's value in this initial period. 'We couldn't believe he was here because we thought he could have gone anywhere, so that was a boost. The main thing was that he got us playing football, we'd had no ideas before he arrived. In training, he'd show you that you might be able to beat a couple of men in a dribble but with an intelligent pass, you could beat four or five. He liked to mix it up, give you that variety. He was a short ball man but he knew the value of the long ball when necessary. When the ball came out in training – and that was a new thing, up until Bill, it had been running, weights and so on – that was when his charisma affected you. Here was a guy who'd done it all, could still do it, and could impart it.'

An early indication of Bill's impact came in February when Workington entertained Port Vale, clear at the top of the Third Division North – they went on to win it in style by 11 points, losing just three times in the process, even reaching the semi-finals of the F.A. Cup where they were beaten by West Bromwich Albion. The visit of Vale seemed sure to plunge the Reds back into the re-election dogfight but instead they won 2-0. 'That was Bill's strong point,' according to Jackie. 'Those teams that were classed as better were the ones he wanted to beat and invariably we would.' The local press were euphoric, running the headline 'Reds Greatness Has Been The Talk Of The Town'. Derwent wrote that 'surely now Workington have established themselves as the most improved team in English soccer'.

Bill's ebullience was perhaps the central reason for the rapid improvement in Workington's fortunes. However, his driving commitment could occasionally force him to regret his behaviour under pressure, as he did after the Port Vale game. Noel Hodgson was fifteen when Shankly took over.

'He could be a bit frightening at times, walking around in his crombie and his Anthony Eden hat. One of the lads had told him he was getting married and he went mad. "What? You don't get married to play football! You eat, sleep and drink football!" So we were a bit wary of him. Anyway, the club was excited because Port Vale were coming and I looked on the team sheet on Thursday and I was in the "A" team for the Saturday. He'd put everybody's name down and I was seventeenth man. It was away at Frizington and I thought I'd learn more by watching Port Vale so I missed the "A" team game and went to Borough Park instead. As the team came out, Bill passed me.

"What are you doing here, you should be at Frizington!"

"I was seventeenth man, Mr. Shankly."

"You've no interest in the game, boy. Get off home and don't come back," and he chased me out of the ground. I was crying 'cos I'd been down at the club for years, but I kept away. Two weeks later there was a knock at the door and I could hear my mother talking. "You've a nerve coming here."

"Where's the boy? I want to talk to the boy." I ran through and he put his hand on my shoulder. "I was a bit harsh, get yourself off down there tomorrow," and I was over the moon. As a young lad, it was incredible to think he'd admit he was in the wrong and come and get me back.'

Bill was enjoying life at Workington. He and Billy Watson would go to local games including one at Cleator Moor. 'Just a little place with a rope around the ground, no stands,' as

Billy describes it. 'Our "A" Team were beating them and Bill was shouting away on the touch-line when this old woman came across and started hitting him over the head with her walking stick because we were winning. Bill actually said "Calm down, it's only a game of football missus."' He must have been shocked by this outbreak of geriatric hooliganism because saying it was 'only' a game was akin to breaking one of the Ten Commandments. It was also an indication of his improved frame of mind.

No-one was under any illusions as to the permanence of his position in Workington. Consequently, all at the club tried to make the best use of his experience while it was available. For Shankly, it was a nice winding down period after the trouble at Grimsby. He even managed to get on moderately well with the directors, though Billy Watson admits that 'he didn't have much time for them in general'. Bill recognised that they were doing their best in tough circumstances. Money was never going to be available, so he respected the directors' efforts to pay the players a good wage – £14 a week to the full-timers. One director also introduced him to the delights of herbal tea, by which he swore for the rest of his life. George Aitken, like every other player, received 'a pound of this tea because he thought it would keep you fit but I didn't like it. We only drank it if Bill had come round.' The sheer size of the board, which encompassed some rugby people too, made for some lively meetings.

Bill took life a little less seriously at Workington. He was comfortable there and even his natural aversion to directors didn't take such a savage turn as it did elsewhere although George Aitken reveals that 'he wouldn't even give them the team sheet. He'd no time for people that weren't absolute fanatics, couldn't be bothered with them.' Billy Watson saw the way the wind blew very early on. 'They'd lost away and on the way home, he was holding a post mortem and the language was flying. One of the directors asked him if he'd mind turning it down because his wife was at the front so Bill started on him, "If you don't like it, you can get off." He stopped directors travelling with their wives after that.' Since Bill's fascination with the cinema – Jack Palance had become his favourite – and with gangsters continued unabated, in private, he began to refer to one member of the Workington board as Johnny Bunny, one of Al Capone's henchmen. Indeed in a letter to Billy Watson after Bill had left the club, he wrote 'Thanks for the cuttings, even if one of them was by the big fat man [a director] who looks like Malenkov and acts even worse, they ought to pair them when the Russians come over next week. Also in the band could be Johnny Bunny with big Goring [another director] laying down the law. What a procession that would make, it would be worth walking from Huddersfield to see.' Another carried the postscript 'Hope Bunny is well, he will soon be ready for deflating.' Billy adds, 'Bill wasn't dour at all, he was always looking for a bit of devilment to make life fun.'

Shankly and directors could never really mix according to Jackie Bertolini, who felt that 'he was a thorn in their side because he'd say what he thought. Possibly he was a source of embarrassment because he showed up their naivety, a lack of knowledge and ambition. He was an expert, without peer.' In spite of this, Bill never really fell out with the board simply because he wasn't beholden to them. He never expected any money from them, didn't have to go cap in hand to them and consequently was able to ignore them. In that sense, life at Workington was bliss.

Though the shoestring budget made it impossible for the club to look seriously at promotion, it made for a congenial atmosphere. Everyone knew they were working in adversity and managed to draw on these disadvantages for their own amusement. Certainly life at Workington was never dull, and Bill was happy to get among the people who worked for the good of the club. He was parsimonious when it came to spending the club's cash and did not bring anyone in until March 1954 when he splashed out £3,200 on Ernie Whittle from Lincoln City to ensure the club's survival, drawing on the £900 given to the club by the Auxiliary Supporters Association after the Port Vale win. Whittle, an ex-miner, fulfilled Shankly's requirements, banging in six goals in ten games. Bill had more than done his job. The Reds finished 20th, six points clear of re-election and gates had risen from the typical 6,000 to five figures while the team's future hung in the balance, petering out to around the 8,000 mark as their League status was secured. Given that he was at the helm of a club £20,000 in debt, this was something of a triumph and W. Capel Kirby argued that 'if there was a ballot for the Manager of the Year in England, my vote would go to that tough little character Bill Shankly'. Bill was suitably modest, saying 'All I have done towards it is to give the lads encouragement. They've had enough punishment.' His view was sensible for there were good players available if handled correctly. Jim Dailey was an excellent centre-forward for example, Malcolm Newlands a solid 'keeper who had played with Bill at Preston. Shankly made full-back Jack Vitty his captain, used half-back Dennis Stokoe and had the likes of Aitken and Bertolini to call on.

The Shanklys enjoyed their first summer in Workington. Ness remembers that 'the people were kindness itself, they couldn't do enough for us. We had farmers come to the house bringing us eggs or a rabbit, they were lovely, though Workington itself was a hard place to live with the children. There weren't really any amenities there and that made life difficult.' Ness' father stayed with the family though he had still not been converted to football, even by the loquacious Mr. Shankly. Billy Watson remembers that during one game, he came up to him and said '"The man's mad! Come on, let's go for a drink!" This was while the game was still being played!'

The family had a couple of breaks through the summer though, when holidays followed a familiar pattern. 'We'd spend a week in Scotland with the family and then he had to have a week in Blackpool. We always stayed at a lovely hotel, but I never saw him then either! He was out with the waiters playing football! He couldn't help it, it was his living and his reason for living.' He spent some of the time in Scotland looking for players. The perennial problem for any Workington manager was in recruiting new men as George Aitken – himself later Workington's manager – notes. 'It was difficult to find players because you had to travel a hundred miles just to find a game. You had to go on the advice of other people a lot, which is always dangerous and even when you found someone, it was hard to make him come to Workington. The club helped out with houses, but it was tough. Of course, Bill also needed to find ready made players like Ernie Whittle because he hadn't time to bring youngsters on.'

For the first time, Workington were able to look forward to the new season with real hope. Bill's training continued to help improve his squad, while the signings of Wilf Billington as goalkeeping cover for Malcolm Newlands and Jimmy Fleming, a half-back, strengthened things. The only one note of discord came with the departure of Joe Johnson as Noel Hodgson remembers. 'He wanted him training on Sunday morning but Joe said "I go to church, six days you work and on the seventh you rest." "Rest! You rest son and you'll never kick another ball for Workington." At the end of the season he put him on the list with £2,000 on his head. He was thirty-three and nobody would've paid money for him and so Shanks thought he could retain him and stop him playing or force him to change his mind. Joe 'phoned Elgin City and got a game there, playing semi-pro Scottish non-league. After twelve months, the F.A. gave him a free transfer.'

Perhaps this harsh attitude came about because of the few problems of indiscipline that had clouded that second season at Grimsby. Certainly Jackie Bertolini felt that 'he was a disciplinarian though it hardly ever came out like that. He was like your favourite teacher at school, you didn't want to disappoint him, so he didn't have to be heavy-handed.' George Aitken agrees, adding that 'he got close to the players. On the long coach journeys he'd play cards or talk with us, but he always knew when to draw the line, when he had to show he was the boss. He led by example. He was always there first in the morning with his kit on ready to go.' He was quick with his generosity too, as Jackie saw at first hand. 'When I got married, although he told me it'd spoil my football, he gave us a wedding present of £25. I know that Ernie Whittle had had some problems, so Bill took him out and bought a suit for him so that he'd feel welcome at the club.' Billy Watson, who accompanied Bill to the ground most mornings, remembers that 'all the fellas who were on the dole would stand on the corner by the ground but Bill used to stop and talk to them. He'd say how terrible it was that there was no work, maybe give 'em a couple of shillings which was a lot of money then. Bill always had good suits, with his name on the inside pocket. One morning he came to the ground with a suit and said "Give this to old Foster", who made the tea. He was only a frail chap and Bill was trying to look after him. Foster told me "I'll get a couple of pints for this" but I didn't dare tell Bill that. He'd have gone mad.'

Ironically, it was because the players were so devoted to Shankly that Sunday morning training was instituted. Jackie Bertolini: 'We were so keen we'd go in Sundays for extra work, we enjoyed it so much. Bill gave us the ball and we loved that, we learned finesse, how to play. In the week when we'd finished training, if you wanted – and the compliment to Bill was that most players did – we had a game on the field. The spirit was marvellous because of that.' It paid dividends too for as Derwent wrote, 'Workington play a type of football which is a delight to watch. From full-backs to half-backs to forwards, the ball is moved ... the inside men and wing-halves weaving a shimmering Shankly pattern.'

Workington's large complement of part-timers trained on Tuesday and Thursday evenings while the full-timers trained in the day. Inevitably this had an impact on the cohesive nature of the side; it's hard to instil a systematic pattern into a side where the players rarely train together. They had to make up for that with their enthusiasm. Borough Park provided a refuge where they could share their obsession with like minds. Billy Watson recalls those days with affection. 'The place would be full and it'd be coming up to kick-off. Bill would

come up to me and say "Close the gates, Bill. We're all in."
Like he was shutting out the outside world and was ready to
spend the afternoon with people like himself. That became
like a catchphrase around the club.'

The part-timers' training sessions were generally held under
lights. An indication of Workington's plight comes from Noel
Hodgson. 'The stand lights were powered by a petrol engine
from the boiler room. We'd be playing and the lights would
fail and Billy'd have to put more petrol in and recrank it! I
think it was an old bus engine, and we had it next to the fire!
Shanks would still be out there, pitch dark, shouting "Don't
worry lads, keep going! It's a white ball, you can still see it!".'
The white balls were a saga in themselves. Replacing the old
brown leather balls, white ones were all the rage in the floodlit
1950s. Billy Watson recalls that 'we couldn't afford to have
them in training, so we had to paint the old ones we'd got.
They only lasted one practice game and we had to get them
painted again. As the players kicked the ball, flakes of paint
would come off.' Even that was an improvement on the early
days when the club boasted just two match balls. Noel
Hodgson has cause to remember that fact very well: 'The River
Derwent runs behind Borough Park so if anyone kicked a ball
out of the ground, he'd send me off to swim and get it back!'

Noel Hodgson saw that Bill still missed playing. 'First day of
the season, he'd go out on to the pitch before the game and
say "I wish I was playing today."' Embarking on a new term,
he told the *Workington Star* 'my players know what I want
from them is an all-out effort ... we have had tactical talks
and we have drawn up a number of plans to surprise the
opposition. Every player is under an obligation to give good
entertainment to the public. May I stress that we will do our
best to see that [the crowd's] loyalty is well and truly rewarded.'
Bill was already out on his own as a crowd's manager, one of
very few who even acknowledged their existence, never mind
thanking them for their support.

Jackie Bertolini makes it clear that Bill's desire to entertain
was not just paper talk. 'He was the first manager who said

"Go out and enjoy the game". Like Bill, I felt that being able to play football for a living was a gift, but he always stressed that you should make the best use of your ability, you should put everything into your game. As a motivator, I'd never met anyone like him – if he'd been a General, he'd never have lost a war! We came back from one game and I'd not had a good day. Bill sat behind me and started talking in this stage whisper. I was working down the pit at the time and Bill said "That work must be too hard for him." It was all part of his psychology and I went out the next week determined to show him what I could do.'

That Jackie was down the pit at all was the result of another Shankly attempt to pervert the course of National Service. 'When I should have been called up, Bill said "You're not going. You'll go down the mine." I'd not even seen a mine then but Bill said "It's a reserved occupation, I'll get you a job working at the top." I ended up working underground as a pipe fitter. I had an accident so I came out and got called up. Even then, Bill said "Right, in the Tank Corps." They were based at Carlisle so it meant I could play on Saturdays. I went up to Edinburgh for my medical, and as a boy I'd dislocated my shoulder and it sometimes still popped out. I failed the medical, so all that time down the pit was wasted! Bill was delighted that I wasn't fit of course.'

Bill was still heavily involved in the training at the age of forty-one. Billy Watson remembers the pure joy he got out of it all. 'Bill would be first out and Jim Dailey, the centre-forward would boot the ball high up into the air towards Bill. He'd watch it, take it on his chest and drop it dead. Then he'd look round to say 'What d'you think of that?' George Aitken felt there was a purpose to Bill's enthusiasm for training because 'he played in lots of all-star games and we had many nights going off to watch him'. Billy Watson recalls that 'he used to have an old Rover, it used more oil than petrol, throwing out smoke behind it. We went to an all-star game for Jim Mac-Laren's testimonial at Carlisle and on the way back for the dinner after the game, he crammed eight of us in there. The bonnet was up, he could hardly see where he was going, but he didn't care.'

Where playing was concerned, Bill still had a streak of vanity. Jackie Bertolini suggests that 'he didn't go looking for publicity, but I think he enjoyed it as most people would. It was nice for his ego.' George Aitken remembers him bringing in 'Charlie Buchan's magazine one month. He'd picked his all-time Scottish side and Bill was in there at right-half. Bill had to show everyone. "Isn't this great?".' Billy Watson agrees that 'he liked people to make a fuss of him. We went to a benefit game at Brunton Park. Bill wasn't playing but someone was late and Tom Finney asked him to play. He told me to sit in the trainer's box. All the players came out one by one, they were announced over the speakers. Bill got a marvellous reception, there were about 14,000 there. At half-time, as they were off up the tunnel, Bill came over to me, put his hand on top and said "D'you hear that roar for me?" I couldn't help smiling at him, he was so pleased about it.'

He was rarely generous when returning for a League game, though. George Aitken remembers that 'we had to beat the teams he'd managed. They were the worst places he'd seen in his life!' Billy Watson remembers one trip to Carlisle very well. 'Their stand had burned down and the teams had to change at the public baths and get on a bus to Brunton Park. Carlisle were on one side, we were on the other and Bill started clowning around with this old fashioned bowler hat he'd got from E.D. Smith, the Chairman. He gave it to Kenny Rose, one of the players, and he put it on with his strip, ready to get on the bus. All the players were laughing and joking. Bill came over and said "They're beat now." I looked over at the Carlisle team and they all had long faces. Bill shouted over to Paddy Waters "No change today Paddy!" We were two up in ten minutes.'

This was typical of Bill's attitude to the game, feeding the players' egos, as Jackie Bertolini admits. 'We never worried about the opposition, he'd already done that and we played accordingly. He kept saying we were the best, that we wouldn't let them play, they couldn't play if they didn't have the ball. He gave us this incredible confidence. We'd be getting a drubbing but we'd come out after half-time thinking we were the better side. On the coach going to a game, he'd work through the team, have a chat with every player which made you feel part of it all. He didn't belabour our losses but extolled our wins and strengths. He was a forerunner to Muhammad Ali really, he wasn't averse to showing his bias and he believed we were the greatest.' He turned Workington's isolation to his advantage again, telling George Aitken and the rest that ' "I've just seen 'em. They look sick. It's that road from Keswick, they're finished. No trouble today boys." And we believed it. He always had us on our toes, everything was a Cup Final, nobody got blasé. We were complete believers in him.' Promotion was never a realistic goal for reasons of finance, not simply because they couldn't bring players in but because it meant they could rarely travel overnight to away matches. Bill noted later that 'the travelling was too much, we would have won more otherwise'. Jackie recalls getting home 'at three or four o'clock on a Sunday morning quite often'. Such was the time spent away, Bill often asked Billy Watson 'to look in on Ness and the girls to see that they were all right'.

If promotion was out the club looked forward to a good Cup run. The 1954/55 competition began with a routine home win over Hyde United, 5-1, the prize being an away game with Leyton Orient in the second round. Orient were unbeaten in sixteen games, about to finish second in the Third Division South and so Workington's prospects weren't rosy. Bill secured overnight accommodation and the players set off on the train. On the way, he discovered that they were sharing the train with the Hungarian national side who had just beaten Scotland 4-2 at Hampden, featuring many of the same players who had unceremoniously ended England's unbeaten record at Wembley the previous year. Sitting together on the train, Bill indulged in his favourite pastime, talking football. Language was no barrier, for Bill quickly employed coins, matchboxes and whatever else he could lay his hands on to illustrate free-kicks.

On arrival at the hotel, Bill imposed a ten o'clock curfew and most went out to a show, 'Cinderella On Ice'. Billy Watson recalls that 'at ten past ten he was outside the hotel walking up and down, looking to see if any of the players were about'. The players, needless to say, were all in their rooms. Taking the field at Brisbane Road, the players had a typical Shankly team-talk ringing in their ears – Workington were invincible. He was right for the Reds went through thanks to a Bertolini goal. The *Workington Star* reported that 'this victory is the story of team spirit. It cannot be stressed too often that whatever the class of a team it could not fully succeed unless every man was pulling his weight. And that is Bill Shankly's ace card. He has no time for slackers ... supporters have never experienced such a thrilling time ... when it comes to the finer points of the game, well, there's not many to beat Workington's master.' The victory was completed a couple of days later as Billy Watson recounts. 'I used to have a cup of tea in the boilerhouse and he'd come down for a drink and we'd sit on these upturned crates talking. This day he came in "Look at this", rushing down the corridor like a young lad. He'd got a postcard from the Hungarians, signed by all the team.' The card read 'Congratulations on your historic victory'.

In the next round they were drawn away at Luton, an excellent side, fast improving who won promotion to Division One that season. There was to be no repeat of the miracle of the Orient and the Reds were hammered 5-0. Even in defeat, Workington won admirers for their refusal to simply lie down and accept the inevitable, and had Luton 'keeper Ron Baynham not been on top form, the score could have been different. Shankly received many letters from Luton's supporters club in appreciation of the way they had played. Writer Reg Drury was vociferous in his praise. Bill of course had no time for sympathy in defeat, as he wrote to Drury, tapping out his reply on the office typewriter as he always did:

'This being good losers, is being exaggerated. We were good losers at Luton, but although outwardly I took the defeat well, inwardly I was boiling, I have no time for losing Reg, and I'm possessed with a killer instinct, which in my playing days paid dividends, without using shady tactics, I made sure that my immediate opponent drew a blank. I used to think that it would be better to die, than lose. To enable me to reach the top and keep there, I went to all extremes, no women, no smoking, early to bed, good food, this went on for years, but it was worth while. If all players in the game did the same, the game would improve, and would reach such a high standard, that it would really be an honour to be defeated.'

Though the season still had four months to run, it was effectively over for Workington who never threatened to win the promotion battle despite the directors unveiling an ambitious 'Prepare For Promotion' blueprint which required £10,000 worth of ground improvements. At the end of the season they were forced to ask the players to take a pay cut of £1 per week to help the club through financial difficulties. Even so, their final position of eighth, with fifty points, was comfortably their best to date and a credit to all at the club. Jackie Bertolini remembers 'from rank outsiders, we were in the frame'. If rugby league was too strongly established to be brushed aside, he at least put the round ball game on an equal footing. Borough Park in all its guises was now home to the entire town. Rugby wasn't the only other diversion that took place there. Billy Watson saw 'the Bishop of Lancaster hold a service on the ground. There were a few thousand there one Sunday morning and me and Bill stood on the edge of the pitch watching. Afterwards, one of the priests asked me if they could leave the incense burners at the ground and they were there for about six weeks. I told Bill one day, "We haven't lost a game at home since that Bishop had that service." He turned to me and said "I wonder if we could arrange a friendly with him"!'

The new season started brightly, though inconsistency cost them a place among the challengers. Bill had taken a collection of players that had been going nowhere and wrung every last drop from them. To take Workington further would require money the club didn't have. Bill already had his ear to the ground looking for other opportunities in the game for much as he enjoyed Workington he was itching to take another step up the managerial ladder and get involved with a top side.

Huddersfield Town were struggling in the First Division, scoring just six points in their first fifteen games to lie bottom of the table. Andy Beattie was manager of the club. A close friend from Preston, Andy's career had taken a similar course to Bill's, though he had had a head start as a manager, beginning a couple of years earlier. Beattie was clearly in trouble, a problem not eased by his own desire to get out of the game. The previous season, in which Huddersfield had achieved mid-table security, he had tendered his resignation only to be persuaded back into office by the board. His own uncertainty could not have helped performances.

To help him out, he looked to Bill and in October, offered him the post of assistant manager. After some deliberation, Bill accepted. There's no doubt at all that he was swayed by a desire to team up with Beattie in what he hoped would be a formidable partnership. With Beattie at the head, Bill was sure that he would be given the freedom to do what he enjoyed best – training with the players, teaching them new ideas, motivating them through the week – leaving Andy to deal with the drudgery of football management, the directors! To make the move yet more attractive, Beattie suggested that he would still like to get out of the game in the near future. It was for that reason that he was so keen that Bill should accept his offer, reasoning that with such a successor in place, the board would give him a more sympathetic hearing should he want to leave. Bill was within reach of his greatest ambition – managing a First Division club.

No-one at Borough Park was particularly surprised by the news, though of course they were saddened. Jackie Bertolini says 'he was a god in Workington. When he left, it dropped off, an era had passed.' Billy Watson recalls that 'he did the right thing. I didn't want him to go but he had to go on to somewhere better.' The Workington board realised just what they had and one of the directors, Joe Mason, even offered

Bill a house to stay at the club, but the die was cast. He accepted
the Huddersfield post on 22 November, leaving Workington
on 10 December. He maintained contact with the club, even
going so far as to stay in touch with Mason, while Billy Watson
remained a close associate. In a letter to Billy a few months
after the move, he took 'this opportunity of thanking you for
your friendship and loyalty to me during my stay in Workington ... the only regrets I had on leaving were for such as
yourself, the players'. Talking about current form, he revealed
that the affection he maintained for the Reds was in sharp
contrast to his feelings for Carlisle, Workington having beaten
them 4-2 at Brunton Park: 'I see the lads gave Carlisle another
dose, I was really pleased about it, actually Carlisle are not in
the same class,' adding later, 'It's time Emery [Carlisle's
manager] and co. gave it up, as they will never have a team
with the present set-up at Brunton Park, truly a great pity, as
the support is there. If we had moved over to Carlisle from
Borough Park, with our team of the past two seasons, we would
have attracted 20,000 gates, and might have won the League.'
In return for the club's friendship, he had put them on the
map and ensured that in the years to come they would be able
to compete, numbering such figures as Joe Harvey and Keith
Burkinshaw among their alumni. Sadly league football
couldn't be sustained in such a small town and in a later letter,
Bill made one of his poorer predictions: 'I think rugby league
died in Workington more than a year ago and will never rise
again.'

Workington had been an important chapter in his career
and remained, along with Huddersfield to a lesser degree, the
only club that he left without any bitterness. He would not
have been able to work with the crowds and harness the
enthusiasm of the Kop if he had not learned how to deal with
them in the lower divisions. Had he not been forced to work
with little money, been required to get the best out of players
that weren't always good enough in these footballing backwaters, he would not have enjoyed the success that was to be
his later on. The experience also taught him to have the

greatest respect for the lower divisions and without that, he might not have swooped to buy Clemence, Keegan or Heighway.

His grasp of human psychology was his greatest weapon and he had honed that skill at Carlisle, Grimsby and Workington, developing it into a fine art. George Aitken points out that 'he always wanted the best for his players. He would never humiliate you in front of the others, he'd pull you aside if he wanted to have a go at you.' Harking back to that comment that prior to his arrival the players had 'had enough punishment', that was the central thrust of his philosophy. Treat the players well and you would get the best out of them. Denis Law, who worked with both Shankly and Matt Busby, argues that 'great managers treat players not as numbers but as men'. Bill felt that 'you must treat players like human beings. They have to be spoken to individually, some need to be spoken to strongly, others sympathetically. You use your brain; when I had a player injured, I'd tell the boy that I put in "Listen son, you're a better player than him."' At Borough Park, such positive thinking was all that he could offer; the team as a whole were perhaps not up to executing elaborate tactical plans. By stoking up their enthusiasm and creating a unified force that was working towards one goal, he could turn ordinary teams into good ones. If he'd been presented with the manager's chair at a side blessed with top class performers, he might never have had to develop that talent and might not have become the great manager. He often said that 'managers would benefit from a few years at the bottom of the game'.

A whole section of Bill's life was coming to a close, for things would become more serious now that he was moving in higher circles. Just as childhood in Glenbuck had taught him decent human values, so his time scrimping and saving with the smaller clubs taught him how to run a football club efficiently and how to maximise its resources. These lessons equipped him for the life on which he was about to embark.

chapter thirteen

A FRIEND IN NEED

Teaming up with Andy Beattie was exciting for the two had remained close. Bill was convinced that they could salvage something from Huddersfield's miserable season and put the once great club back on track. Having accepted the job in the final weeks of November, he was joining a club that was bottom of the First Division with a mere eight points from sixteen games. Rather than taking up a position with the first team as he had envisaged, Bill found himself working with the reserve team while Eddie Boot fulfilled the role of first team coach and trainer. This came as a disappointment for he felt sure that, with his effervescent influence in the dressing room, he would be able to help the side avoid relegation. Beattie was looking to the longer term. He refused to entertain the idea of relegation for he felt that the club had sufficient playing strength to survive. His fears were for the future, worrying that some of the team were too old for the top flight, a problem exacerbated by a lack of quality in various positions and a shortage of hard cash. Huddersfield's strength was in their youth policy. Beattie was keen that Bill should take them under his wing and mould them into top class professionals. He knew only too well how suitable Shankly was for this role for on his arrival at Preston from a junior side in Aberdeen, it was Bill who had helped him to settle in the town and schooled him in the ways of professional football.

Ray Wilson was in the reserves. 'Andy brought Bill in to give him a bit of backing because things weren't going well. There weren't the same rigid tactics that there are now, the game was about freedom, so Bill was always keen on getting the players going. His training was a revelation after the run a lap, walk a lap business before. We'd never see the ball before

Thursday because that was supposed to make you hungry for it on Saturday. The lovely thing about Bill was that you played small-sided games every day because he was so enthusiastic and he wanted to get out and play.' That enthusiasm was endemic among young men already excited at the prospect of playing football for a living and whose number included other impressive talents such as Denis Law and Kevin McHale. Sandy Kennon, who joined the club a little later, adds, 'Bill was great with younger players, he had an empathy with them because they were willing to work their guts out to break through.'

While spirit in the reserves was improving, all seemed lost for the seniors. Four wins in April lifted them off the bottom but the task was too much. Aston Villa won their final game of the season to condemn Huddersfield to relegation. Inviting Workington colleague Billy Watson to Huddersfield during the summer, Bill wrote, 'We were unlucky to go down at the finish, the effort started too late, it was a blow to me as I'm not used to being with unsuccessful teams.' Watson remembers that stay with the Shanklys with affection and it's indicative of Bill's liking for the real foot-soldiers of the game, the people who put in the hard work at the grass roots without any recognition, that he stayed in such close contact. On arrival, Bill took him to meet Raich Carter at Leeds, a tremendous thrill for any follower of the game, an example of his thoughtfulness.

Huddersfield looked forward to immediate promotion the following year. Beattie looked to Bill to recommend which reserves could play in the first team, simultaneously looking to strengthen the squad by bringing players in from outside. One summer signing was Sandy Kennon, a South African goalkeeper who came to the club after some promising performances in Rhodesia. 'I'd played a couple of games against an F.A. touring side that included people like John Bond, Ted Burgin and Bill McGarry. I had several offers after that from Brighton, one of the Bristol clubs and from Huddersfield, I think on Bill McGarry's recommendation. Andy Beattie said that they were looking to get promotion right away.'

Sandy's view of Andy Beattie is interesting for it illustrates a man of similar views if different personality to Shankly. 'It's a long flight, 5,000 miles, and your mind plays tricks. I was asking myself "What have I done?" I only had £2 with me. But Andy was there to meet me. He was a very kind, generous man and on the way to Huddersfield the following day, he gave me a big, white £5 note – I didn't think it was real money, but he told me it would "look after me over the weekend" once I was in digs. On the Monday, my first day at the club, he had me in his office and introduced me to the main players and staff at the club and Bill Shankly was there, though I don't remember him too clearly at that meeting.'

Shankly stayed in the background on such occasions for he had no intention of stepping on Beattie's toes. In a reversal of the roles at Liverpool, Bill was living the lesson that those on the staff should always give their unequivocal support to the manager. This musketorial attitude was a principle in which he believed with absolute conviction and which he put into practice. Kennon's real introduction to Bill came on the training pitch. 'I nearly died, I was exhausted. It was late August and the others had already gone through their pre-season work, so I was behind them. Bill was a stickler for fitness and I'd never been particularly fit because I'd had rheumatic fever as a boy which left me without any stamina. Bill wanted you to run, run, run and at that stage we had lots of little clashes.' If Shankly was the hard man on the training pitch, Beattie was more careful with his charges. 'He pulled me aside to tell me that I'd start in the reserves, making it clear that it was a big step-up from what I'd been used to. He treated me with a lot of kindness and that helped me when it came to competing with the other 'keeper, Harry Fearnley.'

Unhappily, the new season hadn't started well and by early November, the club were ninth in the Second Division, eight points adrift of leaders Leicester City. In contrast, the reserves were unbeaten in their first fourteen games and Shankly's young side were a revelation as Ray Wilson explains. 'We were in the Central League and we had to play First Division reserve sides, so there were a lot of good players in there from the big clubs. For us to get a draw away from home would be a good result. We went to West Brom the year before and they ripped us apart, 4-0 up in twenty minutes. We stopped on the way back and I heard Bill on the 'phone to Andy Beattie: "After the first twenty minutes, we paralysed 'em. We ran 'em off the park." He just couldn't see the other side playing at all; he knew they were better, yet he'd kid himself they weren't and he'd have you believing it as well. He wasn't a hard man in that way, he'd never go over the top, shouting at us even when it was deserved. The only time he was annoyed, and it was disappointment more than anything, was if you hadn't performed and hadn't given everything. He'd be quite happy, though upset, if you'd competed and lost.'

Wilson graduated to the first team early in 1956/57, becoming a regular by October, another example of Bill's influence. 'Wages were poor because of the maximum wage, so the club could afford a massive squad of 40 or 50 players which made it hard to break through. I was an inside forward or a wing-half and by accident I ended up at full-back in practice games because the regular back, Laurie Kelly, lived in Wolverhampton and wasn't available for training. Bill must have spotted something and started playing me there for the reserves. Before too long I was in the first team.' Another to benefit was Mike O'Grady, a winger. Bill said of him 'he was shy, reserved, lacking in confidence ... I wouldn't play him in his own wing position at first. I stuck him in the juniors at full-back where he'd have to fight and tackle for every ball.' O'Grady became a full international.

Despite the elevation of Ray Wilson, things were not going well and the failings of Beattie's side were shown up by Shankly's lads. It was no great surprise when on 3 November Bill Shankly became manager. There was some confusion over the appointment as Bill pointed out in his autobiography. He received a call from Bernard Newman, the club chairman, who arranged to meet him that night at Leeds Road. He offered Bill the manager's job. Bill assumed that Beattie had tendered his resignation, yet when he went to speak to him, he never mentioned the subject. Shankly was upset that he might have taken the job before Beattie had left office and that Beattie's dismissal might have been conditional on Bill taking the job. He wrote that 'how I got the job is one of my biggest regrets', an ample illustration of his desire never to let friends down. Happily their friendship endured and Beattie became a scout at Anfield.

For local consumption, Beattie told the press that he had resigned his post as he had wanted to do a year earlier, secure in the knowledge that the team was in safe hands. For his part, Bill told the *Huddersfield Daily Examiner* 'I expect to get 100% effort from all the players. I am making no promises or predictions. I will work hard and do my best for the club. I have devoted all my life to football. Everything has been thrown overboard for it.' Whether Beattie jumped or was pushed is a tough one. One observation from Ray Wilson is especially pertinent. 'Just before he took over as manager, when he was still coaching the reserves, the first team threatened to go on strike because they were fed up doing the stereotyped training and they wanted a share of Bill. He made training ever so enjoyable. He wanted to be involved so the warm-ups were over and done with as quickly as possible so he could play.'

Whether training is fun or not is a personal matter. While English pros like Wilson enjoyed what they saw as a major shift in emphasis, Sandy Kennon was still troubled by the changed environment. Shankly may have cut down on the physical side of practice but he still made sure that his players were fit. 'I didn't think that a goalkeeper needed all that running,' remembers Kennon. 'I needed lots of short, sharp work, running backwards, lots of gym work. In those days, the goalkeeper was just one of the team. I wanted specialist training and Bill wasn't prepared to do that – I remember we threw medicine balls at one another quite fiercely in the gym one day! The others didn't mind the running but it was terribly difficult for me. I couldn't do it. Bill was never abusive towards me but he took the mickey and I resented that. He was trying to make the point that everything was about the team rather than about individuals. Once Bill became manager, Eddie Boot supervised the training and he wasn't so hard on me.'

Bill's outlook changed out of necessity. It was his responsibility to get that club back on its feet. He had little time for any obstacles that might be in his way. Though Sandy Kennon has nothing but respect for him and fully understood his motives, the two continued to clash. 'As a newcomer to the country, I wanted the boys to sling crosses in at me, especially in the wet, so that I could get used to that and to wearing gloves. Bill refused to let the groundstaff boys do that in normal training time so they had to come back in their lunch hour to do it, which upset them.' Whether Bill viewed this minor confrontation as a threat to his authority is impossible to answer though certainly he was still keen on maintaining discipline. He wanted to make it clear that he would treat all players as equals on the training ground and so Kennon was required to do all the work that the others did. If you wanted to do extra training on your own initiative, fine. Oddly however, this willingness to stand up to the boss helped endear him to Shankly. Ray Wilson had similar experiences because 'we fought so hard on the training ground. I'd argue with him which he didn't seem to like, but later on he told me he admired that because it was the kind of thing he'd have done. He wanted people who'd die for it.' Shankly agreed, adding 'when Wilson and Law played each other in training, it was worth ten bob to watch it because they had ability, dedication, guts and ambition. A world-class player is one who does everything he should do.'

Early results were excellent, opening with a 5-0 win at Barnsley. The game had been prefaced by a ninety-minute talk, with Bill making it clear that 'I want the players' ideas as well as my own. We must get down to this business together ... the players must have the will to win.' Pilgrim wrote: 'The new appointment has been a popular one with the players. Mr. Shankly has amply demonstrated an abundant enthusiasm for the job and, perhaps more important, a remarkable capacity for passing on his enthusiasm to those under his supervision.' Unfortunately in the higher leagues, enthusiasm is not enough on its own and Huddersfield returned to their inconsistent ways, taking just ten points from Bill's first ten games. Bill didn't think he had a team capable of promotion and had his eyes on the following season when players like Wilson and Kennon would have greater experience. He set about the task of introducing more of those young stars. Ray Wilson feels that 'he was pushed into a corner there. We had some good young players and the board wouldn't give him any money though I know he pleaded for it. It was an old side that went down, they'd aged together and we had to play much earlier than he might have liked but we came on rapidly.'

Denis Law was just sixteen when Bill gave him his debut at Notts County on Christmas Eve 1956. Law had already created a stir and Matt Busby had offered £10,000 to take this prodigy to Old Trafford when Andy Beattie was still manager. A slight youngster, Shankly instantly took to him when he had been looking after the youngsters as he recalled on Radio City. 'Skinny little boy, I saw him one day eating in the café next to the ground. I went in and he was eating beans on toast for lunch and I thought "Christ son, you'll not get strong on that" so I told the man in the café to get some steaks into him to build him up.' The fiery temperament that was such a part of Law's game also forced Bill to defend him off the ground: 'His landlady sent for me because he'd hit Billy McDonald, another boy at the club. I went down and Billy had a black eye so Denis said, "If he says that to me again, I'll hit him again." So I turned to Billy and said "Right, let that be a lesson to you!"' However hard he tried, Shankly still had his favourites, though in fairness no football fan could fail to be enamoured with Law's genius. Bill's faith was absolute and during his first season in the first team 'I saw him play against Jimmy Hagan of Sheffield United in the F.A. Cup and I told one of the writers, Waverley, to go away and write that Denis would get eighty international caps.'

Even the advent of new boys Law and his right wing partner

McHale along with Wilson, Low and Massie was not enough to transform the season. Law's excellent form provided Bill with a headache for Denis, not seventeen, was still an amateur and was being courted by a number of teams. Bill gave Law the benefit of his extensive powers of persuasion, reminding him and his family that Huddersfield had given him his big break, that it was a club that had a bunch of exciting young players maturing together and that Denis would be the fulcrum of that side. Within a couple of months of his debut, he agreed to sign full professional forms for the club, days after his seventeenth birthday. Shankly had made his most important signing for the club and knew that he could approach the following year in good heart. Though he had a good team in the making, Bill was unhappy at the response from the local people and he later admitted that 'they're nice people in Huddersfield but not football minded. It's a rugby area,' an assessment that's borne out by the front page of the local newspaper of the time. Saturday evening's late edition was split equally between rugby and football, all the more dispiriting after his spell at Workington when rugby had loomed so large. He noted 'the competition from rugby league is just as strong, gates are a constant worry and money is tight'.

There were pockets of like-minded fanatics in the town and Bill managed to find them. James Castle was a neighbour of the Shanklys at Oakes in Huddersfield. 'Nearly every Sunday, come rain or shine, Bill would come out and play football along with about 30 of us on a field in Crosland Road. We spent many happy hours out there and Bill would still get stuck in whether he was tackling a ten year old or a fifty year old, which was the age range of the players. Bill would set off for goal and even if it was a kid in goal, he wouldn't hold back.' Bill was extremely popular in town for when he and Billy Watson went to the cinema while Billy was staying with the family, 'somebody spotted him and they weren't bothered with the film after that. All these kids were after him and he spent all the time giving autographs and handing out sweets.' Huddersfield suited the family and Ness was very happy there, not least because it meant that 'Barbara could settle down in one school for a period. In the years before that, we'd moved around so quickly that she'd never had that chance and I felt very sorry for her but then that was his job.'

Unfortunately, although Bill enjoyed life in Yorkshire and was able to put together a promising side, he was never able to take them further and the next two seasons were extremely frustrating on a professional level. Their inconsistency was summed up by a bizarre game at Charlton Athletic in December 1957. Huddersfield, missing the injured Denis Law, were 5-1 up with half an hour remaining before a Gerry Summers goal blitz put Charlton into a 6-5 lead. They snatched an equalizer with two minutes remaining, only to be beaten with virtually the last kick of the game; to make matters worse, Charlton had played the last twenty minutes or so with ten men, centre-half Derek Ufton going off with a dislocated shoulder. Sandy Kennon was in goal that day and remembers it as 'one of those afternoons where every shot went in. Gerry Summers was a little one-footed as a player but that day, he could do nothing wrong, scoring with both feet. I felt I'd had a reasonable game, the goals were unstoppable.' This was one occasion where Shankly did rant and rave in the dressing room afterwards. His mood was not improved when 'we heard this roar while we were getting changed. The Charlton players were waving to the crowd from the directors' box!'

Money and the lack of it was a constant thorn in the Shankly flesh as Robin Taylor, a young Huddersfield player, relates. 'I'd played through the 1957 season in the Town third team after he had spotted me playing for the District League XI. The next season I went into the Army and got a 48-hour pass after basic training had finished. I phoned the club, reversed the charges, and asked to talk to Bill to see if I could get a game that weekend. I heard him muttering in the background and after he'd confirmed I could play at Hull, he gave me a sharp lecture on how expensive it was to run a football club and not to reverse the charges again as I was now a qualified soldier!' Robin Taylor's experience is significant in that, while he admits

'I was never a brilliant player, he always made you feel an important part of the club'.

The family atmosphere he fostered was enjoyed by young and more experienced players alike and helped get the best out of the team. Dave Hickson had joined the club at the same time as Shankly and admitted 'he created a camaraderie that made you want to win. When we went away, he liked to keep us together. The lads that didn't drink often went out and one night at Blackpool, he took us to watch the dogs just so we could be outside. "Lovely fresh air boys, take it in, better than being in a theatre." He was mad about the fresh air.' He remained mad about winning too and, in the absence of fresh faces at the club, tried to generate enthusiasm in his team meetings. 'We looked forward to it,' recalls Ray Wilson. 'It was a comedy half-hour, like watching Dave Allen. It was wonderful. He never mentioned the opposition because I suppose Alf Ramsey was the first to introduce solid tactics, so he'd just talk. "We're at home to Lincoln. One horse race. We'll get a point at Walsall, then Grimsby at home. No bother." By the time he'd finished, we'd be unbeaten for the next six weeks and in third place! He staggered me, I couldn't believe that anybody could be so besotted by just one thing. Perhaps having missed out on playing during the war, management was compensation. That comment about football being more important than life and death wouldn't be planned, it'd come out and he'd mean it. He couldn't stay away from the ground, he'd come in on Saturday at nine in the morning and if a shirt wasn't hanging right in the dressing room, he'd straighten it, or he'd move a towel somewhere, just something to keep busy.' Sandy Kennon recalls that 'in team talks, he'd invite you to have your say but before you'd finished talking, he'd taken over. He'd chip in and make sure it remained his meeting.'

Possibly at other clubs, he had been a little too close to some of his players, as concerned with their welfare as that of his club. At Huddersfield, those priorities underwent a subtle shift as Sandy Kennon discovered. 'We got talking on the way to a game and he found that I knew a lot about boxing – I took *The Ring* magazine and had boxed at light-heavyweight. When he discovered that, we had a meeting of minds which eased things between us, even though he was always niggled by my inability to do the training. I could understand that and I was pleased to find a way we could communicate more easily. I had to do the training but if I was flagging, I wasn't shouted at. We went to a few tournaments together, always at his invitation of course, some in Leeds, one where we saw Brian London in Blackpool. There was no awkwardness there and Bill always paid, which was nice!'

'I had elderly parents back home who weren't well. I went to see Bill to find if there was any way the club would help me with a loan for a return air ticket. Bill wasn't interested because he thought I wouldn't come back, so he must have thought I was unsettled. That upset me because I had no intention of staying out there and in a bit of anger, I said "I'm going back at the end of the season" and he said "In that case, I'll have to leave you out of the team," which was understandable. He didn't allow any personal feelings to cloud his judgment, it was always what was best for the team.' Even then, Bill was keen to do what he could to help a man who he had come to regard as an honest pro doing his best in the game. 'I only had a couple of games in eight weeks and I was getting very frustrated. Bill said "We're going to Preston tomorrow, they're interested in you. What d'you think?' By then I just wanted to get away to play some football. We arrived at Deepdale and Bill told me to get changed because he thought there'd be a practice match. I went out on my own and a few minutes later Bill came out and said "Get changed, we're going. They want you to have a trial, see how you handle yourself in goal with the kids taking shots at you. You're a first-team player, I'm not having you go through a trial." Tremendous respect grew from that because he didn't want me to be demeaned and that was wonderful. After that, Norwich City came in for me. I'd been playing as a winger in practice that day but once Bill had spoken to them, these youngsters arrived out of nowhere to knock balls at me. Bill knew I was on my way and he wanted me to regain my confidence.'

With Kennon set for a transfer, he was delighted with his final conversation with Shankly. '"Good luck, if you want to train with us any time, you're very welcome. I'm really pleased for you, you're a good goalkeeper. Your dedication to goal-keeping is great, your dedication to training isn't!" He gave me quite a pep talk, "Don't think any the worse of yourself for going to a lower club," filling me with confidence. After that, he told me he was giving me a free transfer and that any signing fee would be mine which was a lovely gesture. A couple of years later when he was at Liverpool, Norwich went there and I was so pleased and proud because he greeted me like a long lost friend, "Lovely to see you boy, hope you don't play too well," and he made a point of seeing me afterwards to say I'd had a good game. When someone behaves like that towards you, you can only hold them in very, very high regard in spite of our few differences.'

That was typical of Bill's regard for footballers who had played for him. Five months after he'd left Huddersfield, Ray Wilson won his first cap for England, against Scotland at Hampden Park. 'Bill sent me a letter, couple of pages, all about pulling your shirt on, walking out in front of the crowd and you could feel his genuine delight that I'd been capped. It was a wonderful letter. He said "I've been capped for Scotland but being capped for England where there's 75% more people to pick from, that's a great thing." Nowadays, if any of the players that I know do particularly well, I always drop a line to say "pleased for you", because of that letter from Bill.'

All was quiet on the directorial front. He maintained his policy of washing any dirty linen behind closed doors and there was never any hint of any disenchantment with the Huddersfield board though there must have been some. With players like Denis Law on the books, Huddersfield were always going to threaten opponents but it was apparent that there were gaps in the side yet Shankly spent much of his working week denying that Law was about to be transferred, a problem

which could have done little for his humour. While Bill wanted
to strengthen the team in the transfer market, some members
of the Huddersfield board were pushing him to cash in on
their greatest asset. This was all the more galling since his
scouting work had identified the two players who he believed
would take Huddersfield up. 'If we had got Yeats and St. John,
as we might have done, with the others in the team, we'd have
won the League five successive seasons,' was his considered
judgment.

It was painfully obvious though that Huddersfield could not
afford them and it was this that forced him into the final
realisation that he could not stay at the club much longer;
he'd already been spoken of as a possible manager for Leeds
United in November 1958. With the 1959/60 season under-
way, Shankly was already looking for another club. In spite of
Huddersfield's moderate form, his stock as a manager was
higher than at any other time. The youth policy that he
followed was much admired, all the more so since this decade
was that of the Busby Babes who had tragically perished eighteen months earlier. A manager that could bring through outstanding prospects was attractive to any club.

Having toiled in virtual anonymity Huddersfield was a
platform. His successes on the field were more noticeable
to the wider footballing public, but it was his indomitable
enthusiasm that was winning more attention. Everyone in
Workington knew how committed Bill was to his club and
how devoted he was to football but his engagingly eccentric
passion for the game was news to those in the higher echelons
of the game. As Ray Wilson says, 'Bill had worked hard, done
his apprenticeship and was ready for a bigger stage than he
could get here. We were disappointed that he was going to
leave because were becoming a reasonable side, but without
more money we couldn't make that last step. He had to move
on.'

Certainly, Bill left with regrets. On tendering his resignation
in November, he told the press, 'I'm leaving a fine bunch of
players behind – players of class and young players who I hope

I have been able to help along ... our insistence on putting football first is beginning to pay dividends.' The people of the town were sorry to see him go too as James Castle records. 'Just before he left, the lads and dads from the games at Oakes held a farewell party and we gave him a caricature of all of us in the field playing football. It was shown when Bill was on *This Is Your Life* and he said that it was one of his prized possessions.' Bill relished the vivid memories of that 'hotpot supper in the house of Ken Daly and the signed sketches of all the players which they presented to me will never be bettered'. Still very much a people's man, Bill was off to the city where they lived for the people's game. Anfield was waiting and Shankly was ready.

chapter fourteen

A WORKING CLASS HERO

Phil Taylor might still have been the manager at Liverpool, but after 17 October 1959 he was living on borrowed time for on that day, the Liverpool Chairman, T.V. Williams, travelled over to Leeds Road to watch Huddersfield take on Cardiff City in a league match. 'The game had hardly started when suddenly I found myself listening to it instead of watching it. My ears became tuned in to a voice that was coming from the trainer's dug-out. It was yelling instructions to the players. Egging them on. And it was obviously being obeyed by every man to whom it was directed. I had been long enough in the game to know that the owner of the voice knew what he was talking about. I had no idea who he was but my mind was made up. He was the type I wanted at Liverpool. At time-up, Bill Shankly, then manager of Huddersfield, emerged from the dug-out. By the look of him, I knew he had played as hard as any of the twenty-two players on the field. I put my arm around him and said simply "How would you like to be manager of Liverpool?"'

Shankly was cagey but the decision was made fairly quickly for Taylor was ousted on 17 November, just one month later. Bill played the Liverpool board like an expert angler reeling in the biggest fish. He was desperately keen to go to Liverpool, but after the experience of his job interview in 1951, he had reservations. By playing hard to get, he was able to win concessions. He would select the team without any interference. He would control the playing staff and the coaching staff, decide on the playing and training methods. Money would be available for new players. As soon as he felt he had concluded negotiations to his satisfaction – including a £500 rise to an annual wage of £2,500 – he tendered his resignation at Leeds Road.

How much of a Damascan conversion Williams underwent that day in Huddersfield is hard to tell. Liverpool were a club that had spent a decade under-achieving, for following an F.A. Cup Final defeat in 1950, they had steadily slipped down Division One until relegation gathered them in in 1954. Thereafter, they came close to promotion but had been unable to clinch it. Ray Wilson notes that 'they travelled badly but were a banker at home and that had kept them in contention for years'. Phil Taylor had replaced Don Welsh but he too had been unable to produce the blend that would secure them top flight football. When the first seventeen games in 1959/60 yielded only seventeen points, it was clear that Liverpool needed to rethink. There was little hope of improvement on the horizon.

Williams was under pressure, not least because on the other side of Stanley Park, Everton had remained in the First Division throughout Liverpool's exile. They were top-dogs on Merseyside and for as long as that was the case, their own shortcomings were effectively camouflaged. In any great footballing city, local rivalry is every bit as important as gathering trophies, as Ray Wilson discovered a few years later when he moved to Everton. 'You don't realise how intense the Liverpool-Everton rivalry is. It took me a couple of years to realise that feeling bordering on hatred they have there. I'd be talking to Bill as I remembered him at Huddersfield and he'd be telling me that it was a disgrace I'd got picked for England, I was the worst full-back ever! Anyone from the other side was just totally unacceptable!' With a humiliating Cup defeat against non-league Worcester City just a few months earlier still a vivid scar on their collective memory, T.V. Williams was only too well aware of the demands of the Liverpool supporters, for even in these bleak years, Anfield regularly housed crowds of 30 or 40,000.

With five League Championships to their credit, Liverpool were a big club with a mediocre team and that could be tolerated no longer. Williams felt that he had found a man who could take on the huge task of re-establishing Liverpool, yet Shankly's was not the only name that came to mind. Williams consulted a number of the game's most respected names including Walter Winterbottom who confirms that he had 'a short-list of applicants for the managerial post. From those, I recommended Bill.' To those on the fringes of the game, it was surprising that Shankly should get the nod for in ten years of management he had yet to earn any tangible reward for any of his sides. Those who kept their ear closer to the ground understood however the difficulties under which he had been operating. They knew that his love for the game and his appetite for work was undiminished and that he had learned enough of his craft to be ready for this greatest of challenges.

Bill had no doubts about his suitability. He revelled in the fervour that surrounded the city. He'd played in front of the great Liverpool crowds at Anfield. He'd seen the club pick up trophies. This was a club with as much potential as any in the land. Only a coward or a shirker could have turned down that job. Bill was no coward and he knew how to roll up his sleeves and do a job of work. Liverpool Football Club would become the consuming passion of his life. His reasoning was simple – he loved the fans, they were his kind of people, he knew how they felt, how they thought, what they wanted and he wanted to give it to them. You could no more learn the talents that Shankly had as a manager – in that job's widest sense – than you could teach a child to be di Stefano, Eusebio or Best for Bill was not simply a football manager as it's now defined. He didn't just turn up at the training ground, school his players, pick the team, watch the opposition and chat to the press as most do. He did much, much more. He inspired, he enthused, he cajoled, he moved his people. He was a true visionary, one of a select few. His great friend Matt at Manchester United was one such man, but his ideals were all about football and the pull of Europe. Bill's vision took in his club but also his city. No man, not even Busby, has been so synonymous with his club in the history of the game for he didn't just want to build a side that might win a cup or two along the way. He wanted to provide the people with a club that could continue to be their whole lives way beyond his own time there. He had worked in towns where football was recreation, but now he was in a city where it really was a matter of life and death, the place where he belonged. Why else would he have left a team with Law and Wilson to manage a side which, on first inspection, had no players that could rank with them?

Ray Wilson best sums up the reason for his defection from Huddersfield. 'He deserved Liverpool and they deserved him. You can't compare the Huddersfield area with Liverpool. I prefer to live near Huddersfield but for football, you have to go to Liverpool. They're fanatics. Bill believed everybody should think about football like he did but they don't around here. In Liverpool, he must have felt like the messiah.' With Shankly installed at Anfield, it seems a bizarre, almost heretical sugges-tion, but for the remainder of his life, football was not the centre of his story. It was the vehicle by which he achieved lifelong goals, fashioning one huge community that lived by decent ideals, that followed the creed he had grown up with in Glenbuck. Bill himself would never have seen it in that light for it's already apparent that he could see the whole world in the game of football. There was no distinction.

The key to his life in Liverpool is the realisation that he was a man of the people. That's a phrase that's been over used and hopelessly devalued over the years to describe anyone with a working-class accent who can peddle the right homilies at the right time. Shankly spoke from the heart and directly to his constituency, the footballing, working people. One of Liv-erpool's other great heroes, John Lennon, had a constant love-hate relationship with the working classes. The 'working-class hero' of the Fab Four, he consistently betrayed the political confusion of his middle-class roots. For him, slogan-songs such as 'Power to the People' were as much a by-product of the guilt he felt over the material trappings of his success as any instinctive solidarity with the workers. A classic woolly liberal, Lennon could never identify with the ordinary mass because he was never one of them. His art-school education and subsequent career as an extraordinary songwriter were all testaments to individuality. It may seem inconsequential yet there is real significance in the fact that neither he, nor any of The Beatles, were regulars at either Anfield or Goodison – they were never part of the crowd, they were a crowd apart. This was most apparent in Lennon's later song 'Working Class Hero', an ironic attack on himself for allowing himself to be sucked into the Establishment he had despised and an assault on the working class 'peasants' as he described them, those who wanted to follow the same path to riches that he had taken, seduced by money and abdicating from the need to speak out against the status quo. Lennon felt that the working class hero was mere window dressing, the lottery winner whose very existence kept the underclass quiet as they dreamed that one day, it could be them.

Though in terms of working class politics Lennon was naive and lacking in any intuitive grasp of the subject, largely because he did not have the working class roots that he pretended, and so did not really understand the subject, he was unnervingly accurate with this observation. Yet a working class hero was something to be, if you could achieve it on your terms, something which the Beatles, in their Epstein incarnation at least, singularly failed to do. If you persisted in calling people who you claimed as your class peasants, then you could never understand what those terms should be. Shankly, though not as well educated as the 'intellectual Beatle', had a far better idea of what the working classes were about and how they lived, for that had been his own life. In years to come, Bill would stand on balcony after balcony in triumph, holding court before hundreds of thousands of supporters. He'd keep it simple, the way he kept the football simple. 'You are the people,' he'd say, scarcely a quotation from Sartre, but it struck a chord. The ordinary people knew that Shankly and his team were working all the hours for their benefit, for the good of their city, to enrich their lives, even their economy, to give them something special away from the drabness of the docks or the factory.

John Peel was a Liverpool fan in the dark days before Shankly arrived. On the day they clinched the 1972/73 Championship, 'I was standing in the crowd by the Kop and some kid threw his scarf to him and it landed at his feet. The police sergeant who was alongside him kicked the scarf out of the way. Shankly pushed the policeman out of his way and picked up that scarf and it's that one that he has on in the famous picture in front of the Kop. He didn't do it as a good PR gesture and it's something that certain managers would quite clearly not even understand but it summed Shankly up, the perfect response to that situation.' Other observers say that he told the policeman 'that scarf's the boy's life'. To be a hero to those people was enough, whatever Lennon might have said to the contrary.

Championships were a long way from anybody's mind, except his own, when Bill arrived at Anfield in December 1959, for he found a desolate club that was less the proverbial 'sleeping giant' than a comatose one. His introduction to the facilities had echoes of Workington, but where the inadequacies of Borough Park were a function of their lowly status and were almost endearing as a result, for Liverpool to be so badly served was an outrage. He wrote later that Anfield 'was an eyesore. It needed renovating and cleaning up. I said to the groundsman "Where is your watering equipment?' "There is none," he said. "We don't have equipment, because there is no water." There was a pipe from the visitor's dressing room and a tap. But no facilities for watering the pitch. It cost about £3,000 to put that right.'

Anfield was not the only problem, for Melwood was 'a wilderness . . . it was in a terrible state'. Ness went to see it, just a mile or so from the house where they settled and remembers: 'it was a dump! It was dreadful. The players stripped in a wooden hut. It was terrible!' With poor facilities and a squad that was by no means good enough, all that Shankly had to work with was potential and the fanatical support. Roger Hunt 'joined as an amateur in 1958 and got into the team just before Shanks arrived. I had a great start, scored on my debut, got a couple of spectacular goals soon afterwards and everything was going well for me. The crowd took to me right away and you could see how important they could be to the side. My debut had been in midweek against Scunthorpe United and we still had 32,000 there.'

Roy Evans was a regular on the terraces at Anfield in the late 1950s and feels that Shankly 'brought some sanity back. He put the football to the fore, took over from the board picking the team and turned Liverpool into a professional outfit. He built a rapport with us very quickly because we knew we were foremost in his mind.' Billy O'Donnell's Liverpool connection dated back to the 1920s and he was quick to realise Shankly's impact. 'The place was really going downhill. Liverpool were in the doldrums before he came and you could see the changes he was making, he'd explain them to the supporters. He felt for the people who paid their money to get in to watch his side and right away he told them it was an honour just to work for them and they loved all that. He was a fighter, little rugged character, had been when he played for Preston – typical dour Scot, difficult to beat, Bob Paisley was the same as a player. I'd have loved to have seen him box. You could just imagine him coming out when the bell went, going forward and the punches bouncing off him. He was that kind of fella. They like fighters here.'

With the troops mobilised, Bill's first task was to assess his staff on and off the field. Bob Paisley had had many tussles in direct opposition to Bill on the field and Shankly appreciated his abilities. Joe Fagan had also played against him and had been a transfer target at Grimsby, while Reuben Bennett's talents were well known to him since Reuben had previously worked with brother Bob. He called them together and told them, 'You fellows have been here, some of you a long time. I have my own training system and will work in co-operation with you. I will lay down the plans and gradually we will be on the same wavelength. I want one thing – I want loyalty. I don't want anybody to carry stories about anybody else ... I want everyone to be loyal to each other. Everything we do will be for Liverpool Football Club. That makes strength.' Ronnie

Moran, club captain at the time of his arrival and a member of the legendary Boot Room set-up ever since his playing days ended, confirms that 'he knew those men very well, he respected them. He was clever enough to see he had good men here. Bob, Joe and Reuben had his outlook on the game but they needed that leader, that figurehead. The biggest thing here is that once a manager makes a decision, everyone backs him totally, even if it doesn't work out. I've heard coaches from other clubs come here and talk about their manager doing the wrong thing but that doesn't happen here. We have our disputes, everybody's ideas go in, but the manager has the final say and we back him completely. We stand and fall together.'

Tommy Docherty makes the point that 'Bill and Bob were a team and they owed a lot to each other. That was what Bill wanted, he had a team off the field in the supporters who were fantastic, he had a team in the Boot Room, men who were disciples of his way and who saw the sense of building from within.' It's a distinct possibility that early on, Shankly left obvious gaps in his system so that Paisley and Fagan would have to make contributions. After all, the two had been associated with a poor side and must have been lacking in confidence. Crucially, as Ronnie Moran says, 'Bill made sure everyone connected with the club shared in the credit for success, he knew it wasn't just down to one man.' Bill brought them out as people and exploited the full range of their talents, creating a powerful unit as a result by practical demonstrations which proved that team-work was the best way forward. They were both bright men with keen footballing brains and it did not take them long to appreciate the wisdom of his approach. Bill used them to the full. 'I would allocate them jobs each day, but they would take the training. I was around Melwood all the time, watching what they were doing and what the players were doing. That's what a manager should do, use good men. If I needed to know about a reserve, I'd talk to Joe and what he said would be authentic.' Roy Evans signed for the club in 1964 and had the opportunity to see just how the training system worked. 'Bill didn't want to know the mundane things, didn't particularly want to be bothered with the everyday confrontations in training, he just wanted to play football. He left that to Bob and Joe and Reuben, Ronnie Moran later, and having them he had some of the greatest pros in the game. They could run the daily routine, look after the players, get them ready for Bill to come in as the supreme motivator.' Shankly saw training and the five-a-sides as his reward for all the hard work he put in on Liverpool's behalf. Turning up at Melwood, he could enjoy the game, relieved, however briefly, of his responsibilities. He relished those games and as Roy Evans adds, 'he'd stand there watching us warming up or doing a bit of running, with a ball under his arm, bored – "When are we playing?" It was the highlight of his day, he loved it. If he was injured or ill, there'd be no games anyway.'

However good the staff, it is the players who win the games and so he had to assess what he had on hand. Roger Hunt remembers that 'he called us all together and said we were starting from scratch and that we'd all get a chance. We had 40 players on the books and he was as good as his word. His enthusiasm generated a fresh excitement in the club and he made it clear that the Second Division wasn't good enough. That was very important because we'd just missed out on promotion quite regularly and a few players were starting to accept that. The players they brought in hadn't been good enough either, older players from the lower divisions. The club was going nowhere until he arrived.'

Bill didn't enter the market, concentrating on drilling his existing squad. Although Shankly would never write off a season and still demanded a win from every game, he consigned those final months of his first season to experimentation and to weeding out those players that would not be good enough. The training pitch was where the initial work would be done and Ronnie Moran is clear about his impact there. 'I wish he'd arrived when I was five years younger – I was twenty-five – because I learned more in his first three months from listening and watching than I did in the previous seven years. The manager's the main bloke at the club; players aren't daft. If they've got a bloke in charge who knows what he's talking about, they'll respect him. He didn't have to be forceful, he made it all simple, he liked to play games, it was all about using the ball.' Roger Hunt agrees that 'his ideas were easy to understand, he was a straightforward bloke. All it was was "pass the ball to the nearest red shirt". He made training far more interesting. It was fun, you looked forward to coming in.' Melwood was the base from which Bill Shankly wanted to create his great dynasty, yet he was faced with a facility in a shocking state of disrepair. The obvious facts had eluded those who had come before – if players train on an uneven, untrustworthy surface, they cannot perfect their skills and cannot improve. 'Shanks transformed Melwood,' recalls Hunt. 'He introduced new training boards that we used in various exercises, he got an all-weather pitch, brought it up to scratch.'

The enormity of the task escaped everyone but Bill and his family. For the Liverpool board, his only job was to get them back into Division One. That done, everything would be fine. For Bill, that was the start. Liverpool was his destiny. He had been working in management for a decade, busily accumulating knowledge, tinkering with his own approach to the job in the lower leagues, waiting for the call to take over at a club that could satisfy his own ambitions. He wanted to build a club, not just a team, that could challenge the supremacy of Manchester United, that could go on to surpass anything that they had achieved. A man of true vision, Shankly wanted to build a family that by virtue of its unity, would be unbeatable, indestructible. The directors at Liverpool had not realised just what they'd taken on when they appointed Shankly. John Roberts remembers that 'a lot of the hierarchy said that Bill was an awkward bugger, but of course he was. If he hadn't been, they'd have still been in the Second Division. It needed someone like him to turn the place round. He could be difficult, irascible, irrational at times, but he was generally proved to be right.' Ness admits that 'Bill spoke his mind. It didn't matter who it was or where he was, he spoke his mind. He was very blunt and if he thought a thing, he had to say it whether it hurt or not. Five minutes later you'd be talking away again but he had to tell you what he felt. I thought it could be hurtful but it seemed to work because no-one fell out with him for too long. He didn't bear grudges and they knew that if he couldn't help you, he wouldn't harm you either.'

At board level, some of Bill's home truths caused resentment, for he was taking over their domain. Not only did he take over team affairs: to all intents and purposes, he took over their club and became Liverpool F.C. Tommy Docherty explains that 'Bill hated to see amateurs running a professional sport. People who'd never played, didn't understand the game, don't know what it means to the people, the loyalty to your supporters. When I call them amateurs, I'm paying them a higher compliment than Bill would because he felt they were useless.' Not an attitude to win friends in the boardroom, it was calculated to win trophies on the field. If he had to fight to get what he wanted, he was doing the game at large a great service, for it was people like Shankly and Busby who were wresting control from those who had guarded it jealously for too many years. They put clubs back into the hands of the genuine football people and helped raise standards. Principled men often cause trouble, but change is achieved. For three years, Bill Shankly had to fight as hard with men ostensibly on his side as ever he had to against the nominal opposition.

John Roberts also points out that 'he was very lucky to have a wife like Ness because she was an absolute rock for him'. Ness herself admits that 'I did get fed up of moving, but it took a long time. I loved it at Huddersfield, I did not want to leave, I'd have stayed there for the rest of my days very happily. But Bill got the job at Liverpool so that was it. To be honest I wasn't fussy about coming here to look at houses but I had to. We looked at umpteen places before we decided but it was a real blow leaving Huddersfield. We had some lovely friends there.' Ness and the children were perhaps the greatest victims of Bill's irresistible urge to rebuild Liverpool in his own image. 'The girls never saw much of him,' she agrees. 'I could take it because I was his wife but I think Barbara and Jeanette missed their dad, missed going to the pictures or the baths with their dad because he was working. Liverpool and the people were in his blood. He felt it was all worth it and if it was worth it for him, then it had to be for me too.'

As Liverpool won trophy after trophy in the decades following Shankly's retirement, it became increasingly hard to recall the enormity of his achievement, the hard work that he and his colleagues had to put in to rebuild that club. Similarly, many forget the early years of his reign when he suffered the same frustrations that he had already endured elsewhere. Roger Hunt points out that 'he needed to have a look at what he had and things only developed gradually'. After his first look at the side at the tail-end of 1959/60, hopes were high for the following year. Once again though, things did not work out as he had hoped for he was able to make just three rather low-key signings, the most important being that of Gordon Milne from Preston. Finance was again a problem, though Roger Hunt wonders if 'he thought we'd get promotion anyway with the players we had. We weren't quite good enough and we picked up a few injuries but we were still very disappointed when we missed out on promotion by a few points.' Even so, he had tried to add Leeds United's Jack Charlton to his squad but was thwarted when the board would not meet the asking price of £18,000. As Bill noted later, not only would that have helped Liverpool's cause but it would have made Don Revie's job that much harder when he took over at Elland Road. The directors were beginning to have second thoughts and Walter Winterbottom confirms that 'in those early days when things were not going too well, I urged the Chairman to stay loyal to Bill'.

Bill was beginning to fret over the lack of success. Ness remembers that 'he wasn't settled. One day he said, "Come on Ness, I'll take you to the training ground." We stood in the middle of Melwood which was still in a state. We looked around and he said, "Well Ness, what do you think? Have I made a mistake?" I knew then that he was really worried so I told him "No, you haven't. You want to get into the First Division, this is your chance." From then he threw himself into it even more, he changed everything. He got most of the staff down to Melwood, helping to get it into some semblance of decent shape to play on. It was hard work, but he loved doing it.'

There were further disappointments just waiting down the line. Johnny Morrissey was a young outside-left who Bill felt might go on to become an important member of the side in years to come though he was not yet a regular. Tommy Smith remembers that 'Morrissey was sold behind his back to Everton and he never forgave them'. Understandably livid, Bill came very close to resigning on principle and it was Matt Busby, among others, who urged him to reconsider. Ness also played a part. 'At that time they were still working at Melwood to get things right, he was working with the team and was busy with all the alterations he wanted at the ground. He was very tired but he was also worrying about something. I asked him "Do you want to resign?" but he wouldn't answer. "I'll take things easy, Ness." I said to him "What do you mean by that? Do you mean taking your pyjamas and going to live at Anfield?" He looked at me and said "Do you mean that?" "Yes, you're seldom at home and if you think you're going to change your job, we're not moving any more. We're going to have some roots at last, I'm stopping where I am!" He laughed and that broke the tension and things were fine with the club after that because things started to go well.'

The Morrissey incident 'cleared the air' according to Roger Hunt, after a difficult first few years. 'Shanks made it obvious that he wouldn't allow directors to decide who was bought and sold. It took Shanks a while to educate them properly! I think that brought things to a head because he'd probably been getting frustrated when he wanted to buy players and they wouldn't sanction it. After he'd promised to go, I think they realised that they had to start backing him up.'

The summer of 1961 proved to be the turning point in Liverpool's fortunes. Shankly made it crystal clear that money would have to be found. It came in the shape of a new director, Eric Sawyer. Peter Robinson, who joined Liverpool as secretary in 1965, explains that 'he didn't have a great deal of knowledge about football but he came on to the board. Sir John Moores, the Managing Director of Littlewoods Stores, was on the Everton board but he had a close affinity with Liverpool as well and he wanted both to do well. He persuaded Eric to join the board, though Sir John once told me that that was one of his few mistakes in business because he'd helped Bill make Liverpool too successful! Eric had a clear understanding of what was required and he backed Bill fully. There were a few more scraps over what we should spend on players, but Bill had a great ally in Eric Sawyer. When Bill got here, the club hadn't spent much more than £12,000 on any player when the going rate was £30,000, so the whole thinking had to be changed and those two did that.'

The professional relationship between Shankly and Sawyer was simple as Bill admitted in his autobiography. 'We had lots of discussions ... we would talk over the affairs of the club, officially and unofficially. I told him of players who were available and others who might become available. I told him "these could be the foundations of the success we need". "Bill," he said, "if you can get the players, I'll get the money."'

Mirroring in many ways the way in which Matt Busby used Louis Edwards to finance the creation of Manchester United, Shankly and Sawyer made a formidable pairing. Sawyer was a hard-headed businessman who had the intelligence to see what other directors could not. The club had employed a manager, a specialist in his position. For him to succeed, he should be allowed to get on with his job and given whatever financial backing was required, within reason. Peter Robinson feels that 'the players were rather spellbound by Bill', but it's a comment that could be used about anyone who met him. Sawyer fell under his spell and felt that this man should rule the club. If Sawyer's most obvious contribution was to find the money to buy new players, he was an equally insistent voice when it came to providing both players and fans with the best of everything, taking some of the pressure from a manager who openly despised the weekly chore of attending board meetings and who rarely stayed a moment longer than was necessary. Sawyer ensured that Liverpool continued to upgrade facilities and that they travelled in comfort and stayed in the best hotels.

Eric Sawyer was, as far as Bill was concerned, the ideal director, for as he explained, 'that man was the beginning of Liverpool'. He put his hand in his pocket when necessary, looked after the business affairs of the club so that Shankly didn't need to worry about them and left the football to him. He grasped the realities of the business. With the abolition of the maximum wage, the gulf between First Division clubs and the rest would start to grow. Prior to the lifting of that ceiling, there had been little financial difference to be had whether you were playing for the League Champions or playing for the team seeking re-election to Division Four. Under the counter payments might have been made to compensate for this iniquitous situation but even so, every footballer could make a broadly similar living from playing whatever his status. The only thing to be said for this form of slavery was that it meant that even the smallest clubs could compete with their bigger rivals for it was easier to keep their best players if they could offer similar terms. It was a regular feature of post-war football to see clubs going through the divisions for all but the elite were on similar financial footings. Once clubs could pay players what they liked, the best would inevitably gravitate towards the richest while the rest would be left behind. Once the floodgates were open, other contractual restrictions would inevitably fall and players would enjoy an increasing freedom of movement. Bill could see the implications of such changes and knew Liverpool had to make progress, had to get promotion so that they would be able to compete financially with Everton, Manchester United and the rest when it came to signing the top performers. Sawyer saw his point and acted accordingly.

For the moment however, Bill was liberated by the opportunity to go into the transfer market with a vengeance. His first major capture was Scottish international centre-forward Ian St John from Motherwell. Motherwell were reluctant to sell such an asset but in the spring of 1961, he received an approach from Newcastle United which unsettled him. A few days later, his transfer request was granted and Shankly had his man, in spite of the interest from Newcastle, a First Division club and one so much closer to St John's home. Nevertheless Bill's powers of persuasion made it perfectly clear that Liverpool was the only place to be and St John signed for £37,500. Within days, he played in a Liverpool Senior Cup game against Everton after the league programme had been completed. Though Everton won 4-3, St John bagged a hat-trick and his appearance so enthused a crowd disappointed by their failure to get promotion yet again, that they already began looking forward to the next season. Weeks later, Shankly prised centre-half Ron Yeats away from Dundee United for £30,000. The magnitude of that signing was underlined later when he said, 'Yeats was a fantastic man, he could have played in the Second Division with no other defenders and we would still have won it. Strong as an ox, the quickest thing in the game as a defender.' Bill's main theme was to strengthen the middle of his team – with St John up front and Yeats at the back, he had almost achieved his aim. He wrote later that they were 'really the corner-stone, the beginning of the big march'. Buying Yeats and St John helped the rest of the club realise 'that we were going somewhere', explains Roger Hunt. 'We spent nearly £70,000 in the summer so suddenly it looked like we were a club hell-bent on promotion and that lifted everyone.'

With 1961/62 promising to be a breakthrough season, pre-season training was especially important. 'There's a cautious initial training period of five weeks. Don't tear them to pieces on hills or sand dunes early on. I wanted people to say they were lazy, not doing much. There's a gradual build up – injuries are caused by stretching before you're ready. You can break down at Christmas but it might have been caused by the initial training being too hard. At Liverpool, we look at all the details.'

Ronnie Moran contrasts that with the routine pre-Shankly. 'We'd change at Anfield, run down to Melwood on the road, about half an hour of running at Melwood, maybe play a couple of games and then run back from Melwood to Anfield which is about $3\frac{1}{2}$ miles. We did that for eight or ten days as soon as we got back. I think the most running we did with Bill was twice round Melwood, which is less than a mile and a half. You don't have to do cross-country runs to be fit.' Bill also pointed out that 'I studied how an athlete functions. How much blood your heart pumps through your body every minute. What you could do with a man. How to prepare him. If you can get them as fit as they can be for football, they can do things they couldn't do if they'd been overworked.'

Shankly was never a man to change for the sake of it and since his regime had worked elsewhere, he saw no reason to make any fundamental alterations. Every day's routine at Melwood was tabulated so that in subsequent seasons the staff could see what they should be doing and when, what they'd done the previous season and what the effects had been. Shankly was always there, keeping an eye on things, ensuring that they were going according to his plan. Sensible enough to allow everyone to have their say and to improvise, it was he who laid down the structure that sessions had to follow.

One development which Sandy Kennon might have enjoyed was the introduction of 'specialist goalkeeping training and special tasks for the forwards' according to Roger Hunt. 'We had exercises with the training boards where we had to receive a ball, trap it, shield it, control it, shoot on the turn, all the things that you have to do within a game, match situations, playing under pressure. The defenders would have crosses sent in at them so that they knew who'd be going for the ball. In that sense, it was tactical as well as technical work and that showed up later on. It was all sharp, quick exercises, pressure things in short bursts. We'd play endless five-a-sides but it was only if we were in a bad run that we'd have a practice game so that he could try different players out in certain positions.' The training boards were introduced because 'I saw Tommy

Finney doing a basic thing at Preston, taking a ball, hitting it against the back of the stand, take it in his stride, shield, dribble, hit it again, control it with his other foot. Here was the star of all stars doing basic skills.'

'He liked to play every day,' recalls Ronnie Moran, 'and he wanted players who trained hard. Some days though, that might only be half an hour, but if you do it properly, that can be enough. He wouldn't over-train, you'd get fit in pre-season and then just maintain that level.' Bill's views were such simple, common sense that the only surprise was that Liverpool were almost alone in following his methods. 'We don't have long, boring, training, but little spells, two minutes on, then you're off and back on later. There comes a time in the season when you can go out, play a proper five-a-side and that's all you need. Everything's in that game, dribbling, close control, movement. The laborious thing stops. It's exhaustion and recovery. Take functions out of the game.'

Though Liverpool's training system was exemplary, that was just one ingredient in their success story; they had good players, playing with freedom within a sensible framework. That season, it paid off. Yeats and St John had inspired the crowd and the rest of the players and they stormed to promotion, opening with ten wins in eleven games. The red tide was irresistible registering a total of 99 goals for the season in the league, Hunt scoring 41 and St John 18. Anfield was a fortress, only three teams managing to draw there. Shankly could put up an almost unchanged team sheet week after week: Slater; Byrne, Moran (or White); Milne, Yeats, Leishman; Callaghan, St John, Hunt, Melia, A'Court. Whether this continuity was down to his training system or his naked hatred for any man who had the temerity to be unfit is debatable, but it worked for season after season. Bill called on just seventeen players, of whom three managed just five games between them. For many at Anfield, Bill Shankly had discharged all his obligations. The crowd were delirious, refusing to allow the players to go home when promotion was clinched – they stayed on the field for ten minutes after the final whistle and

were forced back out after they'd changed. Liverpool were
back and as he wrote later, the directors 'were so thrilled about
it that they presented us with cigarette boxes. I told them "We
got promotion, but you don't think that is satisfactory, do
you? Next time we come back for the presents, we will have
won the Big League, the First Division."' The real tests lay
ahead.

chapter fifteen

WITH HOPE IN YOUR HEART

Almost thirty years had passed since Bill Shankly had experienced the exhilaration of promotion with Preston and the bitter-sweet mix of anticipation and anxiety that precedes the journey into the unknown. Having seen his team perform in such lion-hearted fashion the previous year and with such fine players as Yeats, St John, Hunt, Milne and Byrne on board, Bill had little doubt that Liverpool would be able to cope with the rarefied atmosphere of the First Division. Coping was never remotely enough for him and he set about strengthening the team in several key positions. Though he bought Jim Furnell from Burnley towards the end of the season, Shankly saw him as a stop-gap before young Tommy Lawrence had accumulated enough experience in the reserves to take his place in goal. Tommy Leishman was found wanting in midfield and so Shankly bought Willie Stevenson from Rangers for £20,000, a creative mind and impressive long passer who took time to settle. These changes aside, the team remained broadly unchanged though two more young men, Chris Lawler and Tommy Smith, managed to make fleeting appearances before the season was out.

Roger Hunt summed up the mood. 'We were a bit uncertain, you wonder beforehand if it will be much tougher. It took a few weeks to settle but we soon realised that we were good enough.' Hunt and St John provided the firepower that left Liverpool in a comfortable final position, notching forty-three goals. Bill guided his men carefully through the inevitable setbacks in that first year for as Ronnie Moran remembers, 'When we lost, we were upset which was what he wanted but he'd make us feel better by saying "we were the better side, we just didn't play well today". He'd give a rollocking now and then, but not many.'

Liverpool went through a sharp learning curve that year and were happy to finish eighth, an impressive start marred only by the fact that Everton were champions, thereby increasing the pressure on Shankly. The only upset came in the F.A. Cup. Battling past Wrexham, Burnley, Arsenal and West Ham, they were paired with Leicester City in the Semi-Final at Hillsborough. 'We were very unlucky not to get through,' remembers Roger Hunt. 'We absolutely paralysed them on the play but we just couldn't get the ball past Gordon Banks. Never having won the Cup, it was a big thing for everyone. Your ambition is to play in a Cup Final so we were very upset because you never know if you'll get that chance again.'

Liverpool had made their mark. A crisp passing team playing attractive football, their assurance on the ball made them appear mechanical to some, but it was merely the result of a methodical approach to the game on the fields of Melwood. Liverpool had players who could improvise and create opportunities out of nothing. Bill had packed his side with players who shared his outlook on the game. He backed his judgment – if a man was wearing a red shirt on a Saturday afternoon, he could look after himself. He should be a craftsman with enough intelligence to know what he should and shouldn't do. His men were men, not boys. They could handle responsibility.

Shankly felt he could not win against a press that had a pronounced London bias at the time. Because so many of his players were such powerful physical specimens, another trait that he prized highly for it took a rugged frame to handle 50 or 60 competitive matches in a season, Liverpool were accused of an over zealous approach. This accusation snowballed in years to come once the imposing Yeats was joined by the archetypal hard man Tommy Smith, yet it was no more true of Liverpool than any other side. Chelsea had Ron Harris, Spurs had Dave Mackay, Leeds found Norman Hunter to go with Jack Charlton, Nobby Stiles was far from gentle with opponents at Manchester United and every other side you could name had a crunching tackler. Bill merely insisted that the game was played honestly, but as hard as possible. As Tommy Smith remembers, he would tell his players ' "first is first, second is nowhere", and he'd spit it out like a gangster, "foist is foist".'

In spite of his enormous daily commitment at the club, Shankly made time to think of the future, building toward the next challenge. Even in these early years, the workload was enormous, the worries considerable. It was physically and mentally wearing, but he had to keep on top of things. Had it not been for his voracious appetite for the footballing press, he might have missed the small stories which alerted him to the availability of St John and Yeats, might have missed the two men that formed his team's backbone. Players were his stock in trade as Ronnie Moran accepted. 'The first thing I learned from him is that you have to have the right players. As a player you never really thought about the rest of the team, you just did your job, but he got me thinking about how you put a team together. He was experienced and you could see why he was making those decisions – he wanted ability, but attitude too. They had to work, he wanted them to be really upset if they lost, to really feel it.'

Attitude played a part in breaking down the insular nature of players. No longer could a player be content to do his own job, he had to take a responsibility for the team, be aware of the whole unit. The construction work that had been carried out at Anfield and Melwood was instrumental in creating the right atmosphere. Juniors worked alongside Shankly, Paisley and Fagan and having everyone muck in together helped that spirit. His insistence on absolute loyalty was fundamental as were his views on collective play. Later he told Harold Wilson that 'our football was a form of socialism. Liverpool have character, they're never beaten, they can last the pace because we share the work. You don't have to do any more work than me if we're in the same side.' This was Bill paying tribute to his roots, going full circle to the collective spirit he'd grown up with in Glenbuck. It informed his football as it informed his life.

Liverpool had got the measure of the First Division and they set out to take Everton's title in 1963/64. Happy with his team, Bill made one final purchase in the summer, bringing in Peter Thompson from Preston, his second major capture from his old club. 'I'd asked for a transfer because Preston were going nowhere. I went to see him to talk about the move and when I got to the ground, there were hundreds in the car park, TV, radio, press and I thought they were expecting a visit from somebody. I made my way through unrecognised and he met me at the door. "Hello, Mr. Shankly. Is somebody famous coming?"

"Aye son, you. When you sign for Liverpool, I'm going to make you the greatest player of all time. You'll be so fast you can catch pigeons, you'll be a great tackler, a great header of the ball, the fastest player in England."

'So all that sold the place to me in a couple of minutes. You couldn't not sign for him.'

Bill had completed his jigsaw. The signing of Thompson should have come as no surprise to students of the Shankly method, for he was the latest in a long line of tricky ball players whom he doted on – Hogan at Carlisle, Hernon at Grimsby, Whittle at Workington, Law at Huddersfield and finally Steve Heighway at Liverpool once Thompson ended his career. A legacy, perhaps, from his playing days when he lined up alongside the likes of Bobby Beattie and Tom Finney, Bill's view of these men was embodied in a remark he made about Thompson. 'If you're feeling tired boys, give the ball to Peter and take a rest.' Even when his team were having an off day, this high priest of the team-work ideal knew that a gifted individualist could fashion something out of nothing. Not only did they add venom to his team, he enjoyed watching them play.

Opinions differ as to the importance Bill put on tactical awareness. Several players already put forward the view that Shankly was the supreme motivator and that tactics were not really part of the game until post-1966. Others have a different view for Tommy Docherty argues that 'he knew the game inside out. He was clever enough to know what it was that each of his players was good at and played to that. If the opposition had a strength or weakness, he would pounce on it and if he missed it, Bob or Joe would catch it. Between the three of them, they missed nothing.' Ronnie Moran is of the same view. 'Tactically, Bill was far advanced. You hear the experts today and they don't know what they're saying. The game hasn't changed, you still have to control and pass a ball. Bill would combine a lad who was quick in the head but not so fast with a lad who could run. These ideas were way ahead of their time.' So Willie Stevenson might use a raking pass to set Peter Thompson away, their contrasting talents blending together to bring the best out of both. Tommy Smith 'played along with Chris Lawler, one of the most cultured full-backs that ever played the game. He wasn't ruthless, but then I was in front of him to stop 'em and he was that extra bit of class for me, a good mixture.' Tactics doesn't have to mean writing huge dossiers about the opposing side. Tactics can be simplified – Bill's favourite word – so that you deal with what you will do on the pitch, ensuring that each man is comprehensively drilled in his tasks. 'We had a talk before we played Manchester United,' remembered Bill, 'and someone said "Are Best, Law and Charlton not playing then?" That was music to my ears. If we'd had dossiers on Manchester United, we'd have had a whole page just on George Best and frightened our bloody selves to death.'

Tommy Smith confirms the wisdom of that approach. 'Bob would maybe tell us that a certain player would come inside a lot, so you'd be ready for that, but they didn't pound it into you. We never feared anyone, we went out to play. The boss might get on edge but he'd communicate in such a way that he'd make us want to go out and do a job for him. He left it to us. If we came up against the best players, someone who could run the show, we wouldn't man mark him like other teams. We just kept in communication. If he was on the right, the left-back would watch him. As he came across, Gerry Byrne would shout to Ronnie Yeats. Ronnie would watch him, and call to me if he was coming further and then I'd do the same with Chris Lawler, just passing him on. No-one was too frightening. If you fear a player and give him a marker, the poor bloke gets run all over the pitch and the other fellas only got to do one good thing in ninety minutes and the marker's done a bad job. It relieved the pressure, we didn't have to concentrate on anyone long enough to get worried.'

The beauty of Liverpool's play, and possibly a major factor in their continuing success, was that they found a way of playing and bought accordingly. While they encouraged the attacking flair of Thompson or St John, each had to fulfil his primary function in the team. Other teams relied heavily on individuals operating outside a set pattern, men like Best, Osgood, Bowles, Marsh, but Liverpool allowed them to flourish within defined parameters. How could you possibly replace George Best? No-one could. Yet at Liverpool, no-one was irreplaceable for the style remained similar. In the event of injury or loss of form, a reserve could be drafted in and would know exactly what was expected.

Games were all about his Red Army imposing themselves on the opposition which is why there is an undue concentration on his ability to gee players up week after week. Peter Thompson, who walked straight into the team at the expense of Alan A'Court, believes that 'a lot of playing is confidence. He'd knock the opposition down as if they didn't exist. If you go out so full of yourself in front of 55,000 people thinking you're not playing anything, you had to perform. He left me to play as an individualist, but one day he was having a team talk and he said "You're not listening to me Thommo." He had me in the office later. "You're so fast Thommo, you're like a racehorse."

"Yes boss, I'm pretty fast."

"You're also like a cart-horse, you've so much stamina, you can run all day."

"Yes boss, I'm pretty strong."

"You're also like a hobby-horse, you've no bloody brains. Get out." '

Few ever took offence at these barbs as Tommy Docherty agrees. 'He wouldn't say you were rubbish, he'd say "You've a good wee team. Not good enough." Or "You were beaten by a great team today Tommy." ' The addition of Thompson and, later in the season, Alf Arrowsmith who scored fifteen goals in twenty games to lighten the load on Hunt and St John, meant that his fast maturing team were in the title race right through the season. Arrowsmith allowed Bill the freedom to make one key tactical change, the withdrawal of Ian St John from an out and out striking position into a midfield role just behind the forwards. Tom Finney had completed his Preston career highly successfully as a deep lying centre-forward, the position freeing him to arrive in the box unmarked and to create chances for the other strikers. This may well have influenced the move with St John, for his was too great a footballing intelligence to be used purely in the rough and tumble of the opposing penalty area. Roger Hunt says that 'it was a privilege to play with him. He was very unselfish and we understood each other. He was very astute, a brainy player, he could read situations and pretty soon we knew exactly what each other was going to do.'

As the crucial Easter period approached, Liverpool revealed their thoroughbred credentials. Having paced themselves through an arduous season and with a tough run-in ahead of them, Shankly simply gave the team its head and they responded by stringing together seven consecutive wins to take the Championship in their final home game with a 5-0 demolition of Arsenal. Fans had queued overnight to see them clinch the title, the gates had been locked more than an hour before kick-off and the whole day became a carnival once nerves had been settled by St John's seventh minute opener. It was fitting that the League was won at Anfield for it was the foundation of their success, Tommy Docherty conceding that 'I loved going there even though all you ever got was a cup of tea and a good hiding. You came away a bit wiser.'

Once Liverpool had clinched that first title under Shankly, it was clear that they could be a major power in English football for years to come. Most of the side were in their mid-twenties with plenty of football left in them and so it was no surprise when the next season, Liverpool claimed the prize for which they had long been striving, the F.A. Cup. The final was no great spectacle for both Liverpool and their emerging opponents Leeds United were trying to take the trophy for the first time. The approaches of the two teams offered a stark contrast. The Leeds dressing room was sealed off, doors locked, as Revie drilled his team. Shankly had a policy of open house, welcoming friends. The Liverpool dressing room was filled with laughter right up until 'ten minutes before we went out. That's when we hand the axes out.' Bill's attitude was crucial to the result for as Peter Thompson remembers, 'Everywhere we went it was "When are you going to win the Cup?" The story in Liverpool was that when we won, the Liver Birds would fly away. When we actually got to the Final, the pressure was immense.' Bill absorbed that pressure, leaving them free to play.

The game could hardly have started in worse fashion, for within three minutes Gerry Byrne had gone down under a heavy tackle. The result was a broken collar bone. In an aston-ishing show of bravery, Byrne completed the ninety minutes and the half-hour extra time that was required, because there were no substitutes allowed. Shankly recalled that 'at half-time, the doctor tried to freeze it but he couldn't, so we left him. The bones were grinding together but Leeds United didn't know he was injured. That was the main thing. We took the chance and won the cup. He was the hero, he should have got all the medals.' So impressive was Byrne's performance that he even managed to play a part in setting up Roger Hunt's opening goal, overlapping on the left. Though Leeds equalised, Liverpool wouldn't be denied. St John leapt, twisting, to head the winner nine minutes before time.

Gerry Byrne's display personified everything that Bill Shankly wanted from his teams; guts, pride, determination, the will to win. Ian St John feels that no other Liverpool player would have been able to do what Byrne did, not even Yeats or Smith, and possibly that's true for Smith makes it clear that 'Gerry had more bottle than anybody you could meet'. What's equally plausible though is that Byrne might not have been sufficiently motivated to continue for any other manager than Shankly. In a game that has always had its cynical edge, Bill was a confirmed believer in the glory. Money didn't matter, stadiums didn't matter, directors didn't matter. All that did matter was playing the game, enjoying the game and winning. To Bill, football was the glorious glory game.

The football bug that had bitten him on the windswept fields of Glenbuck was never to leave him. In many ways, Bill Shankly remained a boy, for his vision of the game was almost child-like, though never childish. Football had a certain purity for him, even if he was never blind to its faults saying 'not everybody in the game is honest. Quite frankly sometimes you do begin to ask yourself if it is all worthwhile.' On another occasion, entertaining Billy Watson at Anfield one day, they stopped before the memorial to one of Liverpool's great chairmen, 'Honest John' McKenna. '"Honest?" he said. "He wouldn't last five minutes in the game now!"' However, football was still the greatest joy in the life of this granite-tough little Scot and he approached every job at Anfield with the same boyish vigour and dogged determination that three-year-olds bring to all their preoccupations. He was able to communicate that to men like Tommy Smith who, as Ronnie Moran points out, 'was never a boy. He joined us as a fifteen-year-old and he was thirty then, a hard bloke who could play.' Smith and the team 'sat through the same performance week in, week out. He'd come in and tell us "They've been out late, they're in a state, two of 'em are limping." We knew full well they were fit but somehow we'd believe him, go out and hammer three or four goals and come in so he could tell us we'd beaten a great side. You'd sit there and think, 'He's done it again, he's kidded us again,' but you knew he'd be able to do it the next week as well.'

That boyishness endured and charmed his staff as much as it did his players. A few years later, Geoff Twentyman was appointed the club's Chief Scout and took part in a testimonial game with Bill at Anfield. 'It was a warm-up, staff against another side. Bill had always said that a good player never misses a penalty and we got one. Bill was walking away so I shouted "Come on Bill, a good player never misses!" So he had to take it and Bert Trautmann pushed it round the post. He was livid. We came off to get changed and suddenly it went quiet. "Bert," he said. "That penalty. Would've beat the average goalkeeper." It was typical, he couldn't admit he'd lost to anyone but a great player!'

By now Shankly had created a new club in his own image. Liverpool were, in the minds of everyone there, the supreme club, the place to be. You had to die for your red shirt, remember what a privilege it was to wear it, play your heart out for those people for whom the club meant everything. If you couldn't accept those values, you didn't stay too long. Everything that was important about Liverpool F.C. came together the day after the Final, when they brought the Cup back to Lime Street Station. It's widely accepted that half a million people saw Ron Yeats show the Cup to the city at the civic reception. Bill's reaction was predictable but nonetheless genuine. 'There has never been a reception like this in the whole history of the game. This has been fantastic, there is no other word for it. I have been in football all my life and had my ups and downs and played in Cup Finals, both losing and winning. This without doubt is the happiest day of my life.' Later on, the Kop made it clear just how highly they regarded Shankly when they presented him with a solid gold ring; after the presentation, Bill walked to the side of the hall, opened the door and ushered in the whole Liverpool team who proceeded to serenade the Kop's representatives!

A couple of days later, Liverpool played in a game that he considered the best he was ever involved in. Qualifying for the European Cup, they reached the semi-finals, having beaten Cologne in the previous round on the toss of a coin. Inter

Milan were their opponents, then the finest club side in the world. They played a fierce, uncompromising brand of football with a niggardly defence that bordered on the violent. Coached by Helenio Herrera, Milan represented the ultimate challenge in European football. Although they never matched the virtuoso genius that had characterised Real Madrid's run of success, they seemed invincible, beating the Spaniards 3-1 in the previous year's final.

All that Shankly had said about Liverpool, club, players and crowd, being indivisible came to fruition on that golden night on Merseyside, still perhaps their greatest night, in spite of the trophies that were to come later. Roger Hunt explains that 'we were on a high from winning the Cup and it was one of those nights where the atmosphere made a real difference to the result', Peter Thompson adding that 'we were tired after Wembley and they were the unbeatable World Club Champions, but the atmosphere was electric and that helped a lot'. Bill won the psychological battle and with it the game, for with the Italians out on the pitch, he sent out the injured hero Gerry Byrne, to carry the Cup around Anfield along with Gordon Milne who had missed the Final with an injury. They went to the Anfield Road end first, allowing the noise to build to an absolute crescendo by the time they reached the Kop minutes later. With Anfield groaning under the weight of 54,000 ecstatic Scousers, the noise was deafening and, for all the Italians' experience, captain Ron Yeats believed they were terrified before the game had begun. Roger Hunt agrees, adding 'they were a tough, hardened team, very defensive but we just over-ran them for ninety minutes. We swept them aside.'

It was Hunt who opened the scoring after just four minutes, Bill describing it as 'a goal from three feet high. He scooped it into the net. It was all from the training boards at Melwood.' Ian Callaghan's second was anything but rehearsed though, as Tommy Smith explains: 'Before the match, he'd shown us a film of a free kick by the Brazilians, I think. They had a player on the inside of the wall, a player ran over the ball and round the edge of the wall, the ball went into the wall, flicked on and the lad who'd gone on the blind side put the ball in the net. We'd never tried it because we never practised free kicks, but we went out and did it that night. He drummed it into us that set-pieces were "on the day" things. If ideas came up, terrific. People thought we'd been practising it for months!'

Though Liverpool dominated, a defensive error meant they ended up winning just 3-1, Ian St John netting a late third though Chris Lawler had another superb goal disallowed after beating four players and Peter Thompson adds that 'we hit the bar, the post and should have finished it there and then'. Although everyone at the club realised there was still much to be done, Liverpool could reflect on a truly glorious week, the Kop taunting Inter with chants of 'Go back to Italy' during the game's death throes. Certainly the Italian press were forced to admit that their side had been comprehensively outplayed in every department. *Corriere Dello Sport* accepted the efficacy of Shankly's tactics, noting that 'Inter first lost psychologically and then went to pieces in play'. Milan's *Corriere Della Sera* went further. 'Inter were dazed. We lift off our hats to Liverpool. The moving, colourful, picturesque and electrifying support of their fans is not enough to explain the surprising technical quality of their game. It was a miracle, a triumph of athletic soccer, soccer played to win ... when a team which understands football in this way wins, the inevitable bitterness of defeat for the Italians is lessened. Soccer played in this way belongs to all, everyone would like to see it played this way.' Though the Milan press were staggered by Liverpool's play, Herrera, as thorough in his preparation as Shankly, could claim no such surprise. Prior to the game he remarked 'Liverpool are progressive ... they are really thinking about football and I like their defensive set-up tremendously and the way the inside-forwards are utilised. The way to win the European Cup is to pass man-to-man fairly short and then make the fast burst. Liverpool have developed this and have the fitness to carry it out ... I have a great admiration for Bill Shankly.'

That technical ability had been built up over five years. Their style had evolved quickly during the 1964/65 season as a result of their exposure to European football. Their First Round game – having qualified comfortably in a preliminary against K R Reykjavik – had been a demanding tie with Anderlecht, their first real test. Shankly spoke of 'going out at Anfield that night, I could feel the heat of the tension, like getting into an oven'. It was also a game which marked the real emergence of Tommy Smith. 'I thank my lucky stars that England played Belgium at Wembley just before the Anderlecht game and drew 2-2, though Belgium should have won. The boss came back and he looked a bit apprehensive and that's when I started sweeping up with number 10 on my back to kid Anderlecht because as Shanks put it, I was "Ronnie Yeats' right leg". That was really the start of the flat back four in this country. It wasn't until later that Alf Ramsey, who I've a lot of respect for, started to put that together and went on to win the World Cup. Bill Shankly was the first to go for a 4-4-2.' Though Tommy would play as an inside left from time to time, that defensive role was the start of his career.

'We played to a system. It depended on togetherness and we worked on it in five-a-sides. We never moved up, we kept it dead flat so if anyone ran beyond the back four, they'd put themselves offside. We never ran out to catch them. We'd get caught now and again which didn't look too good but it was a way of playing that was hard to combat.' That led to Tommy Lawrence developing the position of sweeper/keeper that Ray Clemence and then Bruce Grobbelaar would take to a logical conclusion. From there, as Ronnie Moran notes, 'things happen on the pitch and you have to let players can get on with it. Don't stifle anyone, allow them to be flexible. Bill let players play what was on.'

Though Anderlecht were overwhelmed at Anfield, St John, Hunt and Yeats getting a goal each, and the Belgians termed Liverpool the 'champions of world physique', the second leg was not a formality. St John remembers watching the game from the halfway line, barely getting a kick as the defence slugged it out, before Hunt scored with a break-away in the last minute. That experience taught the Reds that their passing needed to be crisper and that there was a way to tackle foreign ties as Tommy Smith explains. 'Eventually, we'd go abroad and play keep-ball. All we wanted to do was silence the crowd, that's all Shanks would say. Didn't need anything else. We played the Europeans at their own game and they didn't like it – in the end we played in Dresden in 1972/73 and won the game 1-0 without them getting a kick.' Liverpool were to play with that measured aggression in domestic competition too, with devastating results.

Such mastery was still a way away in 1965 and the return leg in Milan promised to be hard. Sadly, Liverpool's own naivety let them down. Arriving in Italy, the team went to a mountain retreat. 'It was by a church,' recalls Ronnie Moran who had replaced the injured Byrne. 'The church bell was going all the while and we couldn't sleep. The following day, we wanted to move and the Italians put us in a hotel in Milan. The hotel was in the middle of the city, it was noisy, lots of traffic all the time, we couldn't rest. They told us we had to go there because otherwise we wouldn't be able to get to the ground for the game and we didn't know any different. Those were their tactics to unsettle us and they caught us out. We learned quick and after that we picked our own hotels, sent people to check them in advance, took people to cook our food. That was our first year in Europe and we'd never come across anything like that.'

From Liverpool's greatest night a fortnight earlier, the game in the San Siro stadium was to be one of their most disappointing, a game that has passed into Liverpool folklore, the dark mythology that surrounds the game growing. Bill maintained that he heard before the match that whatever happened on the field, Liverpool would not be allowed to win – whether his informer was relaying the truth or an Italian psychological trick will never be known. Tommy Smith's view is simple. 'It was obvious that the referee had been got at. We had a goal disallowed, they kicked a ball out of Tommy Lawrence's hands, they scored direct from an indirect free kick. We were a bit naive in the way we played, we hadn't perfected that style of keeping the ball and taking the heat out of the game but we never had a chance. I remember kicking the ref as he went off at the end and he never broke his step, just straight off the pitch.' Peter Thompson agrees 'that we attacked too much early on and let in a couple of goals' though Roger Hunt accepts that the Italian crowd had a similar effect on the Reds that their own fans had had on Inter back at Anfield. 'It was unbelievable at the San Siro. There were fire-crackers going off and this constant, incredible noise. When they got their two early goals, both of them disputed, we were absolutely demoralised. It was our first year in Europe and these were the biggest games we ever experienced. We weren't ready for Milan.' Shankly brought himself to concede later that 'it was a war, such hostility, smoke bombs, it was awful. The decisions were queer, everything was made awkward.' It was the closest he came to admitting that his mighty team were undermined by external forces besides the referee.

Roger Hunt's realism goes a long way to explain Shankly's bitterness. The refereeing was questionable, but borderline. Lawrence didn't actually have the ball in his hands when dispossessed, but was bouncing it. The goal came into that 'seen 'em given, seen 'em disallowed' category, as George Best's similar, but disallowed, effort for Northern Ireland against England's Gordon Banks demonstrated a few years later. With the free kick, Liverpool had a stronger case for the referee did briefly have his arm aloft, seemingly signalling an indirect kick, though he had dropped it before the kick was taken. In addition, the award of the free kick itself was highly dubious. However, refereeing mistakes do not necessarily mean an official conspiracy though in fairness, recent research has shown that Inter had a history of buying referees, in domestic football at least. Desperate disappointment, frustration, anger with the Italian tactics prior to the game and fury over his side's and his own tactical errors combined to cloud Shankly's judgment of the game.

He could not believe that his invincible team had been so soundly defeated, yet there was no disgrace in being beaten by the World Club Champions. For all the concentration on Italian organisation and cynical defensive play, Inter had a multitude of fine players in every position including Facchetti, Mazzola and Jair. They were a great team run by a great coach. Though Bill did not admire their style, particularly away from home, he knew deep down that they were a good side. He and his club had been defeated tactically and technically by the Godfather of catenaccio and that hurt. Shankly made it clear that 'this terrible word defensive gets my goat. It's never mentioned at Anfield. I ban it almost. We defend our goal in any and every part of the pitch by keeping the ball away from the goal.' To be beaten by the greatest exponent of defensive football was bitter gall.

Inter made it clear that Liverpool still had some distance to travel before they could win a European trophy. Given that Liverpool were a team built on the philosophy that there was no side in the world to match them, Shankly could not admit that Herrera had got the better of them. He was still angry years later, for when Celtic beat Inter in the European Cup Final of 1967, the after-match banquet featured Celtic's coaches shouting abuse at Herrera on Shankly's instructions! With plenty of circumstantial evidence to suggest that the refereeing was less than perfect, he jumped on that as the reason for their defeat. Peter Thompson remembers that after the game 'Bill came in and said "No team in the world can beat Liverpool 3-0. They must be drugged up to the eyeballs and the referee was bribed." That's all, he didn't have a go at us.' What might have been an off the cuff remark became a Merseyside mantra but it didn't prevent Liverpool learning from their defeat and for the following season, their style had evolved further towards the continental model.

They had to take the supporters with them on this journey into the tactical unknown but Shankly knew that would not be a problem. 'These supporters understand the game,' he said. 'They're professionals, something special, in a class by themselves.' The debt the club owed to them was something he never let the players forget and he would continually invoke them in his match preparation. Before that 1965 Cup Final, he told the press 'if our Anfield fans at Wembley can make as much noise as [at home] ... I don't think there's a team in the world that can live with Liverpool'. That was demonstrably true against Inter and it was equally certain that their absence at the San Siro contributed to Liverpool's defeat. With them always uppermost in his mind, Bill lived more and more for the game, trying to think of new wrinkles that would help him present them with an unbeatable team. That Anderlecht game, for instance, saw him unveil the all-red strip for the first time because he felt it made the side look bigger. Team talks would involve references to the crowd for as Tommy Smith says, 'he adhered himself to the Kop more than anything. "You can't disappoint them." Some managers would concentrate on the opposition but he'd say "There's 50,000 out there, you can't let 'em down," turning the screw that way. He was very sincere which is why people took to him. He could relate to a bin man or the Queen.' Shankly also made it clear to Peter Thompson just how important the crowd was. 'Before a game when we were warming up, I used to flick the ball up, catch it on the back of my neck, roll it down my back, flick it over my head, catch it on my foot. I'd had a couple of poor games and he called me in the office. "Read this letter." It was from a man in Wales who came just to see me do the tricks – sometimes he went home without watching the game! Shanks says, "Right son, you're playing on Saturday in front of 55,000. Do you think you can keep two people happy?" "Two?" "Well you know you'll please the man from Wales so just make bloody sure I'm the other one, 'cos if I'm happy, the 55,000 will be."'

On another occasion, Peter remembers that 'at quarter to three there was no sign of Shanks. Suddenly he came in. His shirt's torn, tie undone, jacket hanging off, hair all over the place. "What's happened boss?" "I've just been in the Kop with the boys."'

'He'd gone in with 28,000 of them and they'd been lifting him shoulder high, passing him round, and he loved that.'

Nothing was too good for those supporters but ultimately,

they were placing a terrible strain on him, though it was never a source of resentment, just pride. Peter Thompson recalls that 'when we won the Cup, he went to bed that night and said that he was planning the next few seasons. He could never stop and celebrate.' Where previously he had had to keep an eye on the domestic game, now he had to go further afield too, visiting Europe to watch foreign teams on a regular basis. Ness recalls that 'he said he was tired after they won the Cup that year. There was so much going on around the club and the people, they were killing us with kindness, which can wear you out! We had a beautiful front garden but he could never go out there to mow the grass because dozens of lads would descend on him for an autograph. We had to get it paved in the end! On Sundays, there was a never-ending procession of lads playing football at the top of the road – it's the Shankly Playing Field now – and they'd play for hours until they were plain exhausted. The door would go and there'd be half a dozen little faces saying "Is Bill coming out to play?" He'd do anything for the supporters but it was hard. At the other places, we managed to get some time for ourselves to go out but after we came to Liverpool, we hardly went out at all. Even if we wanted to buy clothes we'd go to Manchester because here he was just surrounded wherever he went.'

Jock Stein noted that 'Bill Shankly appreciates that the main thing in football is the people on the terraces.' They represented his power base, his leverage with the club and the board of directors. With the crowd behind him, he felt he was fireproof. Tommy Docherty concedes that 'no manager has ever had a relationship with the supporters like he had. He loved them, they loved him and they gave him a goal start.' John Roberts argues that 'he knew they came to Anfield for light relief from what was generally a hard life. His philosophy was that "they've used hard-earned money to see us and I want them to know I'm glad to see them". He was so proud of that spirit that he helped to build.'

There was no kind of posturing in Bill's behaviour towards the fans either, for Tommy Docherty agrees that 'I can't think

of any other manager who felt as much for the supporters as
he did. He knew what the working class man standing behind
the goals wanted and he gave it to him. Their money came
the hard way and he appreciated it. Some people who run
clubs think they can run it like their own business. They don't
understand how important fans are. If they stop coming,
there's no club and Bill knew that.' Shankly explained that
'you may never have known what it is like to be without a
penny in your pocket. I have, many a time, and it's not good.
Anything I do for Liverpool Football Club, I do mainly for the
crowd for they know that position. I am outspokenly in favour
of the crowd. I don't court their favour ... any popularity I
have achieved has come through the players.'

John Peel concedes that 'I much preferred it in the days
when Liverpool used to buy players you'd never heard of. I
used to be so impressed by the interaction between supporters,
the team and Shankly, it was a kind of complete circle and it
went on for a while beyond his time. The first time Alan
Hansen played, a gawky lad from Partick that no-one had
heard of, his was the first name the Kop chanted and you
could see him growing bigger as they sang. The religious
comparisons with football are not inappropriate. As a supporter, you don't need to know much about it, you just need
to believe.' At a time when Lennon was saying that the Beatles
meant more to people than God, in the red half of Liverpool,
Bill Shankly meant more than the Beatles. The religious con-
notations are often laughed off, but they bear scrutiny.

It's often said that to Bill Shankly, football was a religion,
but that's a truer statement than the off-hand nature of the
remark generally implies. While Shankly might have been its
greatest disciple, he was by no means alone in his devotion to
the faith for without a similarly devout congregation, his
vision of Liverpool could never have come to fruition. If we
hark back to earlier chapters, when life in Glenbuck featured
a church that was rarely full alongside a football field that was
rarely empty, we see a pattern that could be transposed to
every industrial area of Britain. Liverpool enjoyed the same

feverish love of the game as it transplanted religion as the opium of the masses. Working men did not want to use their precious leisure hours in pious prayer, looking for a better life of which there seemed little tangible evidence. Political activism had supplanted religion in that regard – unions and, eventually, the Labour Party were the instrument by which they hoped to get better conditions in the here and now rather than in a hoped-for after-life.

Politics did create a vacuum. You could engage in political debate, you could believe in your goals, have absolute faith in them, but it did not conjure quite the same emotions that blind religious devotion had done in the past. Nor did it always inspire the same type of communal spirit that the parish church might have fostered. As religion has diminished as a cultural force, it's possible to see in public entertainments a desire for ceremony, to recreate the togetherness of church services that have been left behind. Ultimately the pub, the cinema, the theatre or music hall and particularly television have all proved to be essentially solitary activities.

Music hall was the ceremonial refuge for working people in the late nineteenth century prior to the advent of film and popular though it was, it never took hold of people's lives in the way that football did. Football tended to be cheaper. Then, in music hall, the audience had no influence over events. They might indulge in a little audience participation, but it was all at the behest and under the control of the people on the stage. At a football game, a fanatical crowd could feel genuinely involved in proceedings, feel that they might be able to will their side on to victory. Every game of football was different where music hall performances were often repetitive and variations on a theme.

The crucial advantage that football enjoyed however was that it was genuinely rooted within the local community and remained so through until the 1970s when money began to erode those cultural links. Back in the 1890s, the local football side belonged to the local people, not financially, but emotionally. The players and most of the officials were local people, men who lived in the town they represented. Music hall offered talented stars passing through on their way to another provincial town, football clubs threw up authentic local heroes.

Football could give people the sense of identity that they had lost with the decline of the parish church. That community still existed, one of selfless co-operation rather than the 'you scratch my back, I'll scratch yours' idea which is now the norm. It was a community where people were wedded to one another. Although this had a theological basis – 'Am I my brother's keeper?' – the people had long since turned away from religion. Their communal spirit was in need of a focus and football helped provide that, gave a sense of civic pride which contextualised local co-operation.

Football provided the ceremonial venue for a certain type of blind faith, one that was to become ever more fanatical over the years of this century, often with appalling consequences – terrace battles in the 1970s and 1980s were fought with the same zealous intensity as holy wars, scarves becoming the sacred articles of faith. Things were rather more innocent early on, but the same principles applied. It would be difficult to deny the similarities between a Saturday afternoon at Anfield and a Sunday in church. The crowd or congregation share the same total faith in the object of their adoration. They want to be consumed by some act of worship; someone grasped by rhapsodic religious ecstasy bears a marked resemblance to a supporter whose side have just scored a last minute winner to win a Cup semi-final. They have the same regard for rituals, both sing hymns of devotion be they 'The Lord Is My Shepherd' or 'You'll Never Walk Alone', and both use their chosen religion as a badge of belonging, ecumenical or geographic. Finally of course, both provide the great escape from the mundane world for short periods where nothing else matters, or even exists.

When Liverpool took another trophy to Anfield, Shankly was their messiah, a word used advisedly. He took Liverpool from the wilderness of the Second Division into the footballing promised land. Football did, probably still does, mean more than religion to many. For the football-obsessed Scousers, Shankly was the miracle worker. Look at any film of the Kop celebrating one of his three championship wins and you'll see him standing before the multitudes with his arms raised, 'like a lovable Hitler' according to Tommy Docherty. Perhaps more accurately, he is bestowing a benediction on the crowd, like the Pope. The most arresting feature of the whole display is not how he holds the crowd in thrall, but the curiously egoless nature of such a potentially provocative gesture. There is not the merest hint that Shankly is soaking up the applause, saying 'Yes, I'm bloody marvellous aren't I?' Every movement, each subtle nuance of speech and posture is saying 'We did it. Thank you for your help. I appreciate it. The boys appreciate it. This is our club.' I can think of no other person, sporting, religious, political who could be so sincerely humble in the face of such total adoration.

Shankly's own view of the relationship was simple. 'It's not a club, it's an institution and I wanted to bring the crowd closer to the club. People have their ashes scattered here. One family came when it was frosty and the groundsman dug a hole in the goal at the Kop end and inside the right-hand post, down a foot, there's a casket. Not only do they support Liverpool when they're alive, they do it when they're dead. This is why Liverpool is so great. There's no hypocrisy about it and that's how close people were brought to the club. It was sheer honesty, I brought them in, accepted them in.' Peter Thompson was on hand to witness an example of this unshakeable bond. 'There was a funeral procession in the corridor and Shanks told the players to follow at the back. We went to the Kop. This lady was sobbing, she'd her husband's ashes with her, a Liverpool fanatic. Shanks scattered them on the Kop and turned to her. "He's a happy man now," deadly serious.'

Shankly had many inherent advantages over other managers, notably that he was in the right place at the right time to marshal circumstances and sculpt an entire club, but his own personality was the vital ingredient in the mix. He was lucky in that his reign at Liverpool coincided with the rise of The Beatles and Merseybeat. Liverpool suddenly became the centre not just of Britain, but of the world. Bill was the perfect man to make the best use of the attendant publicity, constantly feeding the fire to stir up a greater and greater frenzy at Anfield. The place rang to the songs of Lennon and McCartney, Liverpudlians felt that they were the chosen people and the players played with a purposeful arrogance, employing a forensic passing game that left opponents chasing shadows. Yet the signs of the times were just icing on the cake for even if Liverpool hadn't been the centre of the universe because of its music, Bill would have made it so for its football and its club.

Everything was geared to the family feeling. Every supporter was made to feel apart of the club. Brian Barwick, now Editor of *Match of the Day*, 'used to go to Melwood in the school holidays and he was just brilliant with the kids. I used to take my camera and he'd come over and say "Do you want a photograph with me son?" and then he'd make one of the players come over and take it.' Tommy Docherty recounts another story that illustrates the mutual affection that existed between Shankly and the fans. 'They came to Chelsea and at quarter to two, Bill asked me for another 50 tickets and promised us another 50 for the return game at Anfield. The place was packed but I got some from the Secretary. Bill took them, went outside and passed them round to the supporters. "Here you go son, you're all right now." Kissing his hand they were! You could see he loved them when he walked about. Never ignored them, never refused an autograph. He will go on for ever for that, the supporters from his time will pass the stories down and he'll become folklore.' Moments like that don't require much effort but they do demand a good heart and an honesty rare in football.

Perhaps Bill really was a man of his time for as John Roberts concedes 'In Bill's day, the players and managers were doing okay for wages in comparison with the ordinary people on the terraces but there wasn't a huge gulf between them. They were similar people unlike today. He followed a path from working man to player to manager.' Supporters could believe that they were close to their idols. They drank in the same pubs after a game, they lived in the same areas, there was an affinity between them. Nowadays, supporters urge their quieter colleagues to 'Sing your heart out for the lads', but the lads out on the pitch aren't like us any longer. With weekly salaries that exceed the annual wages of most ordinary fans, how could you create that same bond today? Tommy Docherty points out that 'the 1960s and '70s were a great time. Life was good, music was great, super years, good players, great support. George would get in the 'papers but that was it, a cleaner game than now because the money was different and thanks to people like Bill who loved their football. Money never bothered him, people, players, supporters did. He talked about the supporters first and then everything else – he kept them happy by producing a great team and he'd do that now.'

To win the crowd's respect, he would not allow players to get away with the behaviour that is apparently *de rigueur* at certain clubs. Players had a responsibility away from the field. They should not disgrace the club or its support. Docherty admits that 'Bill wouldn't have put up with someone like Stan Bowles – great player, didn't give me any trouble – but he wasn't what Bill wanted, didn't want his club to have that reputation. No shenanigans. You can have problems in a nightclub if you're a player so Shanks would say "What were you doing there in the first place? Go to a restaurant, have a meal and a bottle of wine and act in a manner that befits a professional." If anyone stepped out of line they left, and if you left Liverpool you could only go downhill. If you did anything silly, Shanks wouldn't wear it, you'd be out in two minutes.' The fans respected him for it for Billy O'Donnell's view is that 'Shankly wouldn't entertain anybody messing around – "There's the door!".'

Bill was well aware of his responsibilities and felt that the players were big enough to accept their share. Jack Mindel had kept in touch. 'We were at a hotel before a game and some of the players had gone out. A few of them were late getting back. Bill was pacing up and down like a lion in a cage. I tried to tell him they'd just got held up somewhere but he told me "This is a multi-million pound business. I'm responsible to the club, to the fans and to the directors. Everything should be run smoothly and if the players don't behave properly, I'm responsible." Apparently they'd gone to a hospital to see some kids and then gone on for a drink or something but that annoyed and worried him. He was under a tremendous strain all the time.'

Shankly dealt with the club's affairs in microscopic detail. Not only every player, but every official who came to the club was welcomed and treated to a pep-talk. Peter Robinson took over as Secretary not long after the 1965 F.A. Cup Final and 'I met Bill on the morning that I came to Anfield. He talked to me for about half an hour, telling me what a great club Liverpool was and how they'd win everything in sight for the next hundred years. We struck up an immediate friendship. He only wanted to know about football, he wasn't interested in any other matters at all. He said "I'll run the team and I'll leave you to deal with everything else." We spoke several times a day and he'd think nothing of calling me at home too, several times an evening!' Robinson came to a club in good financial health for not only were the club about to finish paying for the Anfield redevelopment of 1962, well ahead of schedule thanks to their success on the field, but things were so secure that that close season saw a further £100,000 invested in Anfield and Melwood, where a new drainage system was introduced.

Roy Evans had come up through the junior ranks and was rated a promising prospect. He was duly signed up and recalls that 'when I did sign, I played a bit of cricket and was ready to go off on a tour, but he said "there's only one game, son, and that's football". He got stripped for training with the youngsters not the first team and on my first day he sat next to me which was quite awesome. Once he knew you had a genuine enthusiasm and love for the game, there was a great warmth that came off him because of his love of life. Anyone who gave 100% felt that from him.' Another piece of psychology, for Bill was insistent that there should be no 'boss-player attitude. By this close contact I get to know the young lads inside out. I've no time for shirkers, cowards with skill. I want a man who'll go through a wall of fire with his leg broken and come out the other end still shooting for goal.' With the constant flow of information provided by Joe Fagan on the reserve team, this interest in the youngsters ensured that he knew the make-up of each individual as well as their ability on the ball, vital when it came to bringing them through into the First Division. That vibrant youth policy also fed this family image as the lads who came through felt a part of the club from their youngest days. Not only were they schooled in the Liverpool style of play, they were Liverpool fans through and through.

With the end of maximum wages, Bill wasn't slow to spot the dangers to team morale. He acted swiftly and ensured that, as Roger Hunt remembers well, 'we all got paid the same as each other with bonuses on top of the basic. It fostered a great team spirit and it wasn't until that side broke up that individual wages were negotiated. Liverpool probably weren't the best payers, I think other clubs paid more just for surviving. I think Newcastle got the same bonus for staying in the First Division that we got for winning it. No-one wanted to leave because in those days if you were with a successful club, playing in front of those crowds, winning things, that was all you'd ever wanted. You really didn't think about moving. It wasn't until later with the big money that came into the game that a player would want to go from a successful club. We all wanted to play football. Anyone who came here was made aware that it was a down to earth place, no superstars. Everybody respected Shanks and his loyalty. He always let us know what was happening at the club.' With players so infected by his desire for the glory of the game, Bill couldn't go wrong.

Pleased to see the end of the maximum wage and to allow players to earn what they were worth, that parity of payment was of paramount importance he felt. As Tom Finney explains, 'He created a happy unit which was his secret. He thought that it was wrong to have one fellow in the side who was earning twice as much as another because if he's having a bad game what do the others do? They think "he's getting more than me and I'm pulling me pan out". Bill's attitude was that they had to pull together and they got the same wage for it.' Used to scrimping and saving in the lower divisions, Bill did not want to see Liverpool's finances destroyed by a wage explosion however. Allegedly, he, Bill Nicholson at Spurs, Don Revie at Leeds and Matt Busby at United got together and decided on a wage structure that no-one would exceed. The four top clubs ensured that there would be no superstar wages in the game, for the best would rarely consider a move to many clubs beyond those four.

As Roger Hunt suggests, Liverpool were not fabulous pay-masters, but the players could earn in the region of £100 per week, still a handsome wage in those days. There was a basic wage of around £35, supplemented by bonuses. They earned £1 per 1,000 spectators in a crowd of over 27,000 so if Anfield was full, that could mean £27. If they were in the top six, that amount was doubled. There was also a £4 win bonus and £10 in appearance money, giving a possible top wage of £103. Bill felt it wholly appropriate that they had to play well before he paid well because if they didn't, they didn't deserve it!

If financial equality engendered togetherness, so did the feeling, continually fuelled by Shankly, that Liverpool were pioneering, doing things their own way and showing the rest of the country that their ideas worked. Lilleshall came in for some fearful stick as he justified his methods to players who knew just how intelligent they were. 'I went to Lilleshall,' he'd start, like a stand-up comic. 'It was an education because everything they did, I did the opposite. I heard some expressions, "workrate", "blind side running", "peripheral vision", "environmental awareness", "working off the ball". God almighty! I could have written a comic cuts book about it! They were trying to tell me that you could make football players! They had a set plan all the time, but when it broke down, there was nowhere to go. Talk in a language the players understand, simplify and clarify, don't use the big words that few understand the way the politicians do. You've to get through to people. We're not too fond of coaching. Coaxing is a better word.' Roy Evans agrees, adding 'he was idealistic. He wanted perfection. He wasn't a coach, he wasn't a tactician, he was an enthusiast and a teacher. He preached simplicity. Pass it and move.'

Men whose opinions had been forged in the heat of the game were the type he wanted which is why Paisley and Fagan were so valued. Another stalwart of the Shankly school is Ronnie Moran. 'When Bill got here, he wanted to play the right way, pass the ball, give it to a red shirt. I was lucky that I could pick up his ideas which helped me stay in the game. He altered my life by offering me a job on the staff. I'd turned thirty-two, didn't know what I was going to do. He called me in and I thought "this is it, end of the season, I'm on my way", but he offered me a job, which took me aback. I started working with the kids along with Joe who kept me playing in the reserves to help them.' Ronnie went to Lilleshall quite regularly with Joe, though Bill only endured a couple of sessions. 'No-one here's got a full coaching badge but we used to go together on a manager and coaches course. Bill wanted us to mix with the others to see if we could pick up any ideas for training and we got a few. At Lilleshall, there's people who think they know how the game should be played and it should be their way. Okay, Bill was the same but they were dogmatic where he allowed players to be flexible and, well, I've had a lot of success doing things the way we do them here. Bill didn't like it. You went away in groups to work on different aspects of the theme and then you'd all come back together for a talk but Bill wanted to get on. He'd be saying "Right, let's put it into a five-a-side," and the older people who idolised him would get up, "Aye, you're right." The people at Lilleshall didn't like that, but to me, it was a sign that Bill was ahead of his time, doing things practically so they were easy to understand.'

At Workington, Jackie Bertolini said that Shankly was like a favourite teacher who you didn't want to disappoint and that position of father figure was one that he adopted at Liverpool. The Liverpool dressing room was filled with strong personalities, yet it was remarkably harmonious, largely because Shankly allowed the players to get on with their jobs. By virtue of his commanding presence, Ron Yeats was their leader initially, and in time Tommy Smith succeeded him as Shankly's chief disciple. No-one would accuse Tommy Smith of not knowing his own mind and certainly he and Shankly had 'a couple of run-ins. There were never any punch-ups but Shanks always told us to stick up for ourselves which I'm thankful for. When I did stick up for myself though it was against him – he left me out, I had a go, he had a go back. The good thing was you could have a bloody good argument one day and it'd be off his chest, forgotten, no grudges. There was never really any conflict, it was a great atmosphere at the club. If something had to be said, somebody would, but most of the lads were decent fellas so you'd work hard for them. Shanks always reiterated that it was a job that you could enjoy, one that millions would like to do. Any pettiness or jibes, once you got out onto the field, they were gone.'

Smith was a born winner. Shankly said Tommy could start a riot in a cemetery, but that never disguised the fact that 'Tommy could play. You can't knock him down. One day, he was so badly injured, he was limping to the centre-circle to toss the coin. I thought "Christ, he'll never get there, the game won't start!" A brilliant man. Ready for the big team at seventeen, he could play, one of the best in England since the war. As a boy, he was always at me, wanting to be in the team. "Tommy son, I can't play twelve because there'll be an objection." We had a five-a-side at Melwood and Tommy caught Chris Lawler on the ankle, real sore tackle and it blew up. As we were coming off, Tommy says to me "Will I be in on Saturday now?" My kind of player.' In return, Smith was as willing a servant as any manager could hope for. A great mutual respect grew between them, such that there was no prouder man than Bill when Tommy 'rose like a brick gazelle', to use John Peel's famous phrase, to head Liverpool's second goal in the 1977 European Cup Final.

However much Bill admired Smith, or Yeats or St John for that matter, Tommy notes that 'he really was interested in everybody, not just one person. He'd have his little favourites but he spread it around, never gave anyone so much attention that it became embarrassing.' Bill was interested in his players as people. 'I told them "when you finish playing, your life's only beginning", and I told them to get ready so that they could go on to something else.' Roy Evans adds that 'he inspired a nice combination of fear and respect. Players weren't on fantastic money then so they had to be a bit more careful with the manager possibly, but he commanded respect.' Tommy Smith remembers the lesson that 'you weren't a great player, but you were when you were with the others, don't get big-headed, you can't play without the other ten. Shanks was all "nearest man, help your mate". Chris Lawler got fifty goals without taking penalties, the goals were spread around, we didn't leave it to Roger Hunt. That's the sign of a team playing with freedom and playing as a team.' There was no finer team than Liverpool, a tribute to Shankly's vision and the family ideal.

chapter sixteen

SHADOWS AND FOG

When Liverpool had begun their defence of the League title in August 1964, things had not gone well. Bill blamed many of the problems on a close season visit to America where Liverpool had played some exhibition matches and even guested on the Ed Sullivan Show with Gerry & the Pacemakers. It left its mark as he pointed out. 'We had injuries everywhere. I blame that American tour, the boys didn't rest properly.' Visiting America, a country that barely knew of the game, didn't understand it, was a trial and he disliked it from the off. The club flew over in two parties, Bill on the second 'plane. Bob Paisley went back to the airport to meet him and asked whether he'd like to go and see Jack Dempsey's bar. Bill looked at his watch and said, 'At this time of night?' Paisley told him that he needed to put his watch back six hours and that it was just seven o'clock but Shankly replied, 'No Yank'll tell me what time it is. I'm off to bed.'

With the Cup won in 1965, Bill wanted to ensure that the forthcoming season would see his side recapture the Championship, their 'bread and butter'. There were no extensive foreign trips during the close season. Players were told to rest. The injuries early the previous season, while irritating, had proved useful, for it had given opportunities for Lawler, Smith and Strong to earn valuable first-team experience. Planning ahead, Bill had a definite line-up in mind: Lawrence, Lawler, Byrne, Milne, Yeats, Stevenson, Callaghan, Hunt, St John, Smith and Thompson with Geoff Strong, a talented defender and a useful utility player, fitting in as required. Strong spent many Saturdays on the bench for this was the first season where substitutes were allowed. Bill decided that he would only use a sub in case of injury, reasoning that his team selection and tactics were always sound. Football was a game of 'patience. Ninety minutes is a long time. It might take 60 minutes, 70 minutes, 80 minutes for our plans to work, but you've to be patient.'

Liverpool were the class act, packed with seasoned pros who knew the game, adding a new dimension with their continental exposure. They won the League by six points, pulling up at the end, so clear-cut was their triumph. Their season included some emphatic victories – 5-0 at home to Everton, 5-1 at West Ham – and rarely did they seem seriously troubled. Remarkably they used just twelve players with two others sharing four games between them at the tail-end of the season. Bill ascribed this to his training system. 'I don't believe in training twice a day. No way. Does them no good at all. We train hard but sensibly. We train for football, little two minutes of torture, half a minute off, then on again. We've a killer using the boards so the game doesn't stop. No breathers. If the ball goes out, we'd throw another on. That's attention to detail. By building it up, what was difficult for players becomes easier.'

The defence of the F.A. Cup ended at the first hurdle at Chelsea, but with the League under control, Europe provided the spice, in the Cup Winners' Cup. The route to the final was a tough one as they had to overcome Juventus, Standard Liege, Honved and Celtic. The Final, against Borussia Dortmund, was held at Hampden Park. To win a European trophy in Scotland would have been the crowning glory for Shankly but it wasn't to be as Roger Hunt recalls. 'It was one of our few poor displays that year. It was just an off night and to make it worse for me, I was struggling with a bad ankle. It was probably the most disappointing defeat over the years because we just didn't play, though in fairness they were a very good team with some of the West German World Cup side.' Even Bill conceded defeat without his characteristic condemnation of the circumstances. 'We didn't play well and we gave away two silly goals. The Germans got the breaks and that was it.'

For the 1960s side, that was it too, though no-one realised

it at the time. They had taken two Championships, the F.A. Cup, reached the Final of the Cup Winners' Cup and the European Cup semi-final. They were never to get as close to a trophy again despite several more years of consistently high quality play. Ironically, the very physical strength of that 1965/66 side had stored up problems for Shankly and his colleagues in the years to come. Where each of the previous seasons had seen the side accommodate a new face or two, those in possession of the fabled red shirts repelled all boarders this time around. Thus they opened the following season with the same side, all a year older and a little more vulnerable to injury, perhaps a little less hungry.

The nucleus of the side, Yeats, St John, Hunt and so on, were all around the twenty-seven mark and Bill believed they should have several years of good football left. He embarked on another year confident that his troops would come home with another prize at the end, possibly even the 1967 European Cup which had been denied them in such controversial fashion in Milan. Having struggled past Petrolul Ploiesti in the first round, they were paired with Ajax. The circumstances of the first leg in Holland reinforced Bill's mistrust of the foreign game. A blanket of fog descended on the stadium prior to kick-off and visibility was down to no more than fifty yards. Following the local convention that games went ahead if you could see each goal from the halfway line, the match was played, much to Shankly's disgust. 'The match should never have been started. The fog was terrible ... we couldn't see much of the game at all sitting on the sidelines. We couldn't even see the ball.' Irritated by the conditions, he was unable to send his team out to play with any coherent pattern and a young Ajax team, inspired by the genius of Cruyff, ripped them to pieces. At half-time, Bill repaired the leaking defence but by then the damage was done, Liverpool were 4-0 down and all but out of the competition. Ajax finally ran out 5-1 winners on the night.

Once more, Liverpool's lack of understanding of foreign football had let them down. It's a wholly different game in

Europe and it does take time to assimilate the rudiments of that style. English clubs have fared so badly since the Heysel ban because they did not enjoy the experience of European competition for several years. Twenty years of accumulated knowledge went out of the window when we were no longer able to match our skills with those of the Germans, Italians or Spaniards. The English domination of the European scene was over. Back in the 1960s, Liverpool were going through that same kind of learning curve.

In Amsterdam, they had been guilty of a surprising lack of discipline, frustration at the conditions running over into a sloppy performance. There was no shame in losing to such a precociously talented team that would soon go on to rule European football in their own right, but there was disappointment over the tactical shortcomings that had been brutally exposed. Bill spotted the weakness early on, though by then they were two down. 'Willie Stevenson and Geoff Strong started raiding. They were stung and went mad and tried to retrieve the game. So I went on to the pitch while the game was in progress and was walking about in the fog, and I said to Willie and Geoff, "Christ, this is only the first game. There's another bloody game at Liverpool, so don't go and give away more goals. Let's get beat 2-0. We're not doing too bad. Take it easy." I walked on to the pitch, talked to the players and the referee never saw me!'

Bill's indignation had got the best of his players and for once the Shankly magic failed to work. Even when they returned to Anfield, Bill convinced the crowd that they could overcome the 5-1 deficit and they subjected the Dutchmen to intense pressure. Cruyff was like lightning on the break however, and that game ended 2-2. In his book, Bill wrote that 'we were too busy to let set-backs bother us. We were examining the team and planning ahead.' Yet for the rest of that season, the old guard remained intact. Bill managed to inspire his men but by now, other teams had worked out their own methods of combating Liverpool. At Anfield in particular, they were often faced by a ten-man blanket defence as opponents came looking for a point. Seven draws at home cost Liverpool any chance of the Championship and they finished a mediocre season in fifth place.

Bill was learning the difficulty of living up to the highest standards, standards which he and his team had set. Liverpool were an ageing side who had already achieved everything they could have imagined possible. They had pushed themselves through demanding training routines, played hard week after week, 50 games a season. The effort was beginning to take its toll. Liverpool's sting had been drawn. With the Ajax defeat behind them, it was becoming clear that Liverpool required major surgery over the next couple of years to refresh and reinvigorate the side.

Until the signing of Emlyn Hughes in March 1967, almost two full seasons had passed without a new face. This was worrying but it also encouraged complacency within the existing team. Though Liverpool never gave anything less than their best, Roger Hunt concedes that 'though we weren't an old side, perhaps a team only has a certain life span. Part of ours was spent trying to get promotion, and then adapting to the First Division the year after. Maybe you're not quite as hungry if you've won things. You still want to win, you hate to lose but it's not the first time any more and perhaps subconsciously you aren't so desperate for it.' Equally, given that the same eleven lined up week in, week out, family life at Anfield might have become too cosy.

1966/67 could have been passed off as an aberration, but the following year was equally dispiriting. Having entered the League Cup for the first time since 1960/61, they were dumped out of that by Bolton in the second round. West Bromwich Albion defeated them in an epic sixth round duel in the F.A. Cup before going on to lift the trophy at Wembley and in the European Fairs Cup, Ferencvaros took both third round legs 1-0. The League form was better but not quite good enough and the club finished third, three points adrift of Manchester City. It was a second successive trophyless season. Bill began to make changes. With Alf Arrowsmith plagued by injuries,

Roger Hunt had to carry too much of the goalscoring burden. With superb flank players like Callaghan and Thompson in the team, Bill felt that an old fashioned target man might do the trick for them. He called Tommy Docherty at Chelsea and said, 'What about this Tony Hateley then?' Docherty replied, 'A hundred thousand wouldn't buy him Bill,' to which Shankly replied, 'Aye, and I'm one of 'em!' However, Hateley was the man he wanted and prior to the 1967/68 season, he signed him for £96,000. Hateley wasn't the answer for he suffered injury problems and while he scored sixteen goals in his first season to pep up the attack, he was never to play regularly for the club again.

Other purchases were lined up but fell through, notably that of Howard Kendall from Preston. 'Preston had sold a few players to Liverpool in the past, Milne, Thompson and a winger called Dave Wilson, and they didn't want to look like they were a nursery club for Liverpool so they turned him down and I went to Everton instead. He'd just signed Emlyn and he said that he thought that with me in the team as well, Liverpool could go through a season without conceding a goal!' Hughes was an inspired purchase, a player that Shankly had been tracking for some time. Feeling that Gordon Milne would be unable to maintain the same industry in his role of 'carrying messages', Hughes' dynamic enthusiasm provided the solution. Bill also felt that his infectious personality might provide a second wind for the core of his team.

Hughes remembers Shankly's determination to win his signature. 'I made my debut for Blackpool against Blackburn and he burst into our dressing room which was unbelievable because you just don't go into another manager's dressing room. He came straight over to me. "Jesus Christ son, I've seen some bloody debuts in my time, but that was bloody explosive!" We shook hands and that very evening he bid £35,000 for me, increased it the next week to £45,000, but Blackpool didn't need the money because Alan Ball was off to Everton. Eventually though, twenty-nine games later, he got me for £65,000. He used to ring me up every Sunday which I suppose was poaching, asking me how I'd gone on and telling me he was gonna sign me. As a young player, that was superb. I started believing in myself and Shanks was 99% of that. When he did sign me, we had a bump in his car – he was a terrible driver – and the police stopped him because he'd lost the rear light in the accident. While he was arguing with the policeman, he said "Do you realise who I've got in this car? The future captain of England!"'

Hughes walked straight into the Liverpool team the Saturday after he signed for the club. 'Never played a reserve game. From my debut against Stoke, if I was fit, I was in the side. It was a big change but for the better. Blackpool were a super club, homely with 18,000 crowds. Going to Liverpool with 50,000 every week was superb. Shanks had me in the office after a couple of weeks to see how I was enjoying things and I told him I loved it.' Hughes was another first-class example of Bill's penchant for signing players who reminded him of himself. Emlyn Hughes was an all-action, ninety minutes player. Strong in the tackle, intelligent on the ball, never beaten, desperate to win. Hughes accepts that Shankly shared some characteristics with his own father who had played rugby league for Wales alongside Gus Risman, Bill's *bête noire* from Workington. According to his autobiography, *Crazy Horse*, as Emlyn embarked on life as a pro at Blackpool, Fred Hughes told his son 'Don't go out. Stay at home. If you feel you must go out with the lads, then drink Coca Cola. If you go to a dance with them, make sure you're in bed at home by 10.30pm. Don't smoke. This is the time to be making your career. Everything you want will come to you in the end.' Advice like that could have come straight from Bill who noted later that 'Emlyn was like Yeats and St John. No risk at all.'

Though Hughes did provide fresh legs and the drive that those without medals provide, it wasn't enough to win Liverpool a trophy. Emlyn was quickly made to feel at home and part of the Liverpool family: 'we felt that aura from the club, that players, staff, fans, Kop, we were all one'. Unfortunately that unique Liverpool strength, drawn from Shankly's unshakeable loyalty to players who had worked hard for him, was to become a source of comparative weakness over the next few years. When a club is built on commitment to one another, when the motivation comes from not wanting to let down your mates, it's very hard to break up that collection of people. Bill was not keen to let men like St John, Yeats and Hunt go. He knew that he owed them as much as they owed him, for they had helped him achieve all his managerial ambitions. They had helped him construct this monumental club against all the odds.

The writing was on the wall before changes were made, because 1968/69 was another disappointing year. Tony Hateley was clearly not going to play much of a part and so Shankly jumped into the transfer market to pluck teenager Alun Evans from Wolves for £100,000. Impressed by Evans the previous year when he had given Ron Yeats a roasting, Bill fell into the trap that had caught him out at Carlisle, spending on the basis of insufficient evidence. Evans was an exciting prospect but the pressure of being the first £100,000 teenager weighed heavily upon him. He started brightly enough with five goals in seven games, but scored just two more in the remaining twenty-six.

For once, Liverpool appeared to be lacking in direction, even though they harried Leeds United all the way for the title, finishing second, six points behind. Leeds clinched the trophy with a 0-0 draw at Anfield on a night when Bill could be particularly proud of his supporters. They gave Leeds a stand-ing ovation and the Kop chanted 'Champions' as Billy Bremner received the trophy for the first time. Liverpool were operating on pride rather than the unswerving belief, arrogant ability and total fitness that had taken them on to glory three or four years earlier. Shankly could still get the side going, but absolute consistency eluded them. Perhaps the players had heard all his stories before and they were no longer galvanised by them, though Peter Thompson remembers one particular example of the Shankly style with relish. 'I was leaving the ground and he said "Thommo, I'm ringing your wife." "Why?"

"Nothing to do with you." So I got home and she said "Mr. Shankly's been on the 'phone. He says you're the greatest player that's ever lived, his greatest signing, when you play well, Liverpool play well. He said 'Do me a favour, love. Promise him sex in the spare room and lock the bugger in.'"
Next day, I went to the ground so thrilled because I was his greatest player but in the dressing room Ian St John was talking to Ron Yeats, telling him that Shanks had 'phoned his wife, told her how great Ian was and to lock him in the spare room. Ronnie said "He told my wife that!" Roger chimed in with the same and we discovered that he'd rung everybody's wife the day before with the same story. We went out, won well and afterwards, Shanks came in and shook everybody's hand and went off to the lounge where the ladies were waiting. "Ladies, I want silence. I want to thank you all for locking them up last night. They were like wild men out there. Tonight is your night and if they perform half as well as they did this afternoon, you're in for a good night."'

Opinions vary as to whether Bill should have stripped down the side earlier. Behind the scenes, Liverpool were working feverishly to create a new side. On the face of things though, Liverpool were hanging on for their lives and the going was getting harder. Of course, pretty well any other club in the country would have been happy with their results, but this was Liverpool. Bill expected more and so did the crowd. Tommy Smith is vehemently opposed to the idea that the great '60s team went beyond its sell-by date. 'From 1963 we qualified for Europe every year, top six every year, three trophies. I thought it was a damned sight harder playing in the 1960s than in the 1970s and certainly tougher than now. It was a harder league, there were more really good players. That 1965/66 side was the best I ever played in, oozing with class. In those years, any one of probably a dozen teams might win the League whereas in the 1980s, it was usually one of three.' Smith's analysis is pretty persuasive, given that a Manchester United team packed with the genius of Best, Charlton and Law and a host of excellent supporting players could only take two titles and great teams like Spurs, Everton, Leeds and Manchester City managed just one each in the decade.

Bill himself felt that 'if the '60s side had had Ray Clemence in goal, they'd have won all the cups under the sun because Ray Clemence is one of the greatest goalkeepers of all time. No one could possibly have beaten us.' He was deeply attached to his players and was perhaps misled by the fact that they were going so close to trophies without capturing them. Among friends, he seemed to be willing them on to one final, glorious swan-song, a last hurrah that might allow them to leave the stage in a manner befitting their massive contribution. His views were coloured by his own experiences as a player for he felt that 'my best years were from twenty-eight to thirty-three. I was a tradesman. I bargained for the players going on until they were thirty at least.' What Bill had not added into the equation was that his peak years coincided with the war and consequently, competition was never so fierce as it was under proper League conditions. Neither had Bill to cope with the exhausting round of European matches that helped sap the energy of his men. In the years since hostilities had ceased, life for a professional footballer had become harder and harder and that had to have an effect on their longevity. If Tommy Smith's argument as to the quality of the League is accepted, then the more intense nature of the competition among high quality, evenly matched sides, would only further test the fitness and hunger of the side. Even the fact that Liverpool players rarely missed out through injury had to mean that those extra games were taking their toll. The likes of St John played forty-plus games a season for eight years at Anfield where at other clubs, some players might have averaged thirty games a year. Injuries would keep them out, but paradoxically, they would keep them better rested and able to go on longer. As the 1968/69 season drew to a close, Bill had to face the unpalatable facts that Yeats and St John were thirty-one, Hunt and Byrne thirty while Tommy Lawrence was causing him anxiety by putting on weight as he got older. These cornerstones of his team all required replacing. Indeed, perhaps one or two of them should have already gone for the team had aged in the key positions down the middle.

Since Bill was allowed to spend big money on Hateley, Hughes and Evans, one can only surmise that he did not want to go into the transfer market for ready-made replacements. Though he might have preferred to grow his own, it might also be that Bill was simply postponing the fateful day when he had to make sweeping changes. The pressure was gnawing away at him as friends like Jack Mindel saw. 'He had his moments of anger when he was strained. The pressures were enormous. Another fellow we knew from our time in the RAF lived in Liverpool. He was a friendly chap and some weeks Bill would see him and sort out a ticket for him but others he'd just ignore him. Of course, he was very upset but I told him that he had to realise that Bill had so many things on his mind, you couldn't take it to heart, you had to take it in your stride. He wasn't being deliberately rude, it was just his mind was elsewhere.' Bill himself noted ruefully that 'managing is a soul-destroying job. You have to have a stomach made of cement to take the blows.'

Bill knew from painful experience the misery of ending your playing career. His had been terminated prematurely, he felt, and he could hardly bring himself to do the same to men for whom he felt so much. So upsetting were the circumstances that there was even a time, in 1968, when he toyed briefly with the idea of leaving Liverpool after Sunderland had approached him with the offer of the manager's job. A little downcast at the way things were working out at Anfield, he gave Sunderland's offer serious consideration but concluded that he couldn't leave Liverpool behind. The club was in his blood and, while tough decisions had to be made, that was his job and he would see it through for the sake of the people on the terraces.

The first inkling that he was ready to do that job came in controversial fashion in a Cup tie with Leicester City at Anfield. Billy O'Donnell remembers that 'they were in a bit of a rut at the time, the whole team were playing badly. Shankly pulled Roger Hunt off, but to be honest, he could've taken any of 'em off. Roger was stood there in the middle of the field and you could see he couldn't believe it. He ran off and he threw his shirt in to the dug-out which I don't think was very popular!' The significance of the substitution was that Liverpool never brought a player off for any reason other than injury so what would normally be a blow to any player's ego was, in this case, especially severe. 'We were fighting a battle for our lives ... Roger wasn't playing well. On the bench we had Bobby Graham, a quick-fire player who might have broken through. We needed a little pace. I could have picked any one of the players to bring off, but I thought Roger was doing nothing by his standards. I sat for five or six minutes and thought "it's got to be Roger".'

Hunt admits that 'I didn't consider leaving until the incident when I was brought off the field. I realised he was trying to tell me something. Things weren't the same after that.' Since both Shankly on the bench and Billy O'Donnell from the stands agreed that any player could have been substituted, it's odd that Bill chose to take off Liverpool's greatest goalscoring weapon with the team trailing. In its impact, it was a move akin to Graham Taylor's replacement of Gary Lineker in his final international in the 1992 European Championships, bringing down the curtain on an illustrious career and an illustrious era. Roger was back in the team right away and scored twice in the next five games but was then left out of the side and was never a fixture again. Bill felt Hunt had to be the first of that great team to go, whatever the implications. Since Roger Hunt, or Sir Roger to give him his full title, was a living legend on Merseyside, it was a risky strategy, all the more so in the light of the bare trophy cabinet. The Kop backed Bill to the hilt, confident that he knew what he was doing and would once again find the right blend for success. Hunt was the obvious choice to go first since in Alun Evans and Bobby Graham, Bill had two new forwards who he thought might develop a partnership.

The manner of his going was questionable though and it was deeply unfortunate that he was substituted in humiliating circumstances. There is no way of knowing, but it's possible that Bill was looking to provoke Roger to ask for a transfer, thereby preventing him having to deal with it himself. Though Hunt was too attached to the club to oblige, it's a theory that gains credence when one considers the demise of Ian St John. The first time he was dropped was in the 1969/70 season when he'd travelled with the team to St James' Park, ready to play against Newcastle United. He was talking to Jackie Milburn outside the dressing room when Milburn got hold of a team sheet and told St John that he was substitute. St John rushed off, but couldn't find Shankly until he came into the dressing room as the team were about to go out. When St John demanded an explanation as to why he hadn't been told of his demotion, Bill told him it was his own fault for not being in the dressing room when he'd announced the team. The whole process was so painful, that he couldn't bring himself to face St John with the news.

That attitude extended to the likes of Hunt, Yeats, Byrne and Lawrence too. Peter Robinson feels that 'he did find it very difficult. He did tend to fall in love with his players and it was only results that eventually forced his hand.' Ness agrees and says 'it was sad when that team ended, they were great lads. He wanted them to be Peter Pans and never get any older. It was very difficult for him to break them up but he had to do it. I know he talked to them and explained his position and the fact that they couldn't carry on much longer.' It was inescapable that he had to part with great club-servants; it did not make things any easier and Bill felt the pressure, as did those great players who had reached the end of the road. Roger Hunt was naturally very upset and recalls that 'when the manager calls you in to say a club had made a bid and they've accepted it, you know you're no longer wanted. It was an awful moment. I'd been there eleven years and had never been called in like that before. When he first dropped me, I thought I was playing well but he'd already made his mind up. To be fair to him, as a player you always think you can go on longer and the results show that he was probably right.'

Losing a man like Hunt was like losing a leg for Bill, for they had become so close as Liverpool had risen from the ashes. When you multiply that pain several-fold to take in the other changes that had to be made, it's little wonder that he sought to dodge some of the responsibility. With Hunt out of favour, there seems little doubt that he was hoping that Yeats and St John might reconsider their futures independently without him requiring them to do so. More than anything else, those few years exposed the hard man image as the myth that most inside the game knew it to be. Peter Robinson suggests that 'he had a bark but I thought he was a softy. One day, for instance, the girl on the switchboard had upset him and he was shouting about her and then an hour later he called me back to say "You won't sack her will you?" He was always interested in people, they mattered a great deal to him.' Roger Hunt picks up the theme. 'In some ways he was a bit soft underneath. He knew he had to break up the team which was going to hurt him a lot. He really didn't know how to handle it. The team he'd had for years, it was difficult for him to say "it's time you went" and so it could take him a while to say he was leaving you out. He didn't like doing it because he was very loyal to the players. That was the spirit of the club. When you play for a club like Liverpool, you want it to go on forever. There's a lot of heartache involved at the end.' Joe Mercer summed Shankly up beautifully by likening him to an old collie who would push his sheep hard but would never hurt them.

The final straw came in 1969/70. With Roger Hunt already gone, the transition was not going smoothly and Liverpool were also-rans in the League. Their last hope of glory was in the F.A. Cup, which Bill hoped would provide them with that great swan-song. It was not to be for on 21 February, an era came to an end. Playing away at Second Division strugglers Watford in the sixth round, a Barry Endean goal finished a number of careers. Shankly was livid. 'Watford were possibly the worst team that ever beat us, the most negative team I have ever seen in my life,' he raged but, in the cold light of day, it had been a result that had been coming. Peter Thompson remembers it as the 'luckiest day of my life. I was injured and missed the game and he really went crackers after that. That was the beginning of the end.' Emlyn Hughes did play and has the same feelings. As one of the young guns around whom Shankly would rebuild, he admits that 'it was sad to see the '60s side go but it was inevitable. They couldn't physically compete with the kids any longer. After the Watford defeat he just came in and said "That's it, a lot of you have just played your last game for Liverpool" and he changed it there and then, bringing in the youngsters he'd had for eighteen months – Hall, Heighway, Lloyd, Clemence.' George Aitken, one of Bill's stalwarts at Workington, was by now on the staff at Watford. He hardly improved Bill's mood when he passed on another great shock result of the day. 'I had to tell him that Berwick had beaten Rangers, his favourite team, in the Scottish Cup. He said "I wouldn't believe that even if it was true."'

Vicarage Road saw the end of one of British football's greatest teams, for in a matter of weeks, St John, Yeats, Lawrence and Strong were all but finished at the club, with Peter Thompson destined to go the same way. The previous eighteen months had been a terribly traumatic time but he accepted the fact that 'if you can't make decisions as a manager, you're nothing, you should get out. We lost that game and I knew I had to start again.' He intimated just how strongly he felt about those men later on when he said 'for me, all my players were the best. They all gave me everything they had and I got as much out of them as I could. We worked for each other. We were a team.' Saying goodbye to those men was probably the most difficult job he'd had in football for Shankly was anything but thick-skinned. It was an ordeal that scarred him more deeply than many beyond his family ever realised and it required him to develop a harder edge to his personality. Certainly when the time came for Peter Thompson to move on, he faced a different Bill Shankly. 'My career really came to an end a bit

later, in 1970/71. I never got injured, went season after season
without missing games. Then I needed a cartilage op, then
another and then Steve Heighway got in the side and took
over. He was brilliant so my days were numbered. I hung on
and played in the reserves but eventually I went to Bolton. If
Shanks had a weakness, it was that when you were finished,
he'd no time for you whatsoever. When I was injured after
400-odd games for him, he'd ignore me, wouldn't speak to
me. I went to see him and he said "You're not earning your
money any more." I was really upset and I said "I've played
400 games for you, I'm injured," and he just replied "You've
had your day son, time to move on."'

Having learned that hanging on to the past was detrimental
to the club, to himself and to the individuals concerned,
Bill was cruel to be kind when it came to his dealings with
Thompson. He deliberately constructed a hard-hearted facade
to get Thompson away to another club largely out of fear of
his own emotions, emotions that had perhaps got in the way
of Liverpool's best interests a few years earlier. If he could
pretend that Thompson was merely a worn-out, disposable
asset rather than a human being, perhaps the parting of the
ways would prove to be easier. Bill had had to learn the hard
way that there were no easy answers, that the disintegration
of close-knit families always leaves an indelible mark. The
end of the 1960s side broke Bill's heart but the construction
of his next great side renewed his spirit. Eventually he was to
confess that 'the '60s team disappointed me in one sense. I
felt they should have gone on longer and that they should
have won more. I don't want the same mistakes to happen
this time.'

chapter seventeen

STARTING OVER

However you judge Liverpool in the late '60s, you are left with two possible conclusions when looking for reasons for their lack of success. It's conceivable that Bill Shankly was a hostage to his own miscalculation. Thinking that the bulk of the team would be able to play on comfortably into the new decade, it's possible that he felt he had more time to groom their successors than was the case. The alternative is that Bill couldn't let go of a team that he loved and let them play on for too long when youngsters were ready for the fray. His curious indecision over that period was, in all probability, caused by a combination of the two. He was naturally reluctant, for example, to see in Larry Lloyd a worthy heir to Ron Yeats, his great colossus. The truth was that until the decision was made, Bill would never believe that anyone could take Yeats' place. Dreading the moment of truth, he was to find that when the change came, things weren't as bad as he'd feared and that Lloyd, Lindsay, Clemence and Heighway were capable replacements. The striking feature of Bill's rebuilding plan was that he was so loath to bring in big money players unless absolutely necessary. In the preceding years as his team had faltered, he had only bought three players – Hughes, Hateley, Evans – for immediate first team service. Bill was happy to use the transfer market, and a number of new men were brought into the club, but these were low-key signings from the lower divisions. There was method in what appeared to be Shankly madness.

Bill realised that much of Liverpool's greatness stemmed from the powerful team spirit that existed at the club, an unshakeable devotion to one another and to the idea of Liverpool F.C. The propagation of such an atmosphere is a delicate task, demanding minute attention to detail, lest that fragile flower be destroyed. That first great team were united by adversity and ultimately, achievement. Most of them had been at the club when they were in the Second Division, they had come to the club with little in the way of reputation, they had been together for the best part of a decade and, having learned to cope with one another's idiosyncrasies, the personalities had eventually gelled. There were worries that by importing players for large sums of money, they might also be importing big egos that could spoil the carefully constructed fellow feeling.

The only way to maintain that aura that existed at Anfield was to build from within. This was clearly on his mind when he appointed Geoff Twentyman as Chief Scout in 1967. 'I'd had some success as a manager in Northern Ireland and then later when I came back to England, we won the Lancashire Combination Cup for the first time at Morecambe. Bill took notice of those things, he obviously thought I knew a bit about the game and he approached me to come back to Anfield as Chief Scout. In fact, the first player I recommended was Francis Lee who was at Bolton then, but Liverpool weren't involved in the market at that time.'

Shankly noted that he 'couldn't buy £100,000 players and then play them in the reserves', so he clearly had visions of his great side going on into the future. He lavished attention on the youth policy. Perhaps he did foresee a day when, having built a fabulous reserve side, he could make wholesale changes in the first team, drafting in all these new men who had learned the Liverpool style. 'The first result I wanted to know after the match was from the reserves. Get the boys into the habit of winning, it's a good habit. It doesn't matter how you win at first, but as you start getting results, you gain confidence and can change your pattern. You entertain as well as win. I didn't want them in the first team until they could do both. I want a side to bring character and excitement to their performances, this is what gives me enthusiasm and energy.'

Geoff Twentyman acknowledges Bill's preference for 'getting

them young so he could mould them into what he wanted'. Working on them in training and letting Joe Fagan and Ronnie Moran mould the side on Saturdays, it was essential that Liverpool's future be drilled in their comparatively technical style. 'Collective play, whereby we play from the back, came in more with the new team. We learned in Europe that you can't score a goal every time you get the ball, so we play in groups on the right possibly and that can leave room for others to sneak in. It's cat and mouse, waiting for an opening. It's been built up over the years. It's improvisation, using players that can adjust. To play sixty or seventy games a season, you can't run flat out. It's designed to lull and confuse the opposition and to be economical. Everyone at Liverpool does their share, they're all in the pattern. At kick-off, the main aim is to give everyone a touch as quickly as possible. If everyone's done something simple and done it right, you're off on the right foot. They can all do the basics, control and pass, control and pass, so there's no delay, which gives us more space and time. Liverpool don't encourage players to run from one half to the other or one side of the field to the other. At Liverpool you have options, two or three players willing to take the ball, somebody to help you. You're forcing the opposition to chase and change their pattern. You don't run into no man's land. Terrible waste of energy. When you've passed the ball, you've only started, you have to back up. In three passes' time, then you could be back in the game again. Improvisation is the big word.'

Tommy Docherty saw this gradual turnover in personnel as further proof of Shankly's preeminence. 'There's a saying in football, bring in your clean linen before you get rid of the dirty linen. Shanks would bring in the new faces and then, when they'd proved themselves, he'd get rid of a couple who were coming to their sell-by date. It's the way to do it because if you let players go, you're held to ransom when you want to buy replacements. He had the wonderful knack of doing it the right way. No-one ever left and slagged him or the club, they always appreciated what he'd done for them and went with his best wishes.'

Just as bringing in big names to a club has an element of risk, so too does introducing raw youngsters from the lower division, albeit of a different nature. Again, Bill adopted a system designed to ease that acclimatisation period that goes on at any new club. Geoff Twentyman remembers that 'we concentrated on Lancashire and other places nearby and we picked up Alec Lindsay and Steve Heighway. Steve had real pace, hard to play against, could skip past tackles. Bill wanted locally based lads and even fellas like Clemence and Keegan weren't from too far away. We didn't bring them from hundreds of miles away, and that helped them settle.' It also helped give the side a northern identity which in turn pleased the crowd who were happy to see lads from their own area making the grade. Phil Thompson was to be the ultimate example of that, a boy who came down from the Kop to eventually captain the club.

There's always a shortage of really good players, but Bill was adamant that Liverpool would not take short cuts to sign those who did have ability. Jack Lindsay from Carlisle had stayed in contact with Bill and 'he asked me to do a bit of scouting in this area. There was a lad lived outside Carlisle who was supposed to be brilliant so he asked me to see him. I went to his house and saw his mother, told her I wanted to see if the lad would like to sign forms for Liverpool. His father walked in and I could see he wasn't genuine. He changed the conversation – "There's a vacancy coming up outside Liverpool with my company. Could Mr. Shankly fix it for me to get the job? There's a lot of clubs after the lad." So I 'phoned Bill and he says "Can't do that, it's blackmail. The boy can go somewhere else."'

At Liverpool, his success rate improved because he had a little more money to spend and because it was easier to lure men to Anfield than it had been to bring them to Borough Park. Now, he could get the men he wanted. By scouring the lower divisions, players could come to the club cheaply and if they failed to live up to their potential, they could be shipped back out without incurring massive losses. To a man who had been raised in an environment where every penny counted, who had managed clubs in that situation, there was no reason to be profligate just because he had the means.

As with so many of his rules, much grew from his relationship with the Kop and with Liverpool generally. Bill wanted those red shirts to be filled with Liverpool players, people solely identified with the club. If, in 1970 for instance, he'd been able to buy Alan Ball, Ball would have been 'that bloke from Everton' rather than a Liverpool man. That did not fit his vision of the collective family. Essentially his relationship with the crowd was that of father and son or favourite uncle and nephew. Shankly always wanted to please them, surprise them. Suddenly putting out a team on a Saturday that included this complete unknown by the name of Kevin Keegan, for example, was like doing conjuring tricks for them on Christmas morning. As the crowd looked on in stunned amazement, Bill could stand back, take pleasure and satisfaction as he enjoyed their delight and say 'What do you think about that then?!'

There were excellent financial reasons for bringing young players along too. With the end of the 1960s team, which had had wage parity for so long, Liverpool were entering an era where they had to accept a change in their wage structure so that they could enter the market place. Bringing in established players with greater wage expectations would have shattered Liverpool's carefully laid wages framework much more quickly than they would have liked. Bill was particularly keen on maintaining equality for as long as possible because of the beneficial effects on team spirit but he knew too that he had to adapt to modern times. Gradually as Yeats and company were phased out, individual wage agreements were negotiated. Young men from lower clubs had fewer demands and so Bill had another reason to chase them.

Ray Clemence was an example of this. The story of his signing for the club says much about Liverpool's meticulous approach to the market and about his personal hold over his players. 'He watched or had me watched eleven times before he decided to sign me. He took time over the fact that I was left footed and right handed. He said later on that if I'd been left footed and left handed, he wouldn't have signed me because he felt that all-left sided goalkeepers were unbalanced! I was never aware of the interest until the last time he watched me, last game of the season at Doncaster. I saw him in the club before I got changed and had a very poor game. We lost 3-0 and I thought my chance had gone out the window. Thankfully a few weeks later, they agreed a fee and I went to see him. I was a shy eighteen year old and to actually meet the great man was something special. He took me to Melwood, 'the best training ground in the country', impressed on me how lucky I was to play for the greatest supporters in the world. He was obsessive about that. Anybody who put that shirt on had to be proud of it, had to give everything they physically could to make sure they did not cheat the fans who were prepared to give everything they could to support the team. By the time he'd said all that, any doubts went. Money didn't come into it, I just wanted to sign.'

Clemence joined Liverpool from Scunthorpe in June 1967, Alec Lindsay joined him in the reserves two years later from Bury, as did Larry Lloyd from Bristol Rovers. Clemence revelled in the new surroundings. 'I had a couple of years in the reserves, which was a great learning curve. I played the odd senior game, travelled with them in Europe and it was great to watch Tommy Lawrence as the first sweeper/keeper so I could pick up that art. Joe spoke to me about that a lot, but Shanks always wanted players with a football brain so he didn't have to show them the ABC of their job. That's why they don't do the coaching exercises that other clubs do because they get good players who play within the basic system and can improvise from there because they've got brains. The last half season, I felt I'd gone as far as I could and needed regular first team football to prove whether I was good enough, because I was an England Under-23 by then. I had a discussion with Shanks and thankfully for me, they had that poor result at Watford and he decided to play the youngsters to the end of the season. He liked people to be ambitious so my going to talk to him wasn't a problem. He'd had good reports from Joe and I think he felt I was ready anyway.'

Other youngsters had come through the Liverpool ranks, such as Phil Boersma, John McLaughlin, Doug Livermore and Brian Hall, giving Fagan control of a very impressive reserve side. Hall came to the club via a fairly circuitous route and was not the typical Shankly signing. 'I'd played for the county for three years but I'd turned down several opportunities for trials at various clubs because I just wanted to go to university. Liverpool was my first choice, probably something to do with The Beatles rather than the football, and I got a place there in 1965 reading maths. A friend wrote to Liverpool asking them to give me a trial – I didn't know anything about it until he produced a letter inviting me to Melwood. I didn't even take that seriously but I was coming back from a lecture and was persuaded that I could get a bus from the halls of residence at the top of Penny Lane over to Melwood. They signed me on as an amateur that night. Right up until I was twenty-one, playing in the reserves, I still never considered becoming a professional. We had a careers day at the university and I thought I might give it a couple of years after I'd graduated. Billy Liddell was the assistant bursar at the Student Union and I asked him if he'd any contacts at Tranmere or Chester that would offer me a contract because I never envisaged that I'd have an offer from Liverpool. A week later, Joe Fagan offered me a contract. I held on until after I'd done my exams and felt that I'd done well enough in them and then went to see Shanks and signed a contract.'

Knowing that his great side was coming to its end, Bill stepped up his observations of the reserve strength, making notes as to who had the ability and the gumption to survive at First Division level. Brian Hall's attitude to playing in the first team was precisely what he wanted. 'I got a few games as a sub in 1968/69, had a poor season the next year and had a few more appearances as sub, but it was 70/71 when we all started to come through. It was a fabulous experience, I enjoyed it because it was so unexpected. Why be worried about that?'

Hall also has some vivid memories of his first few months at the club when he was schooled in Shanklyism. 'In the summer, I worked as a bus conductor as well as doing some pre-season training. The first time I went to Anfield, I went in my uniform because I was doing a shift in the afternoon. I went in and Ronnie Yeats turned to Ian St John and said "Bloody hell, looks like we've signed Jimmy Clitheroe!" I was directed into the away dressing room where the apprentices changed and I was next to Shanks. "Hello son. Great. Aye, you're the boy from university. Tell me son, do you need a degree these days to be a clippie?" Later on, because I came from Preston, he'd talk to me about Tom Finney and the club and I never got a word in.'

The introduction of Hall and Steve Heighway was a change in Bill's policy. Wherever he had been, his stalwarts were drawn from men with similar working-class backgrounds to himself, for whom football was an escape route to a better life. Hall and Heighway were products of social change, as well as confirming the rise of the footballer in society as a result of the abolition of maximum wage strictures. While not suggesting that Brian Hall joined Liverpool for purely financial reasons, for he still wasn't earning a fortune, would many mathematics graduates have become footballers if they could earn a maximum of just £25 a week?

Understanding Hall and Heighway was a new challenge. Brian Hall admits that 'in retrospect, I think he was puzzled by me. I don't think he understood the education thing and I felt at times that he was a bit suspicious of me because I came from a very different background. I hadn't come in as a fifteen year old and perhaps I didn't always appear to him to be totally committed to football. In my second year as a professional, my game went to pieces a little bit and I couldn't understand it. I went to see the club doctor because I was lethargic. He asked what I did after training and I told him "I do what the boss tells me, I put my feet up and I rest." So he said "You've spent twenty-one years of your life using your brain. You can't just switch it off, you've got to do something to keep that active." Joe Fagan fixed me up with a part-time teaching job and I did that in the afternoons for half a season to get me going again. I always had to be doing something other than football. Whether he couldn't understand someone who wasn't 100%, twenty-four hours a day, thinking, talking football I don't know but that doesn't bother me. I knew that if I performed, I was playing. That was all that mattered.'

For the 70/71 season, wholesale changes were made as in came Clemence, Lloyd, Lindsay, McLaughlin and Hall on a regular basis. Alun Evans had begun to disappoint, finding it difficult to fit in with the training schedule to the obvious exasperation of Bob Paisley. An unfortunate incident in a nightclub where Evans sustained facial injuries further jarred his confidence and it was becoming apparent that he was not the replacement for Roger Hunt that Bill had hoped he would be. These reverses were only to be expected and Bill took them in his stride, delving into the transfer market again. In November, Bill spent £110,000 to secure the services of John Toshack from Cardiff City. Another powerful header, Toshack could lead the line well. His arrival signalled the introduction of the quicksilver Steve Heighway who had come to the club from non-league Skelmersdale. By December 1970, most of his new team was in place and the typical line-up was Clemence, Lawler, Lindsay, Smith, Lloyd, Hughes, Callaghan, McLaughlin, Heighway, Toshack, Hall. Seven new players had forced their way in.

Tommy Smith was one of the few survivors, unsurprisingly since he was still just twenty-five. Nevertheless, he had accumulated an awful lot of experience in a short career and Shankly recognised just how valuable his presence was in the dressing room. Shankly relied on Smith keeping any youthful over-exuberance in the dressing room in check. Smith for his part was Liverpool through and through and committed himself completely to the cause. As the most voluble link between the old and the new, Smith was always on hand on the field to steady the ship when necessary in tight games or to hand out a volley of condemnation if any of the youngsters weren't maintaining the highest standards.

Bill himself was never a great one for confrontation as Roy Evans concedes. 'There was no stronger character than Bill. He didn't talk to you, he made statements of fact, made his opinions known. If he wanted to give you a hard time, he'd go through somebody else. He'd talk to Bob while you were there. "He was awful today Bob, he didn't turn up." He wouldn't say it directly and in the end he'd goad you into having a go back.' Bill was harder on the new boys than he had been on the previous side, Brian Hall confessing that 'he was the hardest taskmaster I ever worked for but he placed the same demands on us that he placed on himself. Inevitably there were times when I didn't particularly like him because of that and obviously if you were left out, you weren't happy but he always had your respect. He treated you like an adult, you wore a red shirt and you had a responsibility. In any dressing room of eighteen highly charged young men, there are going to be clashes of personality, of temperament and so on. As an adult you had to deal with it and if you couldn't you wouldn't be in the dressing room very long. I can't remember a player being fined here. You went down that tunnel and it was all for one and one for all chaps. No clashes ever went on the pitch because that was how Shanks wanted it.'

Shankly knew the score as far as his new side went. He knew only too well the strain that he personally was under. He had to drum a lot of learning into these young men very quickly so that he could have a further shot at glory himself. Though he had no retirement date in mind, he was starting to realise that even he could not go on for ever. Matt Busby had recently stepped down as manager at Manchester United and that clearly had an impact on him. His requirements were now greater, though as Ray Clemence points out, 'he didn't rule by fear but by respect. We knew that whatever he said was right, just a total belief in the man. He got annoyed if people were ignoring the principles, giving away a fifteen-yard pass, because he couldn't believe that a Liverpool player couldn't pass the ball fifteen yards after training all week.' Even so, while Ronnie Moran admits that Shankly rarely savaged the team in the 1960s, by now, according to Brian Hall '90% of the time we got rollockings because he had to be like that, he had to drive us on and on and everything we did wrong, we had to be reminded of that. He rarely complimented us but that was the way he was, he wanted perfection.' The consummate psychologist, Bill was able to turn even that to his advantage as Hall remembers. 'The whole philosophy was simple, you were the best and you never questioned it. The self-belief and confidence was endemic. No-one could question you. Shanks would have his press conference outside the dressing room after the game and the press boys could hear what was said before he went out to see them. He'd come in and blast us and the press lads would take that as a cue.

"Brian Hall didn't play too well today, Bill."

"Great, what a player, what a performance." So we knew damn well he'd defend us in public.'

Bill also introduced a new face into the back-room staff in 1970 with the appointment of Tom Saunders as youth development officer. Saunders speaks with an authority and dry humour that clearly appealed to Shankly and he has gone on to make a huge, if unpublicised, contribution to the club over many years. 'I'd been involved in coaching and was manager of the Schools international team and Liverpool schoolboys. I was a headmaster at the time but the idea of working here was very appealing and coming here was one of the best decisions of my life. Mr Shankly was at the interview with Peter Robinson and he felt I'd have some problems with the industrial language used in football after teaching but I pointed out that I'd been a Company Sergeant Major during the war and was well versed in that. He didn't interfere with what I did. In this business the manager's total commitment is to the first team players so he allowed me to get on with my job.'

Saunders' appointment was a great addition to that powerful

engine room at Anfield, the Boot Room. This great institution was where so much of Liverpool's preparatory work was done and yet Shankly himself spent comparatively little time there. Tom Saunders confirms that 'Bob Paisley, Joe Fagan, Ronnie Moran, Reuben Bennett and myself would come into the Boot Room on Sunday and talk about the matches we'd been involved with but he didn't come in. He knew it was good to let us exchange ideas and to thrash it out without him there and again, he was using his men superbly well, never playing one off against another. He got the most out of that team.' The absolute loyalty and commitment of that team was never in question and their contribution to the club, individually and collectively, is legion. Ronnie Moran points out from personal experience that 'you can't do the manager's job on your own, it's a big job and it's a hard job'. Shankly's strength was to realise that, accept it and divide the responsibilities among his men. He was never insecure, never worried about any plotting behind the scenes that might take his job from him, for he knew that he could trust those five with his life.

Tactically, a lot of Liverpool's work was done in the Boot Room. Ray Clemence feels that 'Shanks was basically the motivator. Bob was tactically very good and then Shanks simplified that, got it over to us very well. Reuben was a great trainer and a character and Joe with the reserves helped me as much as anyone. He was first to pull me aside if things went wrong and boost me, say things would come right.' With a management team of five, players knew that if they had a problem, they did not have to go directly to Bill. Paisley often operated as the player's confidant during these years, a vital role, for despite Shankly's approachability, suggesting that you were unhappy to the manager had all sorts of implications even if, as Brian Hall notes, 'he was always willing to listen if you were worried about anything'. If you could talk the matter through with Bob first, a solution might become clear without bothering the boss.

Paisley had a close relationship with most of the playing staff, something which Bill encouraged for it allowed him to avoid some of the 'dirty work' that he was so uncomfortable with. If he tried not to become as close to his players this time around, he could find it hard to leave them out or read the riot act, even if Ray Clemence does point out that 'if he felt you needed cutting down, he had the vocabulary to do it!' Tom Saunders observed Shankly at close quarters. 'He impressed with his work output. He never left the place while a player was about which I thought was tremendous psychology. I'd turn up in the morning at 8.15 and Bill was often there in his track suit, positioned by the dressing room so he could watch them come in. He'd look at them very carefully and he'd say to me: "Tom, that fella's been out too late." He had a wonderful insight into the players. He'd call Bob in then because though Bill made the bullets, Bob fired them.' Brian Hall adds that 'he had a grapevine with information coming in so that he'd know if players had financial or marital problems or whatever'. When Shankly did get involved, he'd use his unique logic to put a gloss on matters so that ill feeling could not fester – 'an argument's just a heated debate' he'd say in an attempt to put the dispute firmly behind him. Tommy Smith admits that 'his logic was often stupid but it was a way of keeping you unsure of what would happen, to the point that it was enjoyable.'

Emlyn Hughes maintains, with some justification, that 'we were playing "total football" from 1970, when we learned how to win everywhere. Everyone in that side could play.' To suggest an English club side played total football four years before the Dutch national side captivated the world with their displays in the Munich World Cup is tantamount to heresy in some quarters but depending on your definition of the term, it stands up to scrutiny. Liverpool may not have been equipped with the genius of Cruyff, Neeskens, Haan or Krol, but in the domestic context, they had enough. Back in 1965, Herrera had been forced to confess that Liverpool had played continental football. Able to mould the new intake, Bill and his staff had Liverpool move further down that road. Every Liverpool player was comfortable on the ball, many could play in several different positions, Clemence was continually involved as sweeper/ keeper, Smith at the back had total command on the ball, Lawler was simply a delightful, composed player. Each man played the full ninety minutes by using his brain, even when he hadn't got the ball, Brian Hall commenting that 'you need talent, collectiveness and bite. Even the front lads would work back to channel the ball into certain areas so that the rest of us knew where it would end up.' Liverpool always had options, they had movement, they played one touch football. Only the intensity of their pressure in many games obscured this for they did not have to play the free-flowing game. If the 1974 F.A. Cup Final was not a shining example of total football, what was?

Bill explained: 'All the players got international caps by playing collectively for each other. Every player in my team has to play for the team. Not himself. We do things collectively. Specialist players in specialist positions. We didn't complicate them, they had a simple job to do. Teams need a system, they should be able to play, know what should be done. Players should be on speaking terms, not strangers. When they can do that, they have freedom to play.' Where Bill scored extra points was in finding players who could not only play but who had a special kind of hunger to accumulate trophies year in, year out. So raw were their training sessions that Ronnie Moran recalls 'when they had the big games, the six-a-sides after training, we'd sometimes have to stop them early because the tackles would be flying because nobody wanted to lose'. Tommy Smith was the inveterate hard man and winner but he also gives credit to Ian Callaghan who he says was 'one of Liverpool's greatest players ever. Dirty little so-and-so as well, but he got away with it because he was so quiet and he always apologised.' Liverpool could handle themselves on the pitch if the going got rough.

For this untested combination, 1970/71 was something of a triumph. They were unbeaten at Anfield in the League, though a lack of craft meant they drew ten of their twenty-one games. Blanket defences seemed impenetrable and the side managed a paltry 42 goals in 42 games. Nevertheless, they finished fifth and brighter finishing would have elevated them further. Understandably perhaps, the inexperienced side fared better in Cup competitions where the need for consistency was not so great. In the European Fairs Cup, they defeated Bayern Munich, Beckenbauer and all, 3-0 at Anfield in a performance reminiscent of that great victory over Inter, Alun Evans enjoying his final fling at the club with a stunning hat-trick.

The side were progressing well in the F.A. Cup too, having reached the Semi-Final and an appointment with current champions, Everton. That tie, at Old Trafford, was to be played at the end of a week in which they had to travel to Munich to defend that three-goal lead. John Roberts travelled with the party and illustrates another side of Bill's character, the compulsive worrier. 'There's no doubt Bill could be difficult but if you approached him in the right way, he would be helpful. He could be very unreasonable, stubborn, but he could be brought round by someone with real authority, he could be in awe of them. Everton were in Greece the same week to play Panathinaikos and they were due to get home a day earlier which was aggravating him before they even left. The Aer Lingus pilot came up to introduce himself and, with his broad Irish accent, Bill thought he said "hame on Friday". He exploded. "Hame on Friday? Hame on bloody Thursday!" The pilot had to stop him and say "No, Mr. Shankly, that's me name, Eamon Fereday." He was so tense, saying "Harry Catterick will be having tea in his own house" while he was in Germany. There was a heavy snowfall overnight and on the day, they had to postpone the match. Bill got the players to pack and he was ready to take them home, revelling in the fact they'd be home before Everton. Peter Robinson told him that UEFA rules said they had to stay for twenty-four hours to see if the game could be played later but Bill wouldn't have it until Peter got hold of the Secretary of UEFA on the 'phone and persuaded Bill to speak to him. He'd been adamant he was going home but after the conversation he turned round to everyone and said "Come on, we've got to stay, we've got to stay" as though the others had been trying to persuade him to go home!'

Having won their passage to the next round with a creditable 1-1 draw, Shankly turned his attention to Saturday and the battle with Everton. In the interim, he'd got wind of ill-health in the Goodison camp as Joe Royle remembers. 'We'd just been knocked out of the European Cup in midweek and we were low from that. Harry Catterick was taken ill on the 'plane and couldn't make the game. Bill knew of course and as we walked into Old Trafford, he was waiting at the door, greeting everybody. "Hello boys, how are you? Shame about midweek." Then he kept saying "Is Harry not here?" He knew he wasn't and when we told him he was ill, Bill said "They'd have to put a window in my coffin rather than miss this one."' His players obliged, coming from behind to win 2-1 and book another day out for the fans at Wembley.

Victory against Everton with such a new team was sweet, particularly as the 'School of Science' had been picking up plaudits while Liverpool had had such a relatively lean time. The 1970 Champions, built around the midfield of Harvey, Ball and Kendall, were a strong side, though one which strangely failed to follow through with more silverware and quickly broke up. In 1971 however, Everton held the balance of power on Merseyside, a problem that exercised Bill's mind as much as any. The battle between Shankly, the tracksuit manager and Harry Catterick, the great tactician was one of fascinating contrasts. Bill was often needled by Catterick's more withdrawn persona and was obsessed with getting the better of him. Even his domestic arrangements exercised Bill's feverish mind as Brian Clough explains. 'We'd just done a very good TV programme and I took Bill to Luton Airport to fly back to Liverpool while I drove home up the M1. We were leaning on a barrier at the airport waiting for his flight and Bill suddenly said, "What's getting me down tonight is that bloke Harry Catterick. He'll be sitting down in front of the TV with his slippers on and that's where we should be!"' That semi-final victory announced another shift in Merseyside's power structure, one which has never really been reversed despite Howard Kendall's success in the 1980s.

The Fairs Cup was to elude them as Leeds eked out a single goal win at Anfield to take them through. The excitement of a Cup Final in the first full season for most of the team sustained their spirits and it was with great anticipation that they approached Wembley. It was Liverpool's misfortune to encounter Arsenal on that day, a side that was one game away from the historic double of League and F.A. Cup. Just as in 1965, the pressures of the day got the better of both sides – Arsenal, understandably buckled beneath the weight of history while Liverpool, filled with so many youngsters, found the atmosphere hard to deal with. A stultifying game reached extra-time before Steve Heighway produced a moment of magic to put Liverpool ahead, but that merely tumbled Arsenal from their torpor and eventually a Charlie George goal sealed their triumph after a bizarre equaliser from Eddie Kelly. Emlyn Hughes concedes that 'Arsenal were the better side, we didn't deserve to win'. Equally frank is Ray Clemence who admits 'I froze on the day and so did a few of the other lads. I don't remember a thing about it, it was all too much for me. Most big games, I remember certain aspects of them but that one, I only remember the goals. To this day, I still don't know what happened with their equaliser and the game just came and went. I remember sitting in the dressing room afterwards thinking "Christ, I've played in a Cup Final, it might be the only one, and I don't remember it." '

The following day, Liverpool had booked the traditional open-top parade through the city. Once again, that remarkable rapport that formed that unbreakable circle around Shankly, the team and the fans came to the fore. What might have been a wake was turned into a party. Brian Hall recalls that 'I wasn't looking forward to the tour because frankly I didn't think anyone would come out. It was unbelievable. Hundreds of thousands of people greeting us and when we came back for the following season after the disappointments, that had buoyed me up. We hadn't lost really, we were a new team, we were re-emerging and they understood that.' Bill had never doubted the depth and sincerity of the response and in turn, he gave the crowd what they needed, making a simple but effective speech. 'At Wembley we lost the Cup. But you – the people – have won everything. I have always drummed it into my players that they are playing for you, the greatest public. If they did not believe it, then they will now.' Once more, Bill was brain-washing his players, instilling in them the paramount importance of the people who had lifted their spirits. The juxtaposition of that speech and the sea of faces had a powerful impact on the young men that would represent them for the next few years.

For Brian Hall, it was an unforgettable day. 'When I was a student, we got to see these limited release films and they tended to be political ones. We saw a Nazi propaganda film from the 1930s, might have been 'Triumph Of The Will', one of the finest pieces of film I've ever seen. The way they developed the theme was phenomenal. The final fifteen minutes was all about Adolf Hitler leading the National Socialist party, the Nuremberg rallies, hundreds of thousands of people. There were these fabulous sequences of this little man and the response of the crowds and you could feel the control that he had over these people. In 1971, we got onto the balcony with all the dignitaries, crowd of 300,000 there, it was staggering. They were singing, chanting, making an incredible noise. The Lord Mayor went up to the microphone but you couldn't hear a thing. Somebody else tried, somebody else tried, but it was deafening. Shanks went up to the microphone, put his arms out for quiet, that's all, and there was absolute silence. It was just like that film. Hitler was a malignant force and Shanks quite clearly wasn't, he was there for the good of the people and I'm quite convinced he believed that. The empathy he had with them was astonishing. In that context, he's the most powerful man I've ever met in my life. If he'd been a politician, he'd have been frightening.'

Hall's comparison is well made, though possibly Shankly might have preferred to be ranked with Aneurin Bevan or Billy

Graham. Nevertheless, it is entirely true that before a crowd, Bill Shankly was in his element. John Roberts points out that 'he persuaded people, they believed in him, liked him, empathised with him, felt an affinity for him. He could sway crowds with the weight of his personality.' Brian Barwick certainly concurs with those sentiments having seen this charismatic man at first hand. 'I was at Liverpool University and every month the Law Society would invite someone to speak, a barrister from a famous case or something. They invited Shankly and it was the biggest attendance they'd had. They started by mocking him, because they thought they were educated and he was this typical thick football manager. Within ten minutes, he had them eating out of his hand. He was there two and a half hours and you could hear a pin drop. It was astonishing.'

Bill's skill was that he instinctively understood the chemistry of crowds. Just as he used his own experience of the game to communicate with footballers, he used his experience of life to speak directly to working men and women. Shankly would never dress up his speeches with fancy phrases or highflown rhetoric. He spoke in everyday phrases, spoke to them rather than at them, articulated the feelings they themselves had about their city and their football team. Tom Saunders accepts that 'his ability to communicate was second to none. As a schoolmaster, I often thought what a wonderful schoolmaster he'd have been. He could paint graphic pictures with his language, there was an intensity and enthusiasm about it which you listened to. You went away and might even disagree with it later on, but he'd said it with such confidence that you hung on every word.'

It is possible to learn the art of public speaking. There are certain tools of that trade, little rules that will help you do a serviceable job. What Bill had was something entirely different, an electricity that few are destined to have. The source of it is one of the great imponderables. Was he born with the gift? Certainly his supreme self-confidence lent an assurance to everything that he said which made it sound all the more convincing, yet such confidence can often antagonise an audience. Bill was never short of enthusiasm nor intensity, yet raw passion can also act as a turn off to a crowd. Somehow, this relatively uneducated man managed to strike a winning balance that few could match. Even politicians, schooled as they are in speech making, rarely enjoyed the same warm reception that generally followed Shankly. Perhaps that was the key – sincerity. Bill Shankly never tried to pull the wool over people's eyes, wasn't trying to sell them anything, was clearly trying to give them something they wanted, honest rather than calculating.

Shankly has been called a demagogue in recent years, such was the power of his personality. In ancient times, that was not a pejorative term, for it described any popular leader and Shankly was certainly that. In more modern times, it has become a term of abuse, implying power-crazed leaders who whip up their audience's prejudices for their own ends. Bill's prejudices were broadly positive ones, a belief that Liverpool was the greatest club on earth. In stressing that, he never fell into the trap of attacking other clubs for even Everton were only insulted in the course of a sly joke. Under Shankly's rule there was rarely anything aggressive about their support.

The interesting thing about Shankly, when compared with other demagogic figures of recent times, is that he was rarely disliked even by those who opposed him. Again, perhaps this is down to the fact that Shankly's speeches were genuine, his actions were honest. The communion he shared with the Kop when Liverpool took a trophy was unaffected and, therefore, affecting. Whatever he said at the close of the season came from the heart and went directly to the hearts of his supporters. Those watching at other clubs could only wish that they had such an inspirational figure at the helm of their side. They might have the odd chuckle at his lapse into harmless extremes of language, but they certainly envied Liverpool their manager.

Brian Hall, now working in public relations for Liverpool, has had good cause to study Shankly's ability to communicate. 'As with all great people, you have to try to learn from them because you cannot emulate them. There are certain aspects of his performance that I've tried to work on in my position at the club. The change in the pitch of his voice, building up slowly to a crescendo. He'd hit people with these one-liners that he'd zap out at them, slap them in the face with, something he knew they wanted to hear. It's dead obvious, but punch it out. Use very simple philosophies, keep it simple, be practical.'

To compare footballing personalities with politicians is rather like comparing tortoises and crocodiles but it can be instructive. Margaret Thatcher was an almost exact contemporary and she too built a reputation for her oratorical skills. The clear difference between the two – other than the message itself – was in delivery. As Brian Hall suggests, Shankly employed all the tricks of the trade in his speech, the simple, big idea, changes in pitch, building to a climax. Thatcher did the same but it was readily apparent, even to her supporters, that she was acting, putting on the caring voice, moving into the strident attack and back again. Hall's comparison with Hitlerian manipulation was far closer to the truth here, for she and her advisers knew very well that she was pulling the strings, pushing the audience's buttons to elicit the right response. If you agreed with her, there was nothing wrong in that, for it was the most effective way of getting her message across to the maximum number of people as quickly as possible. If however you were not in sympathy with her beliefs, she presented a robotic spectacle, quite obviously running down a check-list of Pavlovian prompts. Insincerity was her stock in trade, her distaste for the mass of people quite tangible.

Politicians are always going to divide opinion. That after all is their job. There is however a great difference between the natural speaker, people like Bevan or Churchill, who are admired on both sides of the divide for their integrity and sincerity and those, like Thatcher and 95% of the current crop of politicians, who are manufactured for public consumption. Shankly fell into the former category for he was as natural a speaker as he was a footballer and manager. He could relate to the people in the crowd and spoke with feeling. Over time he assimilated certain tricks of the trade, but these were never allowed to interfere with his simple passion for the people. That was the secret of his hold over them, not simply the success he brought to the club.

Another factor which endeared him to the public was his genuine humility. Not for him tiresome, dishonest platitudes invoking the spirit of St Francis – though he might talk of the spirit of St John. He shared everything with the crowd. Nor did he suggest that the Liverpool way was the only way, a characteristic that persists, Ronnie Moran merely making the point that 'it works all right for us at this club'. Accused of arrogance as a manager, Shankly might have had to plead guilty because he felt that that was a useful weapon in getting results. As a man though, Sandy Kennon believes that 'I don't think Bill ever thought of himself as being anything more than just a football manager. He was proud of it, proud of his club, but I don't think he ever had any thoughts that he was anything out of the ordinary as he walked around. In his own eyes, he wasn't a legend, not big headed at all. His importance to himself was quite minimal.'

As an orator, Bill's greatest stumbling block was his natural flair. In his way, he was as tricky a speaker as Peter Thompson was a winger. He spoke without a safety net, relying on his intuitive understanding of the people to get him through. At certain events, this was to prove a liability as Brian Hall observed. 'I've seen him go too far. There were formal dinners where people thought they were laughing with him when they were really laughing at him because what he was saying wasn't meant to be funny but it was so extreme they thought it was. That would start him and then he'd really let go with the funny lines. There was one big dinner and he started banging the table. It was pre-season and it was "you are the people, we will produce teams for you and we will win" and he just went over the top and killed it.' A passionate man who was compelled to say what he felt, he didn't have the diplomat's wit to tone down when the occasion demanded it. Crowds were his forte, not select gatherings.

Having charmed the crowd once more, there was planning to be done for the year ahead. His new players had bedded in nicely for as Ray Clemence remembers, 'the big names had been supportive and there were three or four of us coming in together which helped. That first season we did well, got to the Cup Final and because of that, we had tremendous confidence. People said "you'll never do what the '60s side did", which was an extra impetus and Shanks knew that was driving us on.' After the near misses of 1970/71, Shankly knew better than anyone that his side was missing that vital spark of invention that could transform them into winners. What even he didn't realise was that the young man who would make that difference was already at the club.

chapter eighteen

SHOW OF STRENGTH

There was now little doubt that within a period of twelve months, Shankly and his staff had done what few managers have ever managed to do. They had broken up their first great team and replaced it with a side that promised every bit as much. However, with just 42 goals in 42 league games, it wasn't hard to see where Liverpool still had problems. Alun Evans' time at the club was drawing to a close but John Toshack had not as yet repaid the club's faith in making him their record signing. Continually casting around for players, in the week prior to the Cup Final, Shankly had gone back to Scunthorpe United and had bought Kevin Keegan. Bill had received progress reports on Keegan from a number of other sources. 'Andy Beattie told me about him. He'd watched him for nine months, talked about him incessantly. Peter Doherty was on about him too so we concentrated on Kevin after Andy came to work for me.' There was no mistaking his potential, though after Paisley and Fagan had run the rule over him, they felt he would be a long-term buy, looking to replace Ian Callaghan on the right-wing a couple of years down the line after a schooling process in the reserves. Bill wasn't so sure for Callaghan was to become a lynch pin in the midfield. Anyone replacing him had better be something special.

Keegan's father had been a miner and his grandfather had saved many lives during a pit disaster in 1909. These roots immediately attracted Shankly as Keegan admits. 'I can only think he related to me because I was from the same mining stock. Maybe he saw something in me that was in himself. I'm sure he went into my background because he'd try to find the key to you – who needed a kick, who needed encouragement, who he needed to say very little to. He'd come out with just a phrase, the only thing he might say to me in three or four days, and somehow it would be enough. "Hello son, how are you?" That'd be it.' His first training session came in pre-season when he trained as a reserve. 'The training was no problem. I was a fit lad, I'd always done extra training, so that was never a worry.'

Bill kept Keegan with the reserves while the first team went away to play some friendlies, but a new plan was clearly developing in his mind. As he admitted later, 'Kevin was a fantastic man. We had to simmer him down in training, he was first in everything. He was out to prove a point. Same background I had, he was a winner.' Keegan was revelling in his new surroundings. 'It was easy to settle in. He made me feel welcome from the word go, I felt he was interested in me as a person, not just as a piece of merchandise that he'd paid £33,000 for. When he talked, you listened, he just inspired you. I'm sure the things he said didn't make sense to some, but to me they always did. I hung on every word, it was precious. I wasn't in awe of him, but I respected him. On the football side of things, when you're with good players, you're a better player yourself. I'd make a good run at Scunthorpe and the ball wouldn't come to me until it was too late, if it came at all. At Liverpool, everybody could find you at the right time.'

Evidence of Bill's plan came prior to the new season. 'Kevin played in a final practice game before the season which is crucial to us and he played in the big team. They're usually hard matches but he switched it around to a big score, six or seven goals. Ian Ross couldn't tag him and he'd handled Beckenbauer before.' Arriving at Anfield at the right time, he concedes that 'Shanks was looking for a spark from some-where. On the Thursday after the practice game, he asked me did I want to play in the first team or the reserves on Saturday so I told him "I haven't come here to play in the reserves". He felt I was ready and he wanted to see if I did. Playing for the first team was just a licence to run riot I felt.' Within twelve minutes of his debut, Keegan had scored his first goal in front of the Kop.

Keegan's introduction meant subtle changes in the pattern of play. Keegan was played in a forward role alongside Toshack. The two hit it off almost immediately, forming the classic striking partnership with the diminutive Keegan feeding off Toshack's power in the air while Toshack enjoyed the extra space created by his colleague's tireless running. At Anfield, Liverpool were awesome, registering forty-eight goals and winning seventeen games. John Peel speaks for many when he says that 'as a supporter, you waited for those flashes of inspiration. The "This Is Anfield" sign must have been worth a goal start. You could see players coming out after they'd seen that, quite literally terrified. The team seemed irresistible at that stage.' Tommy Smith agrees that 'people didn't know what to expect when they came here, they'd heard stories about this strange little fella who dominated everything'. Another of Bill's favourite tricks for unbalancing the other side was to 'get the man on the door to give the opposition a box of toilet rolls on the way in, it lightened up the atmosphere for us. It didn't do much for them.'

Bill took more and more responsibility on to his own shoulders. Having enjoyed his duels with the press, he took it upon himself to extol the virtues of his players still more powerfully, helping to build up their legend throughout the land. If people read often enough that Liverpool were the greatest team in he country, they might start to believe it. Peter Robinson is convinced that 'he did think about his statements in advance. I think he'd rehearsed some of them on himself. He had a very quick wit but he did sit down beforehand and think of what he was going to do. When we played in London – and then it was a distinct London press who didn't come up here as often as they might have done – he used to put that James Cagney hat on, his chin would go out. I was always fascinated to watch him, the way he was going out to prove something to those London 'softies! There was always an extra strut to his step when we went there.'

Always a great psychologist, Bill expanded the boundaries of his role further and further, trying to make the team feel invincible. Emlyn Hughes admits in retrospect that 'some of his statements were the most ridiculous, utterly stupid things you could hear but you believed them because he did. He'd genuinely say that you couldn't get beat.' At the same time, Ray Clemence makes it clear that much of his advice was extremely practical. 'It's nigh on impossible that you'll get all eleven players in that dressing room at two o'clock before a game all feeling great. One or two will have had a sleepless night, an argument at home or something that's upset them, so they won't be 100% concentrated on the game. Shanks' greatest attribute was that he'd come in and watch how everyone was getting ready and just speak to two or three of them. You could guarantee they'd be the ones who weren't quite there. He'd know, just by looking at them, that their mind wasn't on the game – I know because it happened to me on occasion. He'd sit next to you for five minutes and by the time he'd finished with you, you could think of nothing but getting on the pitch.'

In Cup competitions, Liverpool had a very lean year, so all attention was focused on the chase for the League title. From the end of January, Liverpool hit an amazing vein of form to emerge from the pack – they registered thirteen wins and a draw from fourteen games. Defeat at the Baseball Ground in their penultimate match meant that they went to Arsenal for the final game of the season needing to win to deprive Derby County, by then sunning themselves in Majorca, of the title. Emlyn Hughes remembers 'we scored at Arsenal with five minutes to go and the ref disallowed it. I said to him "Do you realise what you've done?"' To this day, Brian Hall insists that 'we felt we did win the League but that goal was disallowed. I'll never forget that. It was a side of Shanks you rarely saw, but there was a great understanding. He did understand, he was a player. Even as a manager he was still a player. We needed a win, it was nil-nil and then we scored with five minutes to go. Fabulous, we'd won the League, unbelievable moment and then the ref disallowed it. There were senior players in tears and despite all Shanks' disappointment and frustration, when he came in the dressing room, there were no recriminations, no shouting or bawling, just an understanding of how we felt, a sympathy. He knew how players felt and he reacted. That night he was very impressive, so much warmth and sympathy from him.'

As ever, Shankly responded in the best interests of his players. On a personal level, he must have been crushed, for taking the title would have been not just the culmination of nine months' work, but of the three-year project of bringing through the new side. Bill had now endured six consecutive seasons without a trophy which was a terrible blow to his own pride. Even though it was obvious that he had succeeded in his prime objective and that his new team would surely start to carry off some prizes in the near future, the ghost of the 1960s team remained in the corridors of Anfield. To put that personal disappointment aside, to go into the dressing room, to go to each player and console them after they'd had the greatest domestic title snatched away by a hairline decision, showed him at his very best.

Later, Kevin Keegan was able to say that 'looking back, we probably weren't ready. At the end it was getting to be fairytale stuff and it had to end somewhere.' At the time, few of the players were able to be so realistic in the midst of such heartbreak. It was a credit to everyone at the club that they came back the following year in such determined mood. This time there would be no mistakes and, as Keegan points out, 'motivation was something we weren't short of'. Many individuals, many teams even have been destroyed by set-backs not nearly so severe as that which Liverpool had had to endure the previous May. Yet here they were, confident that this time they could put both hands on the Championship. This reflected great credit on the men that Bill and his staff had chosen for they were obviously men with a great strength of character, but Bill had also to take the credit for pushing them forward. His words of encouragement at Highbury had not been misplaced and had sent the players away in good heart. Not failures, they had done brilliantly in the last third of the season to get so close to winning. After that, Emlyn Hughes argues that 'he didn't have to lift us. He knew we had the makings of a good side, the club knew how to win big games, how to set about it. We learned from the '60s side and that year we started to dominate the English and European game for fifteen years.' Adversity had served only to intensify that typical Liverpool spirit and will-power still further. Bill had merely to fan those flames from here on in.

Tommy Docherty acknowledges the sheer power of Bill's personality in shaping events to his will. 'If you've a dour manager, the team play dull football. Shanks was bubbling, talking, moving and the team played that way. If anyone was fed up at training, he couldn't understand it. He'd say "Look at the people at work, down the pit, just to buy food." He thought it was an honour and a privilege that the Good Lord made you fit enough and good enough to be a footballer. It's a short life, give your best for as long as you can. That got through to the players.' Tommy Smith is in complete agreement. 'He was very infectious, got you buzzing, kept you interested in the club. Nothing else but football though. You could mention something and he'd equate it to football. You'd say something about the weather. "Aye son, good day for skidding the ball across the grass."'

Despite the loss of John Toshack for half of the season, Liverpool were a more potent force. Keegan's burgeoning confidence brought him thirteen goals, a total Toshack matched. Peter Cormack, who came in from Nottingham Forest for £110,000 because Bill felt he could play in the same kind of withdrawn role that St John had played, added eight as every regular outfield player got on the scoresheet. By now, as Kevin Keegan explains, 'we were playing the European way, we didn't have to change too much and the players were good enough to just change the pace. Shanks always wanted us to quieten the crowd away from home and then he felt we'd have a chance. First ten, don't give anything away. He'd these little rules that were right.' Bill continued to preach the collective gospel, arguing that 'players were brought up not to worry as individuals, no one player had to win the game, we'd to share the work and the worries'.

Keegan recalls 1972/73 as 'a very hard season. We were the best team but the best team doesn't always win. We struggled a bit at the end to clinch it but that memory probably helped us be more dominant in future, not wanting things to go to the end again.' Fittingly, the title was won at Anfield once more on the final Saturday of the season when they fought out a goalless draw with Leicester City. Yet this was just the precursor to an even greater night. Liverpool, by refining their style over many years, were now tailor-made to win in Europe as well as at home. Emlyn Hughes believes 'we learned how to play in Europe from the 1960s side, learning from defeat. Playing in Europe was completely different. We went and slowed it down – the continentals were better passers so we had to match that and then we took that on into the English league. After Ron Yeats, we never played with typical centre-halves and then suddenly we had Phil Thompson and myself who weren't particularly tall but could play on the ground. We took that into Europe and that was Shanks' idea, he made us into a great side.'

After an arduous programme, Liverpool had overcome Eintracht Frankfurt, AEK Athens, Dynamo Berlin, Dynamo Dresden and Tottenham for the right to meet Borussia Moenchengladbach in the two-legged UEFA Cup Final. Borussia were, like Liverpool, one of the coming sides in European football and were West German representatives at a time when that nation was especially strong. At Wembley twelve months earlier, they had destroyed England 3-1 in a match that was far more one-sided than the score suggested. On that evening, Gunter Netzer had pulled all the strings and turned in a bravura performance that left him ranked with the finest players on the continent. Netzer was the central figure in the Borussia side and Liverpool were undeniably wary of him.

Liverpool had had their opponents watched on a number

of occasions going into the final but were at the considerable disadvantage of playing the home leg first. Recognising the over-riding importance of not conceding an away goal, tactically it was a tough game to read. Not only was Netzer in his prime, but he was surrounded by a phalanx of top class international talent, men like Vogts, Bohnhof, Wimmer, Danner, Heynckes and Simonsen. For once, Shankly was caught out by some black propaganda from the other side for Borussia breezed into England promising to attack Liverpool from the outset. Paisley and Fagan had been responsible for vetting the West Germans and based on their reports and Borussia's boasts, Liverpool started the game with a surprisingly defensive formation. The game was played in torrential rain but after the opening exchanges, it was clear that the Germans had duped Shankly and were playing well within themselves, using Netzer in a sweeper role. What was also very apparent was the fact that, as Bill wrote later, 'the German defenders weren't very big and they never came out of the penalty box ... they didn't bother rushing out and none of them was brilliant in the air'. Expressing annoyance at the reports he'd had on Borussia, Bill was delighted when the game was abandoned after half an hour, to be replayed the next day.

The following morning, John Toshack, who had been left out of the side, confronted Shankly in his office. According to his autobiography, *Tosh*, the two had a blazing row in which Toshack accused Shankly of allowing Paisley and Fagan to pick the side and of being conned by the Germans' pre-match hyperbole. Storming out of the ground, Toshack went home ready to make arrangements for a transfer only to get a call from Shankly telling him to rest because he would be playing that evening. Whether Toshack would have played had it not been for the row is debatable, but surely Shankly would have picked up on the Germans' glaring weakness and adjusted accordingly. What was more impressive was the way in which he tolerated Toshack's outburst and was able to ignore what other managers would regard as insufferable insubordination.

Lesser managers would have put Toshack on the list but, as Ray Clemence says, 'Shanks showed yet again that he was big enough to realise he'd made a mistake in the team selection. He spotted their weakness in the air and put John Toshack in.'

Since only eleven can play at any one time, one Liverpool player had to be disappointed so that Toshack could take his place in the starting line-up. Here, Bill failed to cover himself in glory, handling the situation less than perfectly. In a way, this was a re-run of the omission of Ian St John, for though he knew the change had to be made, it took him all his time to bring himself to break the bad news, though at least he did so face to face this time. The recipient of this ill fortune was Brian Hall. 'From a personal point of view that was devastating. It was a tactical switch, it wasn't as if I'd been dreadful the night before. I'd been part of the first choice team and been playing well. My reaction wasn't a very adult one in fairness. From my point of view, if he'd pulled me aside at lunch time and said "Look, I've got to make a tactical change, you're on the bench", I'd have been blazing, just as angry at that moment, but I'd have had several hours to calm down, rationalise, get on the bench and think about playing well if I got on. To do it an hour before kick-off when I was charged up anyway, ready to go, wasn't very good and I snapped, I had a right go and I shouldn't have done, I should have left it to the next day and gone in and blasted him. That was what he wanted, he really did want that because he had to make difficult decisions but he always wanted to see a reaction from you, but not on the night of the match which I thought was a bit unfair. But they won 3-0 so ... '

Indeed they did win, with all three goals coming from Liverpool's aerial supremacy. However, Bill's treatment of Hall illustrates just how difficult the manager's job can be. As Shankly admitted, by 72/73 he had found a great team again. He could send them on to the park and within ten minutes, he'd know they would win. To achieve that, he needed to have hard men as well as talented ones, winners who could squeeze victory from the toughest situations. To assemble that kind of unit and then expect individuals to acquiesce quietly when they were left out of the side was too much to ask. Clearly when dealing with the UEFA Cup Final, the stakes are even greater and feelings run higher, but the fact that he had two rows in a day, one with Toshack, the other with Hall, suggests that such problems were not isolated incidents. One of the few areas in which he did fall from his lofty standards was in the treatment of players such as Hall on these occasions. Had he only thought back to his final days at Preston when he couldn't get back into the side, he would've known the emotions they were going through and might have responded to them more sympathetically. Possibly it was just that with the UEFA Cup Final to be played, he had too much on his mind to worry unduly about bruised egos, but to leave Hall out with an hour to go to kick-off was dreadful psychology. Who knows, an injury could have had a disgruntled player on within five minutes in no frame of mind to make a contribution.

While he never deliberately played men off against one another, he did make sure that he had strength in depth at the club to encourage competition. This was something that he had not paid sufficient attention to when the 1960s side had seemed indestructible. This time around, however well they were playing, he did not want to put out the same eleven week in, week out. To win the Championship in 1972/73, he used a basic squad of fourteen players with Lane and Storton also featuring on occasion. Within that fourteen though, there was a greater fluidity, such that they all played more than a dozen games. Hall was replaced by Cormack for a spell for example, challenging him to come back a better player, a challenge he rose to because he did not want to be second best. Bill was willing to take the risk that that might create unrest because he knew he and the Boot Room staff could handle it. Skilled in brinkmanship, he was seemingly able to change direction at the vital moment at will, as Brian Hall discovered. 'He'd shoot off at a tangent if you wanted to talk to him. I'd go in about my wages and it'd be "Aye son, it's the government, there's little we can do." I had a spell out of the team and I was cheesed off. We were playing Everton on Saturday and I just couldn't sit out a derby, it would have driven me crackers. On the Thursday, I told my wife I was going to ask for a transfer. Thursday night, I hardly slept thinking of all the different things he'd side-track me with, kept telling myself "I've got to keep coming back to it. If he talks about politics, I want a transfer." Friday morning, I marched down the corridor into his office. "Hello son. Sit down." "Boss, I've decided I want a transfer." He stood up and said: "You are playing tomorrow." That finished the conversation. It was the one thing I hadn't thought he'd say!' Powerful egos made for a powerful side because Bill was big enough to keep them in check, just as Revie and Clough were. Other managers were not, as clubs such as Manchester United were discovering.

With a three-goal lead in the bag and the problems with Toshack and Hall smoothed over, the second leg in West Germany looked a formality. It was far from that and for a while it looked as if it would enter the Liverpool Hall of Infamy as a catastrophic evening. Ray Clemence recalls that 'Netzer was at his best, he just ran the show and I very rarely remember us getting out of our own half in the first half'. Bill felt conditions had helped the Germans, saying 'the pitch was perfection then a thunder storm just wet it and it was like lightning. We were down 2-0 in no time. They ripped us apart but they ran themselves out.' As Liverpool trooped in at half-time, disconsolate, they met an animated Shankly who turned their heads around in the space of ten minutes. Emlyn Hughes remembers him saying ' "They've gone lads." We'd been murdered, they'd given us a helluva chasing, but he was saying "They've gone completely, no way they can score in the second half." He was spot on!' Clemence agrees, adding 'Shanks' theme then was they couldn't carry on, that we had to believe in ourselves. They had a go for another twenty minutes but never with the same intensity and you could see them losing heart.'

Losing 2-0 in Moenchengladbach, Liverpool won their first ever European trophy 3-2 on aggregate. For Shankly, it offered special fulfilment. His second side, filled with men still in their early twenties, had conquered Europe at last and had done an unprecedented double of League Championship and UEFA Cup. Bill recalled later that 'it was a great night. The UEFA Cup is as hard to win as the European Cup, extra games and against teams promising to be great. We beat a team with five great players in it.' Characteristically, his greatest joy came from the pleasure they had given their loyal support. 'We got back at one in the morning and Speke Airport was full which was the greatest thing of all. To see those thousands made it all worthwhile.'

As a gesture of gratitude to the players after their hard work, new Chairman John Smith 'came on our bus at the end of the 72/73 season and told us that we were all getting new contracts for the following year, which was a first!' recalls Brian Hall. 'We had to go in to see Shanks individually and tell him what we thought we were worth. I'd decided what I wanted, which was something like a £40 a week rise, which was a lot of money then. Then I thought "Hang on, he's always getting the better of me, if I ask for £40, he'll beat me down to £30. If I go in for £80, he might beat me down to £50 and I'm still winning." So I went in.

"Hello son. How are you? What d'you think you're worth?"

"I think an £80 a week rise boss."

"Fine son, send the next one in."

I went out with twice what I'd wanted but with steam coming out of my ears because he'd done me again! Actually, I found out recently that everyone settled around the £80 mark and that the club were going to give us £100!'

Liverpool were now installed as *the* team in England, but with such a young side, it would have been easy for them to let success go to their heads. Shankly and his team refused to allow them any such thoughts even if he did tell the press that 'we have tremendous strength in players who will go on maturing and improving for the next five or six years'. Tommy

Docherty points out that 'they believed they were only as good as their last game. They could be six points clear and Bill would say "we haven't won anything yet", to keep the players down. No-one got carried away.' Emlyn Hughes is quick to pay credit to Shankly's steadying influence on the side. 'Shanks generated the atmosphere. The fans were the most important people. The lad who opened the door for us when we drove in was more important than the superstar in the team, the women who made the tea were more important than the lad who'd scored a hat-trick the week before,' sentiments with which Kevin Keegan concurs. 'They expected men to be men. You didn't get pampered or spoiled. You wouldn't be allowed to get away with the things some players did at other clubs. The players would knock it out of you too. Tommy Smith and Ian Callaghan always kept us down. Footballer of the Year? Didn't count for much. You always thought "Look what I've got around me, aren't I lucky", not "Aren't they lucky to have me?" It was always accepted that if you left, you'd be replaced.' Old hands at the club, like Ronnie Moran, had already won plenty of medals in their time at Anfield and they had no intention of breaking the spell that existed there. 'You have to be brutal sometimes to get success. You can't pat players on the back all the while even if they've played well, but at the same time you can't keep kicking them up the backside if they're having a bad run. Shanks was the master of doing the right thing at the right time. We don't look back. We're made up when we win but we don't celebrate until the summer, then we enjoy that. But summer's a long time if you've won nothing. Nobody mentions what we did last year and if they do, they get knocked down straight away.'

Even the Yeats team had found motivation to be an elusive force after their purple patch in the mid-1960s and it does take a certain kind of intensity to come back for more year after year. Ray Clemence ruefully recalls that before the 1973/74 season 'we came back for the first day of training and Shanks had us all in together. "Thanks for last year boys. Your medals are in a box over there. Now, forget it, we start at the bottom again." He wanted men with the mental strength to do that and it is difficult to keep doing that every single year.'

Learning from the past, Bill tried to inject as much variety into life at Melwood and Anfield as he could to maintain maximum concentration and commitment from his players. Team talks were often a particular highlight according to Brian Hall. 'We had a talk about the game on Friday morning. One Friday, he had a guy come in with a box full of black puddings. He'd just won the "Best Black Pudding In The World" award. He asked Shanks if the best black puddings in the world could be photographed with the best football team in the world. So we were all there, just before a team meeting, holding black puddings with this guy in the middle, killing ourselves laughing. We went into the meeting and sat there for twenty minutes and he talked about nothing but how great black puddings are. That was it. The thing was, you didn't know if he'd done it deliberately, just to change things a little. You just never knew.'

With his impassive features, Bill was a great straightman and few were ever entirely certain whether he was saying things for comic effect or not. As Hall points out, if the players didn't know what was coming, it kept them on their toes. Even members of staff like Tom Saunders remained unsure of him. 'I'd graduated to watching the opposition on occasion. I watched Chelsea, wrote up what they did. At the meeting, he had a board marked out like a football pitch with magnets on it to show the other side. In he walked and started talking about boxing. I kept waiting for the call but then suddenly he just swept these iron pieces off the board, which made a considerable noise. He said "They can't bloody play anyway," and that was the end of the meeting. To what extent that was an act I don't know, but if it was, it was very convincing.'

He was something of an innocent abroad according to Hall. 'He was so naive for a man that had travelled the world and been involved with football and footballers. We went to Amsterdam, Denmark, West Berlin, but Shanks was still disgusted by a topless picture outside a Brussels cinema. "Disgusting boys, fancy showing that in public by Christ!" and he wouldn't stop, he'd go on and on about it. We told him to come "with us to West Berlin next time, we'll show you the real world!" He hadn't a clue at times. On that trip, we sat down to eat at our hotel and he was into freshly crushed orange juice. He called the waiter over and unfortunately his English wasn't too good. Shanks said to him "Orange juice," but the waiter wasn't sure what he wanted. So Shanks says "Orange juice, fresh orange juice," a bit louder this time. The rest of us had had a drink by then so we were laughing away at their conversation. The waiter came back with this large glass of crushed orange juice, but it was frothy on top. Shanks wolfed it down. "By Christ, that was good Bob. Son, here, another one of those." Brought him another, Shanks sunk it. Bob had sussed it, it was Bucks Fizz, but Shanks didn't realise. We couldn't shut him up, he was telling stories, getting louder and louder, more extrovert. "By Christ Bob, best orange juice I've had, ever. Son, another of these." He never worked it out!'

Though Bill had his moments, any jokes at his expense were affectionate ones for the players knew he had their best interests at heart and would do anything for them. Jack Cross, who joined the Liverpool board in 1971, recounts one example. 'We went to Sunderland for a Cup game and it was bitterly cold. We planned to stop at Skipton for a meal and on the way, the heating broke down on the bus and it was very, very cold. The directors had a rota system to make sure that there was always someone travelling with the team and I was with them on this occasion. Bill came to me and said "Mr. Cross, my lads are not coming back on this bus. As soon as we get to Sunderland, I want it sent back." Peter Robinson organised another for the return but until he had, Bill was living on his nerves, pacing up and down.'

Such an expenditure of nervous energy could only wear down even this power-house of a man but he refused to accept that his physical powers might be waning. He exercised the same techniques as he used on his players when it came to injuries as Brian Hall makes clear. 'Shanks had this mind over matter philosophy on injuries – it's only pain, switch off. Many of the injuries we picked up, we took home and we treated them ourselves. It was bruising really. Some injuries are painful but once you get out there you can get on with it. He wanted men who'd die for the cause and it worked. As a result, a few players have ended up with injuries that they'll carry for life but that was your decision. The competition was such that if you had a knock and felt like a week off, you might not get back in the side again.' Ray Clemence illustrates that Bill's lifelong hatred of injury was still going strong. 'He wouldn't speak to you. It was like putting a bell round your neck and walking round Melwood. His philosophy was that if he made injured players feel like lepers, they'd be back quicker.' Bill continued to wax lyrical about the beneficial effects of training and the work ethic. 'Work, work, work. You can get so fit you are almost immune from most injuries, like a rubber ball.' One story, possibly apocryphal, sums up his attitude. Chris Lawler had played season in season out, amassing more than 250 consecutive appearances on the way. Finally, he picked up an injury in training and on the Friday morning, was forced to tell Shankly that he couldn't play the next day. Bill turned to Bob Paisley and said, 'Bob, do you not think that boy's malingering?'

As they embarked on yet another season, Bill was approaching his 60th birthday and interviewers began to question him on how much longer he would be manager of Liverpool. Bill gave them short shrift, saying that he would be manager as long as he was healthy enough to do the job. Nevertheless, by February 1974, John Smith felt he should make a statement to the press. 'Mr. Shankly's present contract expires on 31 May but I have already spoken to him about his future. Mr. Shankly assures me that he will be delighted to stay with the club for which he has brought so much success and my sincere hope is that it will be for life. I have told Mr. Shankly that he can decide the terms of the new contract and he can decide whatever length of contract he wants.' Though Bill was tired, there was never any suggestion that he would not take up the new offer, though he put negotiations on hold to the end of the season as he absorbed himself in the important business of winning another trophy.

Even though Leeds United had opened the season with a twenty-nine match unbeaten run, Liverpool managed to stay in touch with them and as Leeds faltered following their first defeat, five successive wins for Liverpool gave them every hope of retaining their crown. Finally though, the strain of pursuing the F.A. Cup too and the resultant fixture congestion proved too much for them and they had to settle for second place, a grave disappointment after they had been dumped out of the European Cup early on by Red Star Belgrade. Another F.A. Cup Final appearance was a very nice consolation prize though, and was the fulfilment of a promise that Shankly had made when they had lost to Arsenal in 1971.

This time, Newcastle United were their opponents. Without a Cup win since 1955 and the glory days of Jackie Milburn, Newcastle were looking to another feted centre-forward to fire them to victory. Malcolm MacDonald was the kingpin of a young, but decidedly average Newcastle side. With fifteen goals in twenty-nine League games and seven in the F.A. Cup, he was the main threat to Liverpool. As Ray Clemence points out, Supermac was the difference between the two teams, though not in the way he'd anticipated. 'Malcolm MacDonald won that one. He liked the sound of his own voice at the time and spent a week telling the world what he was going to do to us. From the beginning of the week Shanks just said "let him talk and on Saturday, we'll play". The pressure built up on Newcastle and there was none on us. I think he had two shots which hit the crowd.'

At last, in their third Cup Final under Shankly, Liverpool were sufficiently relaxed to be able to play with the freedom that characterised their League form. Even so, early exchanges were tight and at half-time the scores were level. Jack Cross was told later that 'at half-time he bounced in to the dressing room and said "Well done lads. You'll win three or four-nil." He told them he'd walked round to the tunnel with Joe Harvey, the Newcastle manager, at half-time and said "Sorry Joe, your lads have gone altogether!"' The second-half witnessed a virtuoso performance from the Reds. Alec Lindsay thumped in a wonderful goal from the left only to have it disallowed, but there was no denying Liverpool on that day. They were simply relentless. Bill enjoyed the performance to the full and remembered the whole experience. 'Management's a terrible job, you could see it with Joe that day. I think he had had a few Johnnie Walker's to keep him going. We were sitting together which was unusual but it was how we felt. When we were attacking, he couldn't look, so when the ball came over the halfway line I said "Joe, you can look now, you're getting a kick." He only saw twenty seconds of the game!'

Goals from Keegan and Heighway put Liverpool in the driving seat before, in the dying moments, a sweeping movement of a dozen passes that began with Clemence and involved seven players gave Keegan a tap-in to complete the rout. Liverpool had not simply beaten Newcastle, they had wiped them out with a performance of style and panache. It was a performance calculated to strike fear into the hearts of all those watching for there was little that was typically British about it. Liverpool had, after a decade of effort, finally mastered the continental game. Newcastle were brushed aside with real contempt by a side that simply had too much for them. Yet the indelible image that has come to represent that Final was not any scenes of celebration, nor even the goals. It was a picture of a rugged Scot, sitting on the bench, painting pictures with his hands. With his side in command, Shankly was exhorting his men to keep possession, to play the passing game, to advance up the field in their relays, to demonstrate their absolute mastery of football. He was instructing them to terrify not the nominal opposition on the field, but every side in the country with pretensions towards taking the title the following year. As Shankly gestured towards his players, he was frozen for ever as the puppet master, pulling the strings as his well drilled team did his bidding. With a display that was a peak in English team football and which became a blueprint for the future, John Roberts notes simply, 'I think he was fulfilled.'

Brian Hall is proud to have been a member of that side and puts the performance in a wider context. 'I think that our domination came from the European experiences, that passing game, the control, the way really good sides get a grip. You can't just sit down and decide to play that way, it takes time to evolve. I think that Cup Final was a landmark in the evolution of that game. It was so one-sided it was a joke in the second half but that's what we were aiming for. It was marvellous to be part of that development with Shanks' team which then went on to win the European Cup with Bob Paisley. It wasn't just one team that won that trophy, it was a continual process of refinement and development. Everyone who'd been at the club since Shanks had started had played a part in winning those trophies later on and everyone at the club appreciated that.'

The end of season civic reception had almost become a routine by now, but one that they all looked forward to. Unlike 1965, this time the bus came into the city from the outskirts rather than Lime Street station, enabling yet more people to get a view of the Cup. Ness remembers that 'there were so many people, you could have walked on the hands all along the route'. Brian Hall recalls the convivial atmosphere on the bus. 'We'd had a few scoops on the way back to celebrate. I always thought there were times when Shanks was a bit dotty because he was so committed. As we were approaching the back of St. George's Hall, going through all those thousands of people chanting and waving, Shanks tapped me on the shoulder, cold sober of course.

"Son, that Chinaman. With the wee red book and the sayings."

I thought "What? He's flipped here, he's going". So I said "You mean Chairman Mao?"

"Chairman Mao. That's him. Great. Thanks son," and he went back to waving to the crowd. His first line when we got on to the balcony was "Chairman Mao has never seen a greater show of red strength than today." They went mental and I just thought "you clever so-and-so". While we'd been enjoying ourselves, Shanks had been thinking of a line that he could use on them.'

Shankly never stopped. He was the footballing equivalent of perpetual motion, always looking to the next game, the next season, worrying about his players, thinking about introducing new ones. There was never any rest for him. Yet all the work, the strain, the pressure was surely worthwhile for he was in charge of a side that promised to dominate English and European football in a way that even his beloved 1960s' side hadn't done. Liverpool's future had never looked brighter.

chapter nineteen

YOU'LL NEVER WALK ALONE

With the F.A. Cup in the Anfield trophy cabinet for another year, the red half of the city enjoyed the early months of the summer, secure in the knowledge that Liverpool were, once again, the team to beat. There was further cause for celebration in June when, in the Queen's Birthday Honours, Bill Shankly was awarded the O.B.E. for services to the game. Cards and telegrams poured in from around the world, from supporters and friends who wanted to congratulate him on recognition long overdue. Ness recalls that Bill was characteristically unselfish about the award. 'Liverpool was his life apart from his family. He was very proud when he received the O.B.E., but he said it wasn't for him, it was for the people of Liverpool and the team.'

Most of the messages inevitably wished him well for the forthcoming season, reminding him that he could emulate the feats of the 1960s by winning the League for the second time in three years with the F.A. Cup as the filling in the sandwich. When Liverpool Football Club called a press conference for 12 July, no-one was prepared for what John Smith had to say. 'It is with great regret, as chairman of the board, I have to inform you that Mr Shankly has intimated to us that he wishes to retire from league football.'

Not even the hardened press corps had expected such a revelation for they, like everyone in football, had expected Bill to die with his boots on. A man who had given every waking moment to the football club for almost fifteen years surely couldn't simply retire. Shankly's own body language betrayed what a wrench it was for him to leave the club. Looking like the condemned man who had neglected to tuck into the hearty breakfast, it was suddenly possible to see just how the strain of managing such a big club had had its effect on him. The necessary bravado was gone and the private Bill Shankly, the one known to his family and friends, remained. He finally looked like a sixty year old man as he spoke quietly about his decision to retire.

'This is not a decision that was taken quickly. It has been in my mind over the last twelve months and I feel it is time I had a rest from the game I've served for forty-three years. My wife and I both felt we wanted to have a rest and charge up my batteries again. It was the most difficult thing in the world to make a decision like this and when I went to see the Chairman to say I was retiring it was like walking to the electric chair. I was going to be burned up, frizzled up.

'When I've had a rest, there are plenty of things I feel I will still be able to do in football. I don't think it is time to talk about them. It will be part of my hobby. Whether I can live without it, I cannot answer. I can only wait and see. There is no animosity between the Chairman, the directors and me. These people kept me bartering, putting propositions in my way that possibly even Paul Getty would have taken. In the end I felt guilty, as if I was committing a crime.

'I said some time ago I would go when I got the message to go. My wife felt it was time at the end of last season. In fact she was quite hostile when I said no. I'll be here on Monday to meet the players when they report back for training. It's very sad for me to break away from football. My wife thought at one time that I wouldn't finish with the game until the coffin came in the house but I think I will have years now before the coffin comes. I'm not saying the game would kill you but being a manager is often like steering a ship through a minefield. I shall continue to live on Merseyside. We won't move from here. The Liverpool crowd have been wonderful. When a new man comes in, I will be out. It will be a complete break with Liverpool Football Club. But I'll still come to watch Liverpool and when I do, I'll want them to win. I'll probably go into the Kop.'

The initial reaction was one of stunned amazement. Brian

Barwick remembers 'when he retired, on Merseyside, it caused amazing shock waves. I had to leave work early, I couldn't get over it.' Literally every Liverpool player interviewed for this book has a similar story to tell as Ray Clemence. 'I had to hear it from two or three people and then on the radio before I believed it. We wanted him to stay, but fine, if that was what he wanted, he deserved the chance. He built the club and left it in a position to go on and on.' Tommy Docherty feels 'it was a sad day when he retired because he was Liverpool Football Club,' though even in departure, Shankly stories continued to arise as Docherty relates. 'Adidas wanted to present him with a Golden Boot in recognition of what he'd done. Bob took the call and said, "They want to know what shoe size you take."

"If it's gold, I'm a twenty-eight."'

Tom Finney joined the chorus of tributes and admitted that 'I couldn't believe he'd retired. Knowing Bill, I think he'd retire as a reaction to something on the spur of the moment and then realise what he'd done later.' That, of course, was the direction in which all thoughts turned once the surprise had begun to wear off. Why had Bill Shankly left the game so suddenly? Over the next months, there were more conspiracy theories surrounding Shankly's departure than there had been over John Kennedy's assassination. There is no definitive, incontrovertible explanation. Having discussed his decision with the people closest to him, what emerges is a portrait of a man trying to put off the inevitable but who had eventually to bow to it. The passage of time was not the only reason for his retirement. A number of other factors went into the decision, factors which made it clear that the time had come.

Bill Shankly was just short of his sixty-first birthday when he stepped down, an age when many in ordinary, humdrum jobs are already winding down, looking towards their pension and finding that their work is starting to become a little too much for them. Shankly's job was anything but routine. He was at the head of a huge organisation and, because of the way he set about the job, he was the man who made most, if not all of the key decisions. On a simple day to day level, that is an exhausting role.

In spite of all the huge self-belief, Bill was a worrier. He was constantly looking ahead, worrying about injuries to key players, planning for the following season. During his final season, he had seen both Tommy Smith and Phil Boersma walk out on the side when they were not selected for games. Though he could sympathise with their frustration later, perhaps he began to feel that, as more money and media attention crept into the game, players might be harder to discipline, another source of strain that he could do without.

He admitted to the *Liverpool Echo* that 'my attitude was when I had finished playing one game I began to prepare for the next ... when I think back now, I think I missed some of the fun out of life. Perhaps I was too dedicated. The laughs were there with the players but never away from the players. I was too serious. I lived the life of a monk and I carried it to extremes ... there is a happy medium which I should have tried to find.' Though these were reflections on his playing days, little changed when he became a manager except that the hours were longer. Such a serious existence must have ground down his resolve. He also made it clear that 'my home has always been a haven ... I'm only really comfortable there. It's what every man needs.' Having spent twenty-five years in management, perhaps he felt it was time to see a little more of that home, that he had earned the right to a little comfort. Certainly the arrival of grandchildren had an impact for he readily agreed that 'there's nothing I like more than being with my grandchildren'. He missed out on watching his own daughters grow up and had no intention of doing the same again. Retirement would give him time to enjoy his family, improving his health too.

There were external pressures too, notably the pressure of celebrity. Although he did not have to contend with quite the intense media scrutiny that today's managers and players have to deal with, he was nevertheless a very public face. In Liverpool he couldn't move without being mobbed, though this was a source of perverse pleasure as he revelled in the attentions of the fans. For the rest of the family, his fame had its price. Ness remembers that in 1973, 'when he was on *This Is Your Life*, it was the year of Jeanette's wedding. They wanted to do the programme at her wedding. They were very persuasive but I said "no way". It was her day and I didn't want it taken over.' A surprisingly private man away from the public glare, Bill was as keen as Ness that their family life should not be intruded upon and that his daughters should be allowed to live normal lives. Fame was just another worry that had to be dealt with.

Ness, who had not enjoyed the best of health at the time, felt that 'you can be fit and be tired too and he was. I asked him the year before to think about it and I think he did it for me. I didn't push him to resign. He had to make that decision himself. It must have been very, very hard for him but I'm glad he did. Even then I didn't see much of him, there was always a game to go to!' It's a perceptive observation because outwardly, Bill seemed the picture of robust health, still able to give as good as he got in the Melwood five-a-sides. It was this apparent indestructibility that lead so many to question why he could not continue.

Inwardly, the heavy workload had taken its toll. The rebuilding job that had gone on at the club from 1959 was an enormous task which he had inspired, supervised and driven on to completion. Even then, his work was not done for he had to continue to deliver trophies, unearth new players, devise new tactics. No-one would suggest that he was alone in doing this job, for with men like Paisley, Fagan, Bennett, Robinson and Moran on hand to help, the workload could be shared but it was Shankly who bore ultimate responsibility for the success or failure of his programme. With the reconstruction of the team in the early 1970s, Bill was forced to conclude that the job was becoming too tough. Ness recognised that 'building that new team made him ill. He didn't say anything but he looked shocking sometimes. It had been coming for some time when he retired. He was really tired but he wouldn't give in.' It's a view with which Brian Hall agrees. 'His persona was one of stability, determination, love of the game. It never changed, never wavered. He probably got to the point where he had to finish. You can only carry that persona, that power, that icon business for so long. He was an amazing man but to maintain that drive and determination, the will to win and the ability to come out with these quotes must have been a strain. He knew more than anyone how difficult it was to keep winning, the fine margins you were dealing in.'

Despite protestations to the contrary, football isn't really a funny old game, especially if your livelihood depends on it. Although he was a master of the one-liner, Bill was deadly serious about his work, about creating great teams. That intensity can't be maintained indefinitely. He admitted in his autobiography that 'I had been around a long time and I thought I would like to have a rest, spend more time with my family and maybe get a bit more fun out of life. Whilst you love football, it is a hard, relentless task which goes on and on like a river. There is no time for stopping and resting. So I had to say I was retiring.' There's a trace of regret in that statement to which we'll return, but essentially it illustrates a man worn out by the cares of his position.

A desire to escape the responsibilities of office was not the only reason to go. All through his life, Bill had stressed the importance of duty. He felt that each person should discharge their obligations to their community to the full and to the utmost of their ability. It was a principle from which he never deviated and he admitted that if Liverpool had been struggling, or still in transition, he would not have left the club. Having seen his boys perform so magnificently on football's greatest domestic stage in May, he might simply have felt that he could do no more. Liverpool's display that day was a peak in ensemble play, the team was going in the right direction, they had been rebuilt. He wrote later that after that Final, 'my mind was made up. If we had lost the Final I would have carried on, but I thought "Well, we've won the Cup now and maybe it's a good time to go". I knew I was going to finish.' In that sense, it was almost a spur of the moment decision, the kind that Tom Finney has alluded to. While such decisions are generally regarded as being taken in the heat of an argument, they can be made in a spirit of fulfilment, which must have been Bill's reaction to that win. Liverpool had proven themselves again and it would take a lot to improve on what they had just done.

John Roberts notes: 'I don't think there's any doubt that he was tired but he felt it wasn't the end, something would follow it. He idolised Matt Busby and thought he'd follow in his footsteps, they had great mutual fondness and respect. Bill left Liverpool in a better state than Matt left United. He'd rebuilt the team for the future whereas Manchester United in 68/69 had a lot of players who would need replacing, and he was able to recommend a better successor in Bob than Matt could with young Wilf McGuinness.' In short, Bill had done his duty by his club.

The concept of duty is slightly more complex than that though, for in duty there is often ambition. As Bill noted in his retirement statement, there had been thoughts that having done the double of League Championship and UEFA Cup in 1972/73, that would have been a good time to go. Yet look at what he had just achieved. Liverpool had taken their first European trophy, beating great sides like Moenchengladbach at their own game. Finally, after all those years of working and refining, Liverpool were ready to take on the continentals and win. By winning the League, Bill and the team had qualified for another crack at the European Cup. As one of the game's greatest romantics, one who lived for its glory, the lure of one last, great, valedictory tilt at Europe's premier trophy, one last chance to emulate Matt and Jock, was too great a temptation to resist. That dream perished early on, when Red Star Belgrade took them out at the Second Round stage.

With that gone and Leeds seemingly unassailable in the League, Bill must have begun to toy with the idea of his imminent retirement, the more so once Revie's men clinched the title. If he was a romantic at heart, he was a realist too. If he wanted to win the European Cup, he knew that first Liverpool would have to take the 1974/75 title, a distinct possibility though hardly a certainty. Thus, in the quest for the European prize, he would have to commit himself to remaining Liverpool's manager until May 1976 at least, when he would be approaching sixty-three. By then, given the experience of the 1960s, he knew that he would have to rebuild the side again. Callaghan would be thirty-four, Lawler thirty-three, Smith thirty-one, Cormack and Hall thirty, Hughes and Heighway twenty-nine. On a personal level, breaking up Yeats' team had left wounds that were hard to heal. As Jack Mindel observed, 'I think that having rebuilt the '60s side and created this new one, he wasn't looking forward to doing it again in the future.' Having tried to maintain a greater distance between himself and these players, he could not do it and the thought of having to tell these men they were surplus to requirements was not a task he relished. When you add to that the physical effort required to actually find new players, it was an awesome prospect. With his devotion to duty, he would not hand over the reins until this third team was assembled and that could conceivably take him into 1979 or beyond, by which time he would be in his late sixties. It was too much to ask.

By leaving in 1974, Bill knew that he would be bequeathing a good team to his successor, one with two or three good years left in it. With Liverpool's fortunes paramount in his mind, he knew that whoever followed him would have a comparatively easy season in which to get acclimatised to the role, though the term 'easy' cannot be comfortably applied to an English league season. With Manchester United relegated and in disarray, Leeds having a relatively old side and having lost Don Revie to the England job, Derby still in transition after Brian Clough's walkout, Liverpool's rivals could not claim to be in as healthy a state as they were themselves. It may even be that in such circumstances, Bill felt that coping with retirement offered him a bigger challenge! He noted that 'everything has its time, its era, and as friends like Busby, Mercer and

Nicholson were leaving the stage, perhaps he felt it was time for him to go too. His principles were becoming sadly anachronistic as money flowed into the game. After retiring, he told the *Liverpool Echo* 'when I hear of the money that's bandied about it makes my blood boil. There are men with tennis courts and swimming pools who haven't even got a championship medal.' He could cope with change, but that didn't mean he liked the increasing commercialism. He felt that players would be harder to control as they earned more and he admitted to some disquiet over the implications of freedom of contract which allowed players to change clubs with impunity. He could adapt, but he didn't particularly want to. It was fast becoming a different game.

Again, his duty to Liverpool helped make up his mind. For many years, the Boot Room had been the heart of the club. Bill had worked with good men who knew the game. They had helped him to success and in return he was unselfish with his own knowledge of the game. As the years went by, Shankly sought to establish an Anfield dynasty, drawing on Paisley, Fagan and Moran. With a view to his own mortality, Bill paved the way for his own demise by giving Bob Paisley the confidence to run a club. Shankly laid down principles, principles that his colleagues could understand and which they knew would work. For a reticent man like Bob, this provided a framework that he could rely upon. If he never sought the job of manager – and he actively tried to dissuade Bill from leaving, offering to simply look after the shop for six months while Bill recharged his batteries – the ideals of Shanklyism proved to him that he could do it. Sadly, the only way in which the existence of the dynasty could be proved or otherwise was for the head of state to step down and crown a replacement. It's not inconceivable that Bill wanted to see for himself whether he had achieved this aim, nor is it implausible to suggest that despite their efforts to keep him, the board weren't entirely unhappy to see this Vesuvian temperament go and be replaced with the more equable Paisley.

In the midst of his pleasure at the team's showing at

Wembley, Bill must have felt that he could take them no further and that fresh impetus might be the only way of taking them to the great European trophies on a consistent basis. He was well aware that tactically, Paisley was his equal, probably his superior. The injection of a new approach might be the final spark that his side required. Otherwise it could only come from outside and how many players were there that were better than those he already had? Once again, he was back to the spectre of rebuilding.

On a rather more controversial level comes the suggestion that he was less than happy with his own remuneration, felt that the board had been less than generous in rewarding him for his efforts at the club. In a tribute that appeared in *The Observer* the weekend after his retirement statement, Hugh McIlvanney had this to say. 'According to his own evidence [the directors] did not treat him too splendidly during his distinguished period in their service . . . he was bitter about the meagre financial rewards his accomplishments have brought him. There was no whiff of self-pity in what he said, only a sense of cruel disappointment. He spoke of how he and his wife, Nessie, had managed at last to set their two daughters up in "nice homes". It was, he made clear, perhaps the most satisfying thing he had ever done. "And we did it without any help from those people," he said grimly. "I don't need those people." It seemed poignant that a man like him should still have to feel defiantly independent, isolated in his pride.'

The key to Shankly's vitriol is not necessarily the unfair treatment which he felt he received from directors at almost every club he worked for. The roots of his discontent go far deeper than that, back to his childhood. His anger is that of the ordinary working miner whose job could disappear. His frustration is born of the inherent insecurity that has been a constant companion of the working classes since time immemorial. We've heard plenty about this in the last five years as the middle class, now termed 'the nervous class' by some commentators, have had their job security taken from them, but the press rarely agonised over it when unemployment afflicted blue collars only. Shankly had lived that life, was marked by the harsh realities and, as a result, wanted financial security for himself and his family. Setting his daughters up in their own homes was a way of insulating them from the world outside. With a house, they had security. That he had to worry about finding the money to do so, given the humble, unostentatious way in which he lived, was, he felt, an indictment of the Liverpool board. Without him, Liverpool might still have been languishing in the Second Division, yet, while not a poor man, he did not share in the riches of some of his contemporaries. His pride, as much as his bank balance, was hurt by this.

It's readily apparent that Shankly and directors rarely made ideal bedfellows from his Preston days right through to the end of his career. As the prime mover in Liverpool's revival, one would have expected Shankly to have reaped the benefits of that financially, yet he never made money an issue. So besotted with the game was he that to be in charge of the team and the playing affairs of the club was all he asked. A man from the old school who hated the idea of begging or being on the receiving end of charity, perhaps he was too proud to ask for more and felt that he should have been recognised without the need to ask. Sadly, such misunderstandings were to be rather common over the period of his retirement so it's reasonable to suggest that he and the board might also have been at cross purposes during his tenure at Anfield. In fairness to the club, Bill had to confess that they had made him a very lucrative offer to continue as manager – the Getty reference in his statement – but possibly he thought it was too late and was only offered after he had forced them into a corner.

Speaking to the *Liverpool Echo*, he noted, 'I regret Ness had to bear the brunt of my being away so much. During my time, twenty-five years as a manager, seventeen as a player, I was so single-minded. I never asked for money. I came to Liverpool to make a success of this job for the club and for this city. Maybe I didn't get enough out of it for my family. I regret I didn't give Ness more. We're still living in the same house we moved into when we came to Liverpool. But at least it's a home, not a house and I'm not looking for Buckingham Palace. And perhaps the family are all right after all. They've all got a place to live and something to eat and I've got five bonny grandchildren, all girls and every one with a Scouse accent. Now what more could a man want?' Therein lay the paradox of course, for Bill was the embodiment of Burns' line 'I wasna fou, but just had plenty'. Money genuinely was unimportant as long as he had enough to provide food and a roof over the family's head for he was blinded by the glory of the game. As his mother had told him back in Glenbuck, every day was a holiday. He was never a worldly man and so financial reward was not important, yet his highly developed sense of natural justice railed at the fact that less successful men were earning far more than he. It was a powerful, ultimately insoluble source of tension, particularly when one remembers that it is the job of all employers to get away with paying their employees as little as they possibly can. That is the nature of capitalism and there are few more capitalist industries than football.

Talk of the board brings us to the final imponderable in the equation, the changing relations between himself and the directors, notably the chairman. At the outset it should be pointed out that there is no evidence, not even a suggestion, that Shankly walked out on Liverpool following disagreements at boardroom level as he had at previous clubs. However, what is clear is that things were changing in a direction not entirely to Bill's liking. This was a component in his decision-making process.

Bill worked under four different Chairmen at Liverpool. T.V. Williams was the first, until 1964 when Sidney Reakes took over. Eric Roberts succeeded him in 1966 and reigned until John Smith's appointment in 1973. Bill had plenty of trouble at Liverpool early on, attempting to shift a defeatist approach on its axis and turn the boardroom into a dynamic environment geared towards success. It was a task almost as great as bringing about change in their playing fortunes but eventually, with the help of men like Eric Sawyer, he achieved it. It had been a long-term, on-going education process but when Eric Roberts took the chair, Bill felt that everyone was finally on the same wavelength. As John Roberts notes, 'He was happiest when Eric Roberts was Chairman and Peter Robinson the Secretary. The three of them ran the club, had clearly defined roles.' Ironically, that period embraced Liverpool's barren spell at the end of the 1960's, yet as Bill wrote 'during that period ... everything ran smoothly, everything was right'.

When touching on personal matters in his autobiography, it is as much what Shankly doesn't say as what he does that is crucial. Where Liverpool was concerned, he was still fond of the club and did not wish to do it any unnecessary harm. However, the quote above is significant. 'Everything was right' implies that there came a time when everything was not right, while Bill goes out of his way not to discuss the new Chairman. John Smith himself was a lifelong fan of the club, having watched his first game from the terraces at the age of four, so becoming Chairman was clearly a wonderful personal achievement for him. With such ties to the club, there was never any doubt that Smith would 'be more than just a titular head', according to John Roberts. Such was the case, for Grimsby Town's President Tom Wilkinson confirms that 'when John Smith took over, he brought in a policy that every director had to watch a player before Liverpool would sign him'. (Whether this had an effect on the long drawn out negotiations for Ray Kennedy's signature, completed on the day Bill retired, is open to question.) Such a policy is not one to which Bill would take kindly and smacked of waging a war that he had already won once. He'd made it crystal clear over his time at the club that he was responsible for all playing matters, without interference. This quasi-embargo on transfers in would have been a blow to his authority. It also gives further credence to the idea that Bill knew well in advance that the 1973/74 season was as far as he was willing to go. If he had been looking to stay, it's unlikely that he would have viewed this with the same equanimity. Knowing he had twelve more months at the club, he bit his tongue. The players were good enough and it's significant that Kennedy was the first major signing under Smith's chairmanship. In addition, when Liverpool went to buy twenty-year-old Ian McDonald from Workington, George Aitken, Workington's manager at the time, confirms that the transfer was handled by John Smith.

Contrast that with Emlyn Hughes' version of Liverpool in Shankly's heyday. 'Shanks did everything. He was one of the last managers who ran a club. It was his club – if you had a dispute about your wages or if you were unhappy, you went to see Shanks. You didn't think of seeing anyone else, if he said you got a rise, that was it over and done with.' The balance of power was shifting as Chairmen in general began to take back some of the power they had devolved since the war. As Smith made his presence felt, Bill no longer had the energy to break in the new man, to bend his will as he had with his predecessors. For a man who was already tired and nearing the end of his career, it was a battle too far.

Comments made for the 'Shankly Speaks' record are rather more revealing than he probably intended. 'You fight on the field to win but you've other battles to fight inside the club too, political battles. Candidly it was a shambles here when I came, not good enough for the people here. I'd fought the battles inside and outside and I was only in it to win the games for the people. I left because I was the manager when I left and that was satisfaction. I left when I had conquered Everest, I'd proved my point, there were no arguments left to win.' That line, 'I was the manager when I left', positively groans with significance. Management was his territory and he wouldn't allow anyone into it. In cinematic parlance, Bill was an auteur, a man such as Scorsese or Woody Allen. Shankly wanted to write the script, direct the film, star in it. Liverpool was his widescreen epic and he demanded absolute control over every aspect. His was the vision and he was the man to execute it. Suddenly, his vision was being corrupted by an interloper. That view is reinforced by Emlyn Hughes. 'After he left, I used to go and see him nearly every other day for a cup of tea and a chat. One day, he said "Sit down son and I'll tell you exactly what happened at Liverpool, I want to tell somebody." Just then the door went and it was his daughter and grandchildren. I never got that close again. I wouldn't have said he'd had enough of football'. Obviously then, the scales were tipped by matters beyond simple exhaustion.

The case for Smith's defence needs to be made. Peter Robinson points out that 'I still don't know why he went. John Smith and myself tried in all ways to persuade him to stay. He had on a couple of occasions in previous summers said he was going to retire. I put it down to the fact that he found summers very difficult because his life was totally football and it was boring if there wasn't a match twice a week. A couple of times he'd said that, but it just went away. When he came to us the first time that summer and said he wanted to go, we sort of ignored it hoping it would go away. He then came back and said he was going and then we tried everything. We offered him a position as General Manager, keeping an office at the ground, come in when you want, do what you want but please, please stay because the thought of Bill leaving was horrendous for us. But he was adamant, he needed to have this complete break. I thought I could persuade him and I had several conversations with him – I think he was a bit more distant from John Smith because he was quite new then as Chairman – but I couldn't change his mind.'

Shankly's reaction to Robinson's blandishments was an odd one. Given that he really wanted to rest rather than retire completely, his refusal of the General Managership, especially on such generous and relaxed terms of reference, is strange to say the least. On his own retirement, Matt Busby took the position of General Manager at Old Trafford and given Bill's regard for Matt it's surprising that he didn't choose to follow that path. Such a refusal adds weight to the assumption that there was little warmth between himself and John Smith, though the counter-argument, that Bill couldn't bear to stay so close to the club without retaining absolute control, is equally persuasive.

Bill's principles were focused on recognition rather than on financial reward. Although he had threatened to resign on a couple of previous occasions, and in the light of that Smith and Robinson were justified in their laid-back attitude to his initial announcement, Bill may well have been upset that they did not make a bigger deal of things. We return again to his fractured ego which demanded success not for himself but for his team and people, yet which simultaneously ached for people to make a fuss of him. Their apparent acceptance of Bill's decision may have upset him far more than they knew. When acting with wounded pride, Bill was never the most rational of men. A cool head in those circumstances proved elusive. Rejecting the General Manager's role might have been the result of a fit of pique, regretted instantly but from which he could not retreat.

Jack Cross was on the board at the time and relations between him and Bill were cordial, since Cross came from Workington and was a generous patron of that football club. They had mutual friends at the club, notably Billy Watson, for Bill 'always wanted to try and get Billy to come to work at Anfield'. Cross confirms that 'we were shocked when he decided to go and we spent days trying to change his mind,' but surprisingly adds that 'I think he was looking for another plane. I think if he could have moved upstairs as a director, that might have satisfied him. We bent over backwards to keep him though he was never offered a position on the board.' It's odd that one director should pick up on this yet no-one else followed through with the idea. In mitigation, Peter Robinson explains that 'I discussed a directorship with Bill but he really was not a committee man and we could not see him sat on a board of directors. We hoped he would be a consultant or a General Manager but for him to sit through board meetings was unrealistic. He didn't even do that as manager, he came in, gave his report on the team and left. He agreed, "I'll never be a director, that isn't me." ' Ness reinforces the view by saying 'I don't think he wanted to be a director. He rarely got on with directors wherever he went and he used to hate going to board meetings.'

At this stage, if Oliver Stone were making a movie of Shankly's retirement, a Machiavellian John Smith would be sitting in a dimly lit back room congratulating himself on having removed him. That's the conspiracy theorists' view and John Roberts does make the very real point that 'John Smith was becoming stronger as Chairman. I think he thought a lot of Bob and he did say that when Bill was there, it had been Bob who was in the engine room which deflected a little from Bill who had been at the helm and guided Liverpool to their position.' Perhaps Smith was pleased to have Paisley as manager for he was easier to work with in an administrative sense even though he did have his own very clear sense of direction where the football was concerned. He offered a much more relaxed working environment for the board. But Smith did make every effort to keep Bill.

Unhappily, relations between Bill and the club soured after he left and there were faults on both sides. Brian Hall believes that 'he made two mistakes. He led the team out in the Charity Shield at Wembley and then again at Billy McNeill's testimonial at Celtic on the Monday afterwards. 'He was putting himself back in the frame again, wasn't he? This huge stage at Wembley, then he went into that fabulous atmosphere at Parkhead. I'm convinced that it was back in his blood again and he didn't want to let go. That's why we had the problems with him at Melwood – if he'd just gone, there'd have been no problem, but he was back in. We were at a dinner in Glasgow the night before the McNeill game and Jock Stein got on his feet, very amicable, welcomed Liverpool, talked about Billy McNeill and then said "I'd just like to remind Liverpool that Celtic don't play friendlies." The hairs stood up on the backs of everyone's necks and Shanks got up. "Aye, right. Liverpool Football Club don't play friendlies neither." He was back on the stage, talking, winding everyone up. What was this man doing retiring?'

The problems at Melwood, which Hall refers to, were the start of the souring process. Having retired on the Friday, pre-season training was due to start on the following Monday and, in the absence of a new manager, Bill had agreed to take the session. Peter Robinson has pointed out how miserable he could become during the summer months without his beloved games. All that would have been wiped away when he walked out on to Melwood that Monday. All his energy and enthusiasm for the game flooded back and the doubts set in. Maybe if that press conference had been set for a week later, Bill might have continued as manager, though it's unlikely. Having told the world he was leaving, there was no way he could go back on that, nor could he go back on his word to Ness. He had left football and, having rejected the General Manager's job – probably the biggest misjudgment of his career – there was no way back. That day at Melwood brought home everything that he was going to miss.

Once Bob had taken on the job, he wanted to do it his way. There were no dramatic changes but he was in charge, that had to be made clear. Equally, since Joe and Ronnie had moved up a notch in the Boot Room hierarchy and Roy Evans had accepted a job on the staff, they all wanted to get down to their new tasks without interference. Bill continued to go down to Melwood to keep fit and to keep in touch with what were, to all intents and purposes, his players, but being the kind of man he was, he didn't exactly fade into the background. Instead, he presented a figure akin to Banquo's ghost, casting his shadow over the early days of Paisley's reign – his parting gift to Paisley on the day of his retirement had even been a player that Bob didn't initially want at the club, Ray Kennedy. Further contact with the players was, most felt, undermining Paisley's fragile authority.

When it was made clear that though Bill was very welcome to do some training at Melwood, it might be better if he did so in the afternoons, he was understandably upset. This was yet one more instance of the club he had built treating him badly, for it would be fair to assume that those other grievances still rankled. It would be all the more galling since he had even taken the trouble to help Liverpool find a successor, Peter Robinson recalling that 'he recommended Bob as well as a couple of others if we chose to go outside the club'.

His regular appearances at Melwood were never made out of spite or any sense of mischief. It was simply that that was where he felt he belonged during the mornings. He also wanted to stay fit and alert. As each day passed, the finality of his decision was brought home to him. Peter Robinson believes that 'within a short time he realised he'd made a mistake but he was too proud a man to say so. I think he did suffer from missing the day to day involvement. It was a terrible shame he didn't stay in some capacity. Bob had quite a traumatic period when he took over because he wasn't as well equipped for the job as Bill. In those first twelve months he could have done with Bill's help because he was never comfortable with the press side of things. He grew into it, but Bill would have been invaluable early on.' Emlyn Hughes is of a similar opinion. 'I really don't think he enjoyed retirement. I don't think he knew what to do, he went to more games than ever, all over the place.'

Part of the problem was that because Bill had given himself so completely to the service of the game, 'he didn't have too many hobbies. He kept himself fit but mentally it was harder because he didn't have things to occupy his mind.' For Shankly, it was really a no-win situation. On the one hand, it might have been best to detach himself from it altogether, break the Liverpool habit cold turkey fashion, but on the other, severing his connections with the game meant he had little else to do.

Bill was, like so many of his generation and upbringing, a victim of the rudimentary education system. Let no-one suggest that Bill was the archetypal dumb football personality beloved of tabloid stereotype. Shankly was a man of tremendous native intelligence, of impressive intellect, but who had never had that intellect developed. In a previous chapter, Brian Hall discussed how, on leaving university, his brain went into neutral once he became a footballer, leaving him lethargic. He needed to have his mind stimulated for his intellect had been properly exercised at university. Bill was very much the same, yet had had barely any education to speak of. Nevertheless, he had a powerful, agile mind and razor sharp wits. Without having had that mind stretched academically, Bill was constantly restless, hyperactive almost. In his working life, he was able to keep his brain working with the endless information that he absorbed about players, opposition teams, tactics, dealings with the board, press conferences and so on. His incredible nervous energy had an outlet in his football club. When that was closed down, he was left with a rampaging brain and no good use to which to put it. He read and re-read Burns voraciously, but intellectually, it was too late for him to find a new direction. Like Brian Hall, he was suddenly stuck in neutral.

His feelings were crystal clear: 'Retire is a terrible, silly word. They should get a new word for it. The only time you retire is when you're in a box and the flowers come out. You can't retire because your mind will get sick. If you're bored with nothing to do, then you're dead.' In such statements, he struck an exposed nerve of his own and it was for that reason that he tried to maintain links with Liverpool. Their understandable reluctance to let him interfere with training, coupled with his own distaste for retirement and his annoyance at his error over the General Managership, meant that disenchantment with his lot quickly turned to bitterness, directed at the club he built.

John Roberts spent many days with Bill in that period, working on Bill's autobiography, and knows only too well how he felt. 'There was friction. He took umbrage and a lot of people were sad that it came to that. He felt shunned and he resented it. He felt he was treated well everywhere else but that Liverpool were trying to close him out. He was trying not to sound as bitter as he was in the book but he said enough to infer how hurt he was. He didn't want to slam any doors and of course he still had a deep affection for the club so he didn't want to seem like he'd turned against it.' Included in *Shankly* was the following: 'I thought that if I was away from the pressures of Anfield for a while, and rested, it would make me fitter and rejuvenate me. I felt I could contribute more later on ... I still wanted to help Liverpool, because the club had become my life. But I wasn't given the chance.'

In retirement, there was confusion on both sides. With Peter Robinson having discussed the General Manager's role at length and having been rebuffed, the club may have felt that there was little reason to offer the post again. Yet that statement of Bill's powerfully illustrates the fact that he did not want to sever his connections with the club. He did want another role, he wanted it on his own terms, but his pride prevented him asking for the job. If he wouldn't say when he was ready to return, how could the club know? Initially, it may have been his intention to return to Robinson's proposal after a decent respite of six months or so, time spent with the family that had seen so little of him. By then though, he had become so embittered by his treatment at Melwood, there was never any possibility of him reopening the issue. It's ironic that his stubborn nature, the foundation of his success during his working life, prevented him returning to the game in retirement, all the more so since his relationship with Peter Robinson remained one of great friendship. If Bill could not speak to Peter on the matter, if he could not tell him, even off the record, what he was looking for, there was no way in which he could ever confront the Liverpool board with his requirements.

There's a sense that Bill spent his working life trapped in a cycle, doomed to repeat himself forever more. Even at Liverpool, where he was so loved, so successful, so fulfilled, his stay had to end in acrimony, as if destiny had taken a hand to lend his career a peculiar symmetry. Ultimately of course, pretty well every separation in any form of life is acrimonious simply because the parting of the ways is engineered either by mutual loathing, and if that's not the case, then usually one party doesn't necessarily want to leave, which obviously causes bitterness.

Tommy Smith was able to watch the story unfold at close quarters. 'He'd really had enough. He honestly felt that he'd become a director and his big problem was that he didn't get on with them. He associated himself with fans, players, staff but stuff the directors. He always thought they had a job to do and if they did it, fine. He didn't want to know. He retired and the club turned their back on him – not the players or the staff or fans. After that he could be very irritable, he came back to the club and made a few comments that were pulling away at the place. I always felt a bit sorry for him, he'd made a decision to retire and he should have enjoyed it. The directors possibly were in the wrong as well for not giving him some recognition. If he'd maybe followed in Matt's footsteps, he'd have been happy. He created this path which he was going down and he couldn't change and there was a conflict which nobody wanted but it was always on the cards. There was nothing wrong with the situation except that it wasn't right. Maybe if he'd been a consultant or something, but he cut the cord which was wrong, a mistake by him and the board. Later, he couldn't and wouldn't connive to force people into giving him his way. If they didn't want to make him a director, forget it.'

The idea that Bill wanted to follow in Matt Busby's footsteps on to the Liverpool board is one that simply will not go away, despite Peter Robinson's protestations to the contrary. Jack Mindel for instance is convinced that 'he thought they should have treated him as he deserved without him having to ask for it, he thought they should have known. Bob tried to patch it up but Bill felt if he couldn't get the recognition, he wouldn't go looking for it. I think it was his biggest disappointment. He didn't like some directors. He was outspoken but he knew that the club was more important than he was, which was why when he retired he didn't have it out with them. He bottled it up and took it very badly. As time went on, because of that he seemed to become more secluded, less involved. People tried to involve him with one thing or another, but they couldn't. Probably he felt it was too late.'

That bitterness rumbled on and on, a tragic end to such an illustrious association. There is little doubt that in spite of Bill's own errors and avowed intentions on this subject, he should have been made a director, non-executive if necessary, and been presented with the role as a *fait accompli*. There would have been no need for him to attend the board meetings if he didn't wish to, but he would have had the right kind of status within the club and within the game. He would have been a PR man par excellence for the club, and it would have given him a purpose in retirement. It is here that the club did most damage to their enviable reputation for they let down the man who had never disappointed his club.

There are reasons for the board's reluctance to make such an appointment. Tommy Smith's assessment is very direct. 'It was always obvious to us that they had no intentions of putting him on the board. He'd given 'em so much stick, he ran the club, he'd threatened to go over Johnny Morrissey and then again a few times later, and they had to take a back seat. They didn't like not being in the limelight but he took it all. It never occurred to them to make him a director. I don't think it was a set plan to get back at him or anything, it just happened. It was an accumulation of mistakes. He was an employee, he retired, thanks, goodbye. They didn't realise maybe that he was a god on Merseyside because they didn't mix with the fans and they were a little bit stupid in their assessment of how much of a god he was. Once the time had gone, they couldn't go back to him a year later and ask him again because he'd have told them to stick it. It was a hobby to them, but it was his life. Some directors are on a different planet. They were proud to be associated with Liverpool F.C. but knew nothing about running a club. Shanks would tell them that and they resented it.'

There is a great deal in that that rings true as John Roberts agrees. 'He was single-minded and anyone like that creates ripples. He could be very rude to directors because he was so wrapped up in what he was doing and he felt they shouldn't interfere. Possibly there was some jealousy among the directors about his success, the fact that he and the club were synonymous. Football had started to develop the personality cult. Pre-war, clubs didn't have managers in a lot of cases and the directors ruled the roost. Apart from Herbert Chapman, it wasn't until Matt and the Busby Babes that managers became as well known as their club. The fans identify with some of them and a lot of directors feel jealous that they aren't recognised – it's understandable because there are a lot of good people who put a lot of time and, sometimes, money into the club. Being a director is an exciting way to advance your own image and local reputation. It's more exciting to say "I'm a director of Liverpool" than it is to say "I own a food processing factory" or "I'm a butcher". There is egotism in the boardroom.'

If Roberts is right, and there's no reason why he shouldn't be, few directors would have their egos fed while Bill was in charge for his legend loomed large over the whole club. It's unlikely that after all the trials he had put them through as manager that they would be especially keen to sit down with him in board meetings, for they would wonder whether or not he might take those over too. One of the great contradictions which Bill wrestled with as manager is one which he shares with the vast majority of traditional supporters. Like the fans, he liked the directors' money but had no time for them at the club. After a decade of scrimping and saving amongst the small-fry of the Football League, he was very happy to arrive at a club willing to spend some money. His problem was that it was always someone else's money he was spending, money provided by directors who, in general, he resented after many painful experiences with their number.

Where Shankly was unique was in devising a workable solution to the problem, evolving a set-up where he could live with the contradictions. By virtue of his overwhelming personality, he became the club. He took Liverpool away from the directors. Bill Shankly was the personification of Liverpool Football Club, the two were synonymous. The men who gave him the money to buy Milne, Yeats, St John, Keegan, Hughes et al got no credit because Bill represented the club so completely it was as if he was spending his own money. His persona was so enormous that it dwarfed all else and you just couldn't see the directors fighting to get a little of the spotlight out on the fringes. That was how he and the fans liked it, for by becoming the club, such was the identification between the two, he gave the club back to the people. That way, the knowledge that he was spending money earned by exploitative business seemed somehow more palatable.

The closest current parallel is, unsurprisingly, Kevin Keegan at Newcastle United. Keegan admits that 'no-one will ever have a relationship like he had with the fans, I just don't know how he did it. He didn't try to fool 'em, didn't try to deceive 'em, he was totally honest and upfront with them, something I've taken with me. The fans want to know what's happening – when I sold Andy Cole to Manchester United, I felt that they had a right to know why and so I talked to them. That's what Shanks would've done I think. I just thought he had everything in control, he never made mistakes, he just had it.' It may be a misrepresentation of what Keegan is doing at Newcastle but it appears that he too is striving to give the club back to the people, despite the fact that it's Sir John Hall's millions which are funding the Tyneside resurgence. It's only three years since Keegan threatened to walk out on the club if things were not run to his liking, a move of which Shankly would have approved. Like Shankly before him, Keegan is willing to take Hall's money, knowing that by spending it wisely on the likes of Shearer, Beardsley, Ginola and Ferdinand, he can keep his supporters happy. He can do so in the knowledge that as a footballing icon, he dwarfs Hall in terms of media coverage – it may not be entirely coincidental that Sir John has turned his attention to Rugby Union of late to maintain his profile. The Newcastle supporters like Hall's money, but they love their manager and so the owner of the club is now trapped. Keegan is fireproof, just as Shankly was at Liverpool.

Depending on one's opinion, men like Hall or Jack Walker at Blackburn Rovers are either community-spirited altruists or ideologically unsound egomaniacs looking to get their name in the paper at every opportunity or to boost their own dubious agenda through the publicity. If the latter is the case, Walker has been infinitely more successful. He is Blackburn Rovers, largely because his managers, Kenny Dalglish and now Ray Harford, have no media profile. They do not detract from the owner of the club. Sir John Hall has to live in the shadow of Kevin Keegan, the most famous English footballer of the era that separated Bobby Moore's World Cup win and Gazza's tears. Inspired by his mentor, Keegan has done for the people of Newcastle precisely what Shankly did for the denizens of Liverpool and returned the club to them.

Football has never truly been 'the people's game' as it has been regularly described. It is the game that the people chose to play and watch in the greatest numbers, but it has never really belonged to them. That has never been more blatantly apparent than it is today; Molineux is the seat of Sir Jack Hayward, the footballing Lord of Wolverhampton, David Sullivan the King of St. Andrews. The ambitions of these very rich and powerful men may be entirely benign – Jack Walker apparently has no greater ambition than to see Blackburn Rovers win and continue winning. He has sunk a fortune into that club. While the people of Blackburn were doubtless thrilled at being able to watch Alan Shearer week after week, their club has little or nothing to do with them any more. For all Dalglish's craft and Shearer's brilliance, Walker won the League. Blackburn Rovers, like every club that wants to compete in the Premiership, are a business, not the focal point of the local community. This may not have been the intention, but it is the outcome. It has happened to Liverpool too – around half of their season tickets go out to people living more than fifty miles away, suggesting that the Liverpudlians are losing out or choose to opt out, unthinkable twenty years ago.

To a lesser extent however, this has always been so – Preston North End remained in the safe keeping of Chairman James Taylor for decades. Though the financial investment was rather less extensive, he still kept the fans at arm's length. They had little or no say in the running of their home town club. Where they had greater leverage than the supporters, or should that be consumers, of today was in the fact that their support was important. Loss of revenue at the turnstiles in the 1930s was a very serious matter since that was where much of a club's cash came from. If Arsenal's crowds were to drop this season, it would probably offer them an excellent excuse to slot in another executive box at the expense of ordinary seating. With money now coming into clubs from every angle, the gate revenue is less and less important. If they don't need that, they don't need the supporters, so why should they care what they think?

A club supporter's lot is generally one of anger, misery, depression, sometimes lightened by ninety minutes on a Saturday afternoon; *Fever Pitch* and *When Saturday Comes* sum it all up. Fans are forced to support their team through deep-seated allegiance, geographic or family ties; there is no way out. They might wish they didn't support Birmingham City or Luton Town but they're stuck with it, scarred for life. Fans are accused of being fickle when they sing 'Sack the board', yet those supporters might have been going to the club for thirty, forty, fifty years without the merest whiff of a trophy while the owners might have been in place a couple of years with no previous connection to the club and might have things other than the best interests of the club in mind – the saintly Robert Maxwell for example. Bill Shankly understood that. Such knowledge was subversive, powerful and dangerous.

Ironically, it was the aftermath of Matt Busby's elevation to the boardroom which contributed to keeping Bill from assuming the same mantle at Liverpool. John Roberts points out that their 'reasoning was that you couldn't give someone like Bill a place on the board because he's not going to sit there as a nominal figure, he'd still want to run things. I'm sure they felt it could have been disruptive. He wanted the recognition and he deserved it and they should have given him his due and that hurt him. He reacted angrily. At United, Matt supposedly never interfered but his presence was inhibiting to those who followed him and so Liverpool used that as a precedent.' Brian Barwick makes a similar point. 'When he retired, the club were in an awkward position. Powerful men usually die in office, they don't give up the position and the club didn't know what to do with him. He could have become a problem for them. For them it was survival, to avoid the Manchester United trap. To them, he was just a paid employee when all's said and done.' It was also Bill's ill fortune that 'the Manchester United trap', as Barwick terms it, had, that very season, turned into a trap-door, consigning them to the Second Division for the first time since 1938. It was a potent symbol.

If we look at things totally dispassionately for a moment, one has to say that Liverpool were right in their actions – twenty-three major trophies in twenty-one seasons since Bill called it a day. But if you look at football totally dispassionately, it isn't football any longer. If in retirement Bill could be his own worst enemy, Liverpool should have been above it all and given the man his due. In his autobiography, Bill wrote plaintively that 'it would have been a wonderful honour to have been made a director of Liverpool Football Club but I don't go round saying "I would like to be this and that". That's begging – and I'm not a beggar! No, no – anything I have done and everything I have got, I have worked for.' For a man hidebound by his own pride to say such a thing, even in anger, was painful and, despite some quite vitriolic attacks on the club, it is to the club's shame that they did not then seize the nettle and bring the bitterness to an end by making the appointment.

Shankly had, in his own mind, become something of a prophet without honour. John Roberts makes the point that 'although I was delighted to see the Shankly Gates put up, I think people would have loved to see him walk through them. Matt received his recognition at United in his time – Matt Busby Way, the suite, made President – and I felt that Bill didn't receive his honours in his own time, recognition that goes beyond your immediate presence in the game.' That is the key because Bill Shankly wanted respect and recognition for a job well done. Typically, he believed that the lack of recognition was not merely slighting him, but the supporters for he was their representative. It struck him as odd that he received due reward from his country in the form of his O.B.E., yet got nothing from the club he revived. He took solace from the crowd which still roared its approval whenever he took his seat, while he even received a standing ovation at Goodison Park on the opening day of the 1974/75 season – he joked that they were simply relieved that he couldn't take any more points from them, but in truth, he was moved by the warmth of the reception. He returned to Workington in August 1980 to open their Shankly Lounge, so named after a poll of supporters which proved almost unanimous and significantly, he admitted that 'this means more to me than winning cups'.

Kevin Keegan was particularly upset with the treatment Bill received from Liverpool but he also offers what would perhaps have been the best possible solution, appeasing Shankly by giving him the respect he craved while allowing the club to gracefully dispense with his services and create the breathing space which Bob Paisley needed. 'That was the saddest part, after he left. It's where my argument with the club lay, no particular person, but the club in general. They named a set of gates after him but I think Liverpool should be playing in the Shankly Stadium, I think the fans would accept that. He started it off, that stadium wouldn't be what it is now if it wasn't for Bill Shankly. They might still be a club with no direction as they were when he joined. The gates are not enough, nowhere near enough and the club know that.' Is it too late to put that right?

As time passed, Bill certainly felt that he was being deliberately ostracised by the club. Bob Paisley has made it clear that tickets were always available but perhaps Bill was looking for more. Instead of being just the recipient of another complimentary, he needed to feel wanted by the club and this arrangement did not fulfil that need. Away games became a particular bugbear. 'I would have loved to have been invited to away matches, but I waited and waited until I became tired of waiting. Finally after twenty months ... I was invited to travel with the club to Bruges for the second leg of the UEFA Cup Final. I accepted because I didn't want anybody to think I was petty but it came too late for my peace of mind ... I was put into a different hotel to the one used by the official party. I found that quite insulting.' It was not an isolated occurrence either for John Peel 'went to Paris for the European Cup Final in 1981 and we were on the same plane as Shankly and the board and wives and girlfriends and they seemed to be blanking him out quite consciously. It is in the nature of clubs, insensitivity seems to be their stock in trade.'

Relations remained strained and Bill's agitation with the club increased. Billy O'Donnell often saw Bill at Anfield. 'My grandson was an apprentice at the club and he got complimentaries for the grandstand. Where I sat, Shankly was in front and I've seen Liverpool score and the whole place get up bar him. I felt like saying "Come on Bill, you made all this." ' Ray Wilson feels that 'what would make retirement worse for Bill is that the club rumbled on without him. He was quite naive in that sense and I feel that he'd think the club would stumble. That's not being arrogant or selfish, but he'd just assume that and in a sense, he'd be disappointed when they didn't. The biggest tribute to him is that they could carry on but I'm not sure he saw it that way. I think it broke his heart.' It has to be accepted that a breakdown in communications rather any malevolence on either side had much to do with the strained relations between Shankly and the club, but he would not have been human had he not felt a twinge of jealousy at Liverpool's galloping success.

It is in the nature of competitors – good ones – to be jealous and if that's a deadly sin, good competitors are going straight to hell. By definition, they want what someone else has. Bill Shankly was always fiercely competitive and that is fired by jealousy. 'I want his Preston shirt', 'I want his Scotland shirt', 'I want to take the F.A. Cup from them'. That is what professional sport is about. To see Liverpool going from strength to strength must have created some very mixed feelings. When they captured the European Cup, he was delighted for the players, the staff, the fans but to see someone else taking the glory after all the work he put in to get Liverpool into a position where they could win these trophies would be galling. Paisley was magnanimous in victory, suggesting that he had done little more than put the roof on the house that Shankly built and Bill appreciated that, but as Gore Vidal pointed out 'whenever a friend succeeds, a little something in me dies'. The film footage of Liverpool showing the European Cup to the city in 1977 contrasts vividly with that of three years earlier and Bill's famous 'Chairman Mao' speech. From being the centre of things, he has been relegated to the sidelines. On the extreme edge of the balcony, he looks for all the world like the father of the bride, pleased to see his child grown up and happy, but sad to see her go, realising that his role as the centre of his daughter's universe is over and that he is now merely a well-loved but ultimately irrelevant observer.

He had confirmation of the city's feelings for him in 1975 when Anfield hosted his testimonial in front of a packed house. It was a very emotional night for him, one which vindicated him totally and proved to him that all the sacrifices had been worthwhile. Just as he was fulfilled as a manager at Wembley in '74, so he was as a man on this unforgettable evening. Speaking to the crowd, he said 'I thank these people for their loyalty to me during my years at Liverpool – the greatest part of my whole life. No man can ever feel more proud, no man can feel more grateful and no man could have more friends than me. This means more to me than anything else. God bless you.' Belying the hopelessly inaccurate caricature of the hardnosed, belligerent Scot, Bill spoke emotionally to the *Liverpool Echo* after the game. 'They all have my thanks for contributing so much to make this into what was, quite simply, the greatest thing that has happened to me in all my life ... what affected me most of all, what meant most was that they still came to support me after I had been away from them for months. I'll admit I was near to tears when I walked round the ground before the match. I felt I was walking almost in a dream as I looked at those faces, heard their applause and felt their waves of affection sweeping out of stands and terraces to envelop me. After the game, under the main stand at Anfield, I met three men from the Kop dressed in white overalls with red lettering. On behalf of the Kop they presented me with a magnificent plaque entitled "The Road To Glory" ... a complete record of my fifteen years at Anfield ... I also received a silver tankard engraved "To Shanks, with thanks, A Fan". When I was going round the ground a teenager came out of the Kop and presented me with a greetings card more than two feet square. They had made it themselves ... more than a thousand signatures on the card in red ... I'll treasure these presents for the rest of my life because they come from people who mean everything to me.'

It's a shame that this chapter is so dominated by rancour, for it suggests that Bill's retirement resembled one of Bergman's dourer epics. This was not the case for he derived great satisfaction from the period, not least in spending time with the family and working with the Liverpool Society for the Blind. Yet Bill was still a fit man and the lure of the game remained strong. If Liverpool didn't require his services, there were plenty of clubs that did, though even that presented a bone of contention as John Roberts explains. 'We were working on the book and the phone would go. He'd answer it and come back with a Rothman's Yearbook and say "Jesus Christ, I'm running every club in the country", because another manager had been on to him for advice. At Liverpool, I think they thought he was helping other managers just to combat them, to get back at them. When there's a hiatus like that, all sorts of resentments and problems evolve from it. You're always wondering about the other person's motives. When it's a close family and someone goes away, no-one's ever happy, suspicion grows from a lack of communication.'

In December 1976, for instance, Derby County approached him to be General Manager, to work with Colin Murphy. It took him a month before he finally decided to turn it down. There was a spell advising Wrexham, and further offers from

Bristol City and Blackpool among others. As Ness says, 'He found football. He'd go to Ireland or Scotland. He never sat down and when he was asleep I'm dashed sure he was still thinking about it because he used to jump. I always thought, "Well, he's got another goal!" When he did finish, he still had plenty to do. He had his own chat show on Radio City, he'd go over to see Matt or to John King at Tranmere and talk to John Toshack about Swansea.'

Those two were probably the greatest benefactors from Shankly's retirement for he spent a great deal of time with them. His association with John King dated back to his days as Liverpool's manager. 'I had a testimonial game and was struggling to get a team good enough to pull people in. Bill must have got wind of that and said he'd send his full first team over, the Cup winning side. He appreciated anyone that worked for the game – I was never a great player but I captained all my sides, bar Everton, and worked hard. Later on, Ronnie Yeats came to Tranmere as manager and soon after I became his assistant. Ronnie wanted advice, Bill had just finished at Liverpool and for a couple of years, I had him watching me doing the coaching, just monitoring things. He didn't criticise, he must have thought I was okay. Ronnie got the sack in 1975 and I got the job. Rather than disappear, Bill stayed with me for a while and it was wonderful to learn from a man like that. While he was watching me, I was watching him, picking up on his little sayings. They've got me out of trouble time and again, things like "never make a decision until you have to, because often they're made for you". Many times since then I've sat and thought of the things he set out and he was never far off, he knew the game inside out.'

Bill clearly had recharged his batteries during his year out of the game for in 1975, King recalls that 'he'd been on the phone to me two or three times a day and I wasn't sure why. Then he phoned me at eleven one evening. "I've been asked who's the best young manager in the game and my finger stops at you, son. Go and have a look at Sheffield Wednesday." I went there a couple of times, had an interview and virtually got the job. I said to him "I don't think it's for me." "Jesus Christ son, they might be like a rocket that's bound for the moon and nobody to fly it." They were in the Third Division, they weren't going to give me any money and I had a team at Tranmere that was going to get me promotion. Len Ashurst took the Sheffield job and had a nervous breakdown as a result. Going there, I'd only been in management five months, taking on such a big club was too much. I still think that he wanted me to take it so that he could work alongside me.'

In between visits to Tranmere, Bill continued to play the game that so delighted him. John Roberts 'went to see him in an afternoon when we were doing the book. He'd be in his tracksuit and I'd ask him how he was. "I've got a bit of a strain, but I'll be OK for Friday." He was playing in a little indoor five-a-side thing but to him, he was still a player and he'd talk about this injury as if he was turning out against Arsenal.' Refusing to return to Melwood to train in the morning, he often turned up at Everton's Bellefield ground where he would occasionally meet up with Joe Royle. 'He used to come to Bellefield for a sauna and I still trained here now and again though I was playing for Bristol City. He asked me if I was fit – I said "Yes, cross-country on Monday, squash all day Tuesday" and he started shaking his head. "The best snooker player doesn't swim for practice."' Howard Kendall positively encouraged such visits when he took over as manager at Everton in 1981. 'He'd pop in for a cup of tea. I think he felt awkward at Melwood but we loved seeing him. He'd say "First thing you do each morning is put your tracksuit on," he knew how you could get bogged down in the office and that the important thing was to get among the players. Great advice. It was wonderful to just sit there and listen to him talk about the game.'

Still, it was Tranmere who got the benefit of most of his wisdom, and wisdom it was for John King. 'Everything he did was simple. I was taking a coaching badge so he said "You've forgotten more than they'll ever know. Don't get tangled up with them people." He's right. They don't know what makes players tick, what makes them play. We were playing in London, travelling by rail the day before the game. He said "Have you got the tablets, son?"

"The tablets, Mr Shankly?"

"Sleeping tablets."

"No, we don't have them. We have a job waking the lads up."

"You must get them, son, relaxes the players the night before, lets them sleep." Soon after, we were on the tablets.'

There are few more enthusiastic characters in the game than John King and the two forged a strong bond of friendship. It was Bill's compassion that helped him relaunch his career after he was sacked by Tranmere in 1980. 'I was out for nearly twelve months which was too long. It was Shanks who told me to take the offer I'd had from Northwich Victoria. "Don't get rusty son. Take it and make them the best team in the land." We went to Wembley twice in three years and I really enjoyed it.' Back at Tranmere, King has assembled an attractive side that, against all the odds, could soon be gracing the Premiership.

Although Bill was of pensionable age, it would have been hard to find anyone of his age in better physical condition in 1981. It came as a traumatic shock when in September of that year, Bill suffered a heart attack. He was swiftly admitted to Broadgreen Hospital where he finally succumbed to a second attack on 29 September. Billy Watson remembers his numb, uncomprehending reaction to the news. 'I said "no, Bill can't die."' He had seemed such a tough, indestructible figure that no-one was prepared for the loss. It was a loss that didn't merely envelop football, it seemed to touch the whole country. The Labour Party, whose conference was taking place at the time, rose in silent tribute to him. In Liverpool flags flew at half mast. Thousands upon thousands felt the loss as keenly as that of a member of the family. Bill would have been proud of that response.

The great and the good flocked to attend Bill's funeral. Billy Watson was Workington's representative and was moved by the show of emotion across the city. 'They were lining the streets, it was like royalty. A fella has to be above something to get that kind of response. It was an honour to be there,' sentiments shared by John King. 'I officiated at his funeral and in a funny way, it gave me such pleasure. He was like a second dad. It was a proud day for me.' Canon Arnold Myers summed up the mood in his address. 'Bill Shankly did not live for himself but for a team, a vast family, for a city, for an ideal.'

It was somehow fitting that the first game Liverpool played after his death was against Swansea City, managed by John Toshack. On the Kop a banner was unfurled which read 'Shankly Lives Forever'. In the aftermath of his death, Liverpool decided to erect the Shankly Gates, Ness insisting that Bill should have a memorial that was visible from outside the ground so that the supporters who adored him could visit it any time they chose. The final tribute came in Liverpool's Anglican Cathedral where 1,400 people gathered to give thanks for his life and hear tributes from Tom Finney, Bob Paisley and Kevin Keegan. During the service, Gerry Marsden led the congregation in 'You'll Never Walk Alone'.

With the mourning over, life carried on but football was immeasurably the poorer for the loss of one of its few genuinely remarkable, special men. But Bill Shankly was not simply a great footballing man. He was a great man per se. What is the game's loss compared with that of Bill's family? Ness Shankly: 'I had seven years with him. He should have retired earlier but it was his love for the game. He might have died after a couple of years if he'd retired sooner because he would still have been too active, he'd have had nothing to do. It was a good life. We were very happy. It would have been nice to have had a little longer with him.'

chapter twenty

AND IN THE END ...

Though Bill Shankly's death in September 1981 was tragically premature, it was also symbolic for it brought down the curtain on an era, not just in football but in British society. This staunch advocate of the working classes passed away at a time when the very people he represented were being systematically attacked, divided and conquered by the Thatcherite greed creed. Liverpool was as badly hit by the monetarist squeeze as any area in the country. Unemployment soared, inner city deprivation, a problem for a decade or more, worsened yet further, the whole culminating in the Toxteth riots of the summer of 1981. The spirit of community which Bill so carefully nurtured in Liverpool, was fractured perhaps irreparably.

The Prime Minister made the point later that 'there is no such thing as Society. There are individual men and women and there are families,' a view diametrically opposed to everything Shankly stood for. It was the community that had built Liverpool Football Club and made it special. That was society at work for the common good. Market economics held sway however and as Thatcherism took an ever firmer grip on the nation's consciousness, more and more people came to the conclusion that it was every man for himself. Those that succeeded suddenly felt the need to deny their roots while those that were left behind were left to fall further and further adrift. The values that Shankly stood for were no longer current and no longer appreciated.

John King suggested that 'they do say he could have been a very good politician, he was always talking about politics. If he wanted to do something, he'd do it.' Bill didn't have the education to handle the political forum but it's ironic that he never took up the political cudgels for like Thatcher, he was a great teacher. He also had the same absolute certainty about right and wrong that she had, but his ideals were profoundly different. Bill pretended to have little interest in the world beyond Anfield, yet he was well versed in current affairs. His general refusal to discuss politics came from his deeply held conviction that there was nothing to discuss. His principles were so fundamental to his life and the way he conducted himself that he could see no possible decently held counter-argument.

Shankly's absence has been keenly felt among supporters. He spoke to the fans about football, but he was also talking to them about life, teaching the youngsters about decency, honesty, responsibility. At a time when society and the family were starting to fragment, Shankly was a wise teacher who gave them a set of values. The youngsters were important to him as he told the *Echo*. 'If I can help a kid along I will. They're heartbroken if you snub them and that I will never do. There were always kids knocking around Anfield when I was there. They're the future Liverpool supporters and they're real people to me.' Billy O'Donnell adds that 'I've seen him outside after he'd finished, going in to the game, seeing a couple of kids. "You going in?" "No, Mr Shankly," and he'd give them the money to get in.'

Bill told Liverpool's supporters to behave and to be a credit to themselves, to the club and to the city. Throughout his reign, for 99% of the time, they did just that. Just as the players didn't want to let him down, neither did the fans. Kevin Keegan wrote persuasively in his autobiography that 'if a lad behaved in a way that was likely to tarnish their reputation, [the supporters] would sort him out. First they would try reasoning with him, but if that failed, someone would give him a belt. He would then know not to cause trouble again. This proved to be more effective than any action taken by a policeman.' Their reputation as the finest supporters in the land was highly valued.

In the introduction to this book, Joe Mercer was quoted as saying Bill was 'Liverpool's answer to vandalism and hooliganism because the kids came to see Liverpool . . . [he] was their hero, their football god'. When Bill was no longer manager of the club, his absence took the lid off the more troublesome elements in the crowd while the youngsters coming through were not schooled in the Shankly way. Though Liverpool were not as disfigured by hooliganism as many clubs, they had their share of problems. It might well have been that, with the worsening social and economic climate of the late '70s, intensifying through the 1980s, even Shankly would have been powerless to prevent the outbreak of trouble – though Ian St John made it perfectly clear that he believes Shankly would have saved Liverpool from becoming tainted with the unacceptable face of football. When Bill was there, he was the head of the family and no-one would step out of line. They had too much respect for him.

All of which brings us back to the Shankly ethic, that of co-operation, of collectivism, the whole being stronger than the sum of the parts. The football club that Bill Shankly built was always intended to be more than a vehicle for collecting trophies. Because of that wider vision, more than any other manager, Bill's teams made a statement for him, on his way of life and his beliefs. They played the game the way he lived. 'Football is a form of socialism,' and he was right.

None of his successors forged the same bond of respect with the crowd. Bob Paisley was a great football manager, but that was the limit of his ambitions. Bill was much more than that. When he was manager of the club, the supporters were part of it, a vitally important part. Bill told the *Liverpool Echo* 'I felt that the Liverpool people were my kind of people. What I achieved at Anfield I did for those fans. Together we turned Liverpool into one huge family, something alive and vibrant and warm and successful . . . I thank God for the people of Merseyside. The attitude of the people towards me and my family is stronger now than it ever was. I never cheated them and they've never let me down.'

Liverpool slowly ceased to be a community for in that sense, it was wholly impossible to follow Shankly. The reserved

Paisley did not try and gradually Liverpool, like Manchester United before them, simply became an organisation striving to win football matches. Liverpool still has some of that communal ethos and, on occasion, the family spirit is revived. When the Kop closed for example, there was a tangible warmth about the celebrations. It was significant that one banner featured a portrait of Bill and the legend 'Lest we forget', though inevitably, the supporters are starting to forget for many of those who watched Shankly's teams, and certainly those who recall Liverpool before his revolution, no longer go to the games. The question that remains unanswered is whether it is more important to win trophies than it is to be a part of your club? Each person will have their own view. John Peel's is instructive. 'The extraordinary thing is it wouldn't have mattered if Shankly hadn't been a successful manager because, unlike now, you felt he was your man on the inside, as much a supporter as you were. His feelings would be the same as yours.'

Liverpool was his life's work, though that's not to denigrate the work he did prior to his arrival on Merseyside. With Liverpool, he had the opportunity to put his ideas into practice. John Peel points out that 'there'd be no room in the modern game for a visionary', but in the 1960s the game was ripe for Shankly's brand of magic. Bill said later that 'my idea was Liverpool had potential, the ground, the crowd, the city, to be built into a bastion of invincibility. Possibly Napoleon had that idea. He'd conquer the whole world and I wanted Liverpool to be untouchable because they're those kind of people. Arrogant, proud, cocky and that's what I wanted the team to be so the team and the people would be the same and eventually everyone else would have to give in.'

Tom Saunders believes that 'he transformed this place. More than any one person, he's responsible for the upturn in Liverpool's fortunes. He was the motivating force. The secret was the feeling that he engendered, that this was the place to be, the place where if you had something to offer, you would be successful. How you arrive at that is a mystery to me still but it was that that I saw in the place.'

Though built on the talents of excellent players playing to a pattern, possibly Liverpool's greatest advantage was that Shankly had them believing in fables. Liverpool was powered by a myth, almost by the concept of the Emperor's new clothes, certainly in the early days. His absolute belief in the team's standing in the game was drummed into his own players and the opposition with such complete conviction that people genuinely started to believe it. Teams would arrive at Anfield hoping to keep their defeat down to respectable proportions. As Brian Hall points out, 'it wouldn't have worked if he had played eleven donkeys', but in his first great team he managed to find good players. Good players allied to supreme self-confidence makes for an unbeatable combination. That became a self-fulfilling prophecy. Liverpool were the best, so the best players wanted to go to Anfield so Liverpool got better. Even after his retirement, the place was still fuelled by this total belief in a divine right to win titles, though that never slipped into complacency. Everyone did their work because they knew that if they did, trophies would come. As far as British football went, Liverpool were supreme. Top players from other clubs would go to Liverpool and happily spend a lengthy spell in the reserves while they adjusted to the Liverpool way when they would never have dreamed of doing the same at any other club. If you wanted to be a champion, you had to go to Liverpool.

The Boot Room became one of the hallowed institutions of the game. Anfield was a terrifying cauldron where opposition Christians were fed to the Liverpool lions. Their training system was scrutinised but rarely understood. Their consistency could not be emulated. Bill knew as well as any the fragile nature of the elaborate con trick that he had played on the country in the first instance, but it endured down the years. Gradually though, pieces were chipped away. Bill's death was the first fracture while confidence in the infallibility of the club was further harmed by the horrors of Heysel and

Hillsborough and then, on the field, by Arsenal's title win at Anfield. The Emperor's nudity was finally exposed by Graeme Souness who destroyed the fragile facade by tearing down the tenets of Shanklyism and imposing his own ideas on the club. Suddenly, by virtue of some ill-judged changes, the spell was broken. Liverpool were human again and other sides knew it. They moved in for the kill and it is four years since Liverpool have had a sniff of the Championship, though the side that Roy Evans is building, which passes the ball like a dream and plays the Shankly way, has gone a long way to redressing that balance. 'When I took over, we went back to the Boot Room idea. If you've got a system of work that's simple, where everybody understands their job, providing you do your work and you've got good players, you've got a chance of being successful. Why change the formula? It's evolved over time, but the basics are the same.'

How did Bill Shankly make such an impact? He was a sharp, intelligent man whose ready wit masked a serious nature. He was lucky that he was blessed with such an electrifyingly charismatic personality, but by dedicating himself so totally to the game of football, he turned himself into a larger than life figure. Perhaps his secret lay in his other great passion. He loved life, relished every day he could wake up and take his exercise. Brian Hall recalls many days at Melwood when 'It'd be freezing, chucking it down, blowing a gale and he'd go out and say "Great to be alive, boys. All you need is the green grass and the ball."'

His love of life was the source of his motivational strength. John Roberts admits that 'you could talk to him and you could see how he could motivate people, his enthusiasm was so infectious. I'd leave him after working on the book and go out and feel as if I should do something, even if it was just work in the garden.' Tommy Docherty is in agreement. 'If you spoke to him for half an hour – actually you listened for half an hour – you came away and you could take on anybody. It was like having a massage, you were ready for anything.'

Shankly did not live for football, he lived for people. The

game was the vehicle he used to reach out to them and he missed that as much as anything else in retirement, although the people still loved him. Neighbour Janet Burgin, now Janet Clarkson, recalls that 'my mother had been with Bill to visit Nessie in Broadgreen Hospital and his car failed to start when they attempted to leave. Word apparently spread around the car park about the driver's identity and a large number of volunteers started to push it. My mother's feeling was that if the engine had not fired, the car would have been pushed or even carried back home.'

Bill Shankly was, above all else, a man of the people. Let's give the people their say.

Tom Finney: 'He was a model, a man to look up to.'

Billy O'Donnell: 'He was brilliant, greatest manager ever in this country.'

Tommy Smith: 'On Merseyside, he's a god. I owe him a great deal, he's the number one, he started it all.'

John Peel: 'I once carried his bag from the hotel to the bus after Liverpool had beaten Real Madrid in the Parc des Princes and it was genuinely one of my proudest moments. It was like being able to go up to the Pope. I was just awestruck that I could speak to him. He means enough for one of our children to be named after him – Florence Victoria Shankly.'

Kevin Keegan: 'I'm always thinking "What would he do?" I've a picture of him on the office wall, he comes into the conversation every day of my life. I learned a lot from him.'

INDEX

All Orion/Phoenix titles are available at your local bookshop or from the following address:

Littlehampton Book Services
Cash Sales Department L
14 Eldon Way, Lineside Industrial Estate
Littlehampton
West Sussex BN17 7HE

telephone 01903 721596, *facsimile* 01903 730914

Payment can either be made by credit card (Visa and Mastercard accepted) or by sending a cheque or postal order made payable to *Littlehampton Book Services*.
DO NOT SEND CASH OR CURRENCY.

Please add the following to cover postage and packing

UK and BFPO:
£1.50 for the first book, and 50P for each additional book to a maximum of £3.50

Overseas and Eire:
£2.50 for the first book plus £1.00 for the second book and 50p for each additional book ordered

---

BLOCK CAPITALS PLEASE

name of cardholder .... *delivery address*
.... *(if different from cardholder)*

address of cardholder ....

....

....

postcode .... *postcode* ....

☐ I enclose my remittance for £....................

☐ please debit my Mastercard/Visa (delete as appropriate)

card number ⬚⬚⬚⬚⬚⬚⬚⬚⬚⬚⬚⬚⬚⬚

expiry date ⬚⬚⬚⬚

signature ....

prices and availability are subject to change without notice